PENTAGON CAPITALISM

The Political Economy of War

PENTAGON
CAPITALISM

The Political Economy
of War

Seymour Melman

McGRAW-HILL BOOK COMPANY

New York   St. Louis   San Francisco   Toronto

Acknowledgement is made to the following sources for permission to use material already published:
Martin M. Kaplan, "Communicable Diseases and Epidemics," *Bulletin of the Atomic Scientists,* June, 1960. Reprinted by permission of *Bulletin of the Atomic Scientists.*
Elinor Langer, "Chemical and Biological Warfare (II): The Weapons and the Policies," *Science,* January 20, 1967.

PENTAGON CAPITALISM

Library of Congress Catalog Card Number: 70–109686

Designed by Christine Aulicino

Second Printing 1970

41467

To Jo Anne

Preface

After I published *Our Depleted Society,* I turned to a question that I couldn't answer in 1965, namely: what made the United States deplete so many areas of its life, or did it just happen? The break on this problem came unexpectedly. As part of a continuing interest in the characteristics of military industry and how it is different from civilian enterprise, I visited the Pentagon, asking questions about how its relation to industry might affect the management of private firms. The discussions with Pentagon staff and the documents that I saw indicated something I hadn't anticipated: the Pentagon was operating like a true industrial management overseeing numerous divisions of its *own* firm. From there on, it was necessary to do the homework on the functioning of the Department of Defense, tracing out its impact in several directions. I concluded that the "military-industrial complex" was effectively terminated soon after it had been announced and that Robert McNamara, under the direction of President Kennedy, had made a major institutional change in American society.

In their important volume, *The Weapons Acquisition Process: An Economic Analysis* (Harvard University Press, 1962), Merton J. Peck and Frederick M. Scherer diagnosed many aspects of military industry. However, in 1962, they recorded that "We have not examined directly or in detail the contractual and competitive incentives provided defense contractors and the administrative devices through which the government supervises its contractors—in short, the various policy in-

vii

struments through which the weapons acquisition process is directed" (p. 581). Peck and Scherer portrayed many dimensions of the military-industry system, and characteristics of the military contracting firms. The present volume adds a diagnosis of the new central control system that was installed under Robert McNamara, and the depleting consequences for American economy and society from the operations of that system. I judge these effects to be a major modification in the industrial system; hence the title, *Pentagon Capitalism.*

Professor Gabriel Kolko was most generous in making available to me the full text of the Eisenhower memorandum (Appendix A) which, in 1946, effectively founded the "military-industrial complex." Professor Kolko discovered this document among the Henry L. Stimson papers in the Sterling Library of Yale University.

I am especially indebted to my students at Columbia University for their critical comments while these analyses were being developed, to Eloise Segal and Dolly Gattozzi for improving the readability of the text, and to Nita Hagan and Marsha Dennis for their unstinting labor through drafts of the manuscript.

Contents

PENTAGON CAPITALISM

The Political Economy of War

1

The State-Management

In the name of defense, and without announcement or debate, a basic alteration has been effected in the governing institutions of the United States. An industrial management has been installed in the federal government, under the Secretary of Defense, to control the nation's largest network of industrial enterprises. With the characteristic managerial propensity for extending its power, limited only by its allocated share of the national product, the new state-management combines peak economic, political, and military decision-making. Hitherto, this combination of powers in the same hands has been a feature of statist societies—communist, fascist, and others—where individual rights cannot constrain central rule.

This new institution of state-managerial control has been the result of actions undertaken for the declared purposes of adding to military power and economic efficiency and of reinforcing civilian, rather than professional, military rule. Its main characteristics are institutionally specific and therefore substantially independent of its chief of the moment. The effects of its operations are independent of the intention of its architects, and may even have been unforeseen by them.

The creation of the state-management marked the transformation of President Dwight Eisenhower's "military-industrial complex," a loose collaboration, mainly through market relations, of senior military officers, industrial managers, and legislators. Robert McNamara, under the direction of President John Kennedy, organized a formal central-management office to administer the military-industrial empire. The market was replaced by a management. In place of the complex, there is now a defined administrative control center that regulates tens of thousands of subordinate managers. In 1968, they directed the production of $44 billion of goods and services for military use. By the measure of the scope and scale of its decision-power, the new state-management is by far the largest and most important single management in the United States. There are about 15,000 men who arrange work assignments to subordinate managers (contract negotiation), and 40,000 who oversee compliance of submanagers of subdivisions with the top management's rules. This is the largest industrial central administrative office in the United States—perhaps in the world.

The state-management has also become the most powerful decision-making unit in the United States government. Thereby, the federal government does not "serve" business or "regulate" business. For the new management is the largest of them all. Government *is* business. That is state capitalism.

The normal operation, including expansion, of the new state-management has been based upon preemption of a lion's share of federal tax revenue and of the nation's finite supply of technical manpower. This use of capital and skill has produced parasitic economic growth—military products which are not part of the level of living and which cannot be used for further production. All this, while the ability to defend the United States, to shield it from external attack, has diminished.

From 1946 to 1969, the United States government spent over $1,000 billion on the military, more than half of this under the Kennedy and Johnson administrations—the period during which the state-management was established as a formal institution. This sum of staggering size (try to visualize a billion of something) does not express the cost of the military establishment to the nation as a whole. The true cost is measured by what has been foregone, by the accumulated deterioration in many facets of life, by the inability to alleviate human wretchedness of long duration.

Here is part of the human inventory of depletion:

1. By 1968, there were 6 million grossly substandard dwellings, mainly in the cities.
2. 10 million Americans suffered from hunger in 1968–1969.
3. The United States ranked 18th at last report (1966) among nations in infant mortality rate (23.7 infant deaths in first year per 1,000 live births). In Sweden (1966) the rate was 12.6.
4. In 1967, 40.7 percent of the young men examined were disqualified for military service (28.5 percent for medical reasons).
5. In 1950, there were 109 physicians in the United States per 100,000 population. By 1966 there were 98.
6. About 30 million Americans are an economically underdeveloped sector of the society.

The human cost of military priority is paralleled by the industrial-technological depletion caused by the concentration of technical manpower and capital on military technology and in military industry. For example:

1. By 1968, United States industry operated the world's oldest stock of metal-working machinery; 64 percent was 10 years old and over.
2. No United States railroad has anything in motion that compares with the Japanese and French fast trains.
3. The United States merchant fleet ranks 23rd in age of vessels. In 1966, world average-age of vessels was 17 years, United States 21, Japan 9.
4. While the United States uses the largest number of research scientists and engineers in the world, key United States industries, such as steel and machine tools, are in trouble in domestic markets: in 1967, for the first time, the United States imported more machine tools than it exported.

As civilian industrial technology deteriorates or fails to advance, productive employment opportunity for Americans diminishes.

All of this only begins to reckon the true cost to America of operating the state military machine. (The cost of the Vietnam war to the Vietnamese people has no reckoning.) Clearly, no mere ideology or desire for individual power can account for the colossal costs of the military machine. A lust for power has been at work here, but it is not explicable in terms of an individual's power drive. Rather, the state-management represents an institutionalized power-lust. A normal thirst for more managerial power within the largest management in the United States gives the new state-management an unprecedented ability and opportunity for building a military-industry empire at home and for using this as an instrument for building an empire abroad. This is the new imperialism.

The magnitude of the decision-power of the Pentagon management has reached that of a state. After all, the fiscal 1970 budget plan of the Department of Defense—*$83 billion*—exceeds the gross national product (GNP) of entire nations: in billions of dollars for 1966— Belgium, $18.1; Italy $61.4; Sweden $21.3. The state-management has become a para-state, a state within a state.

In its beginning, the government of the United States was a political entity. The managing of economic and industrial activity was to be the province of private persons. This division of function was the grand design for American government and society, within which personal and political freedom could flourish alongside of rapid economic growth and technological progress. After 1960, this design was transformed. In the name of ensuring civilian control over the Department of Defense and of obtaining efficiencies of modern management, Secretary of Defense Robert McNamara redesigned the organization of his Department to include, within the office of the Secretary, a central administrative office. This was designed to control operations in thousands of subsidiary industrial enterprises undertaken on behalf of the Department of Defense. Modeled after the central administrative offices of multi-division industrial firms—such as the Ford Motor Company, the General Motors Corporation, and the General Electric Company—the new top management in the Department of Defense was designed to control the activities of subsidiary managements of firms producing, in 1968, $44 billion of goods and services for the Department of Defense.

By the measure of industrial activity governed from one central office, this new management in the Department of Defense is beyond compare the largest industrial management in the United States, perhaps in the world. Never before in American experience has there been such a combination of economic and political decision-power in the same hands. The senior officers of the new state-management are also senior political officers of the government of the United States. Thus, one consequence of the establishment of the new state-management has been the installation, within American society, of an institutional feature of a totalitarian system.

The original design of the American government was oriented toward safeguarding individual political freedom and economic liberties. These safeguards were abridged by the establishment of the new state-management in the Department of Defense. In order to perceive the abridgement of traditional liberties by the operation of the new managerial institution, one must focus on its functional performance. For the official titles of its units sound like just another government bureaucracy: Office of the Secretary of Defense, Defense Supply Agency, etc.

The new industrial management has been created in the name of defending America from its external enemies and preserving a way of life of a free society. It has long been understood, however, that one of the safeguards of individual liberty is the separation of roles of a citizen and of an employee. When an individual relates to the same person both as a citizen and as an employee, then the effect is such— regardless of intention—that the employer-government official has an unprecedented combination of decision-making power over the individual citizen-employee.

In the Soviet Union, the combination of top economic and political decision-power is a formal part of the organization and ideology of that society. In the United States, in contrast, the joining of the economic-managerial and top political power has been done in an unannounced and, in effect, covert fashion. In addition to the significance of the new state-management with respect to individual liberty in American society, the new organization is significant for its effects in preempting resources and committing the nation to the military operations that the new organization is designed to serve. Finally, the new power center is important because of the self-powered drive toward expansion that is built into the normal operation of an industrial management.

The preemption of resources takes place because of the sheer size of the funds that are wielded by the Department of Defense. Its budget, amounting to over $80 billion in 1969, gives this organization and its industrial-management arm unequalled decision-power over man-power, materials, and industrial production capacity in the United States and abroad. It is, therefore, predictable that this organization will be able to get the people and other resources that it needs when-ever it needs them, even if this requires outbidding other industries and other organizations—including other agencies of the federal and other governments.

Regardless of the individual avowals and commitments of the princi-pal officers of the new industrial machine, it is necessarily the case that the increased competence of this organization contributes to the competence of the parent body—the Department of Defense. This competence is a war-making capability. Hence, the very efficiency and success of the new industrial-management, unavoidably and regardless of intention, enhances the war-making capability of the government of the United States. As the war-making department accumulates diverse resources and planning capability, it is able to offer the President blue-print-stage options for responding to all manner of problem situations —while other government agencies look (and are) unready, under-staffed, and underequipped. This increases the likelihood of recourse to "solutions" based upon military power.

Finally, the new government management, insofar as it shares the usual characteristics of industrial management, has a built-in propen-sity for expanding the scope and intensity of its operations—for this expansion is the hallmark of success in management. The chiefs of the new state-management, in order to be successful in their own eyes, strive to maintain and extend their decision-power—by enlarging their activities, the number of their employees, the size of the capital invest-ments which they control, and by gaining control over more and more subsidiary managements. By 1967–1968, the scope of the state-man-agement's control over production had established it as the dominant decision-maker in U.S. industry. The industrial output of $44 billion of goods and services under state-management control in 1968 exceeded by far the reported net sales of American industry's leading firms (in billions of dollars for 1968): A.T.& T., $14.1; Du Pont, $3.4; General Electric, $8.4; General Motors, $22.8; U.S. Steel, $4.6. The giants of United States industry have become small- and medium-sized firms, compared with the new state-management—with its conglomerate industrial base.

The appearance of the new state-managerial machine marks a transformation in the character of the American government and requires us to re-examine our understanding of its behavior. Various classic theories of industrial capitalist society have described government as an essentially political entity, ideally impartial. Other theories depict government as justifiably favoring, or even identifying with, business management, while the theories in the Marxist tradition have depicted government as an arm of business. These theories require revision.

THEORIES OF GOVERNMENT—BUSINESS POWER

The classic theory of imperialism explained the behavior of government, in part, as the result of the influence of private industrial managers and chiefs of financial organizations. In this view, a ruling class, located in private enterprise, used the political instruments of government in the service of private gain. Thereby, the central government's political, legal, and military powers were utilized at home and abroad to maintain and extend the decision-power of this ruling class, through sponsoring and protecting private property rights, foreign trade, and foreign investment.

These classic theories of imperialism do not help us understand one of the most important of recent United States government policies—participation in the war in Vietnam and preparation for a series of such wars. At the time of this writing, the United States government had expended not less than $100 billion in military and related activities in connection with the Vietnam war. This excludes the economic impacts of an indirect sort within the United States caused by this war.

No one has demonstrated any past, present, or foreseeable volume of trade or investment in Vietnam and/or adjacent areas that would justify an outlay of $100 billion. The acompanying data on location and size of United States foreign investments speak for themselves.

U.S. Private Direct Long-Term Investments Abroad, 1966 * (In billions of dollars)

Total	$54.2
Canada	$16.8
Western Europe	16.2
Latin American republics	9.8
Other Western hemisphere	1.6
Africa	2.0
Middle East	1.6
Far East	2.2
Oceania	2.0
Miscellaneous international	2.0

* SOURCE: *Statistical Abstract of the United States, 1968*, U.S. Department of Commerce, 1968, p. 792.

Indeed, there is substantial evidence to indicate that an important segment of the industrial corporations of the United States are not beneficiaries of participation by the American industrial system in military and allied production. (Thus, a Marxist political economist, Victor Perlo, has judged that about one-half of the major American industrial firms would gain materially from a cessation of military production.) Moreover, criticism of the Vietnam war by important institutions of the American establishment, such as *The Wall Street Journal* and *The New York Times,* is not consistent with the idea that the war has been conducted to suit the requirements of private finance and industry.

However, the operation of Vietnam war policies by the federal government is quite consistent with the maintenance and extension of decision-power by the new industrial management centered in the Department of Defense—for the management of the Vietnam war has been the occasion of major enlargement of budgets, facilities, manpower, capital investment and control over an additional million Americans in the labor force and more than one-half million additional Americans in the armed forces.

In his notable volume *The Power Elite,* C. Wright Mills, writing in

1956, perceived a three-part system of elites in the United States: economic, military, and political. At different times in American history, Mills wrote, this elite has been variously composed. That is, one or another of these three principals exercised primary decision-power. Mills concluded:

> The shape and the meaning of the power elite today can be understood only when these three sets of structural trends are seen at their point of coincidence: the military capitalism of private corporations exists in a weakened and formal democratic system containing a military order already quite political in outlook and demeanor.

Mills stated further:

> Today all three are involved in virtually all ramifying decisions. Which of the three types seems to lead depends upon the tasks of the period as they, the elite, define them. Just now, these tasks center upon defense and international affairs. Accordingly, as we have seen, the military are ascendent in two senses: as personnel and as justifying ideology. That is why, just now, we can most easily specify the unity and the shape of the power elite in terms of the military ascendency.

In a similar vein, Robert L. Heilbroner, writing of *The Limits of American Capitalism,* supports the Mills analysis that a system of elites wields primary decision-power in American society: the military, professionals—including technical experts—and government administrators. "There is little doubt," Heilbroner wrote,

> . . . that a military-industrial-political interpenetration of interests exists to the benefit of all three. Yet in this alliance I have seen no suggestion that the industrial element is the dominant one. It is the military or the political branch that commands, and business that obeys: . . . the role of business in the entire defense effort is essentially one of jockeying for favor rather than initiating policy.

The analysis by C. Wright Mills was a reasonable one for his time. It was appropriate to a period of transition, whose closing was marked by the famous farewell address of President Dwight Eisenhower.

In his final address as President, Eisenhower gave his countrymen a grave message. "In the councils of government we must guard against the acquisition of unwarranted influence, whether sought or unsought, by the military-industrial complex. The potential for the disastrous rise of misplaced power exists and will persist." (See Appendix B for full text.) Here and in subsequent addresses, Eisenhower did not offer a precise definition of what he meant by military-industrial complex. It is reasonable, however, to see the meaning of this category in the context in which it was stated. Military-industrial complex means a loose, informally defined collection of firms producing military products, senior military officers, and members of the executive and legislative branches of the federal government—all of them limited by the market relations of the military products network and having a common ideology as to the importance of maintaining or enlarging the armed forces of the United States and their role in American politics.

The military-industrial complex has as its central point an informality of relationships, as befits the market form which underpins its alliances. The understanding, therefore, is that the main interest groups concerned tend to move together, each of them motivated by its own special concerns, but with enough common ground to produce a mutually reinforcing effect. It is noteworthy that neither Eisenhower nor anyone else has suggested that there was a formal organization, or directorate, or executive committee of the military-industrial complex. The new industrial management in the federal government is, by contrast, clearly structured and formally organized, with all the paraphernalia of a formal, centrally managed organization, whose budget draws upon 10 percent of the Gross National Product of the richest nation in the world.

The formal organization and powers of the new state-management also bear on the meaning of the various elite theories. It is true that various groups in society obviously have greater power over the course of events than ordinary citizens. But the elites are not equal. Some are "more equal than others." Primacy in decision-power among major elites is determined by the extent of control over production and by the ability to implement policies whose consequences are favorable to some elites, even while being hurtful to the others. By these tests the new state-management dominates the field. It manages more production than any other elite. Its policies of military priority, military build-ups, and the Vietnam wars program have been damaging to the decision-power of other elites. (This will be shown in the following chapters of this book.) In sum, an understanding of the normal operation of the new state-management and its consequences is essential for a meaningful theory of contemporary American economy, government, and society.

During recent years, many writers have been intrigued by the panoply of technological power displayed by the immense and complicated stockpile of weapons fashioned for the Department of Defense. There has been a tendency in some quarters to focus on control over weaponry rather than on decision-power over people. In December, 1967, Arthur I. Waskow told the American Historical Association, "The first major trend event of the last generation in America has been the emergence of what could almost be seen as a new class, defined more by its relation to the means of total destruction than by a relation to means of production."

In a somewhat similar vein, Ralph E. Lapp, in his recent volume *The Weapons Culture,* concluded: "It is no exaggeration to say that the United States has spawned a weapons culture which has fastened an insidious grip on the entire nation." While I admire the excellence of Lapp's analyses of military organization and weaponry and the consequences of their use, it seems to me that to emphasize the idea of a weapons culture, implying a kind of weapons-technological Frankenstein, is less than helpful for appreciating the sources of recent changes in the American government and its policy.

Lapp declared: "The United States has institutionalized its arms-making to the point that there is grave doubt that it can control this far-flung apparatus." He may be correct in his judgment that the whole affair has gone beyond the point of being halted or reversed. But in order to make this judgment, it seems altogether critical to define exactly what it is that has been institutionalized. Where is the location of critical decision-power over "the weapons culture," with several million Americans involved directly or indirectly in military organization and in its support? Should we understand that one person, or one part, of this network is as important as any other?

In my estimate, it is important to identify the crucial decision-makers of the largest military organization (including its industrial base) in the world. Apart from these considerations, I am uneasy about theories viewing man as the captive of his weapons. This is a self-defeating mode of understanding, rather different from identifying the top decision-makers and their mode of control. Men may be captives, but only of other men. The concept of man in the grip of a Frankenstein weapons system has a severely limiting effect on our ability to do anything about it, if that is desired.

Recently, two writers have developed theories of convergence between military industry and government. Better-known are the ideas of John Kenneth Galbraith, as formulated in his volume *The New Industrial State*. Galbraith states: "Increasingly, it will be recognized that the mature corporation, as it develops, becomes part of the larger administrative complex associated with the state. In time the line between the two will disappear." In this perspective, the major military-industrial firms, as part of the larger family of major enterprises, merges with governmental organization. But this theory does not specify which of the managerial groups involved becomes more important than the other. Indeed, one of the theoretical contributions of *The New Industrial State* is the idea of a "technostructure," a community of technically trained managers operating on behalf of enterprises, public and private, with their movements among these enterprises serving as a bond between public and private institutions. But the technostructure idea homogenizes the men of the managerial-industrial occupations on the basis of their skills and work tasks. This bypasses the fact that an accountant, for example, in the state-management participates in a power-wielding institution of incomparably greater scope than the management of any private firm. Being in the state-management amplifies the significance of his work tasks, which may be qualitatively undifferentiable from those in a private firm.

In a similar vein, a former economist for Boeing, Murray L. Weidenbaum (now Professor of Economics at Washington University), presented another convergence hypothesis before the American Economic Association in December, 1967. In Weidenbaum's view,

The close, continuing relationship between the military establishment and the major companies serving the military establishment is changing the nature of both the public sector of the American economy and a large branch of American industry. To a substantial degree, the government is taking on the traditional role of the private entrepreneur while the companies are becoming less like other corporations and acquiring much of the characteristics of a government agency or arsenal. In a sense, the close, continuing relationship between the Department of Defense and its major suppliers is resulting in a convergence between the two, which is blurring and reducing much of the distinction between public and private activities in an important branch of the American economy.

The Weidenbaum thesis is close to the analyses which I am presenting in this book. My purpose here, however, is to underscore not convergence but the managerial primacy of the new managerial control institution in the Department of Defense, and the consequences for the character of American economy and society that flow from this.

When the Kennedy-Johnson administration took office in 1961, the President's aides were impressed with the problem of ensuring civilian White House control over the armed forces. From this vantage point, one of the main accomplishments of Robert S. McNamara was to reorganize the Department of Defense so as to give top decision-power to the newly enlarged and elaborated office of the Secretary of Defense —clearly a civilian control office superior to and separate from the Joint Chiefs of Staff. McNamara obviously drew upon his experience as a top manager of the Ford Company central office to design a similar organization under the Office of the Secretary of Defense. There is a similarity between these two central offices, but the difference in decision-power is very great. The Pentagon's management is by far the more powerful in the industrial sphere, and is tied to top decision-power in the military and political spheres as well.

It is true that the top echelons of the Department of Defense were reorganized in a manner consistent with the goal of establishing firmer civilian control. This result, however, was achieved by methods that also established an industrial management of unprecedented size and decision-power within the federal government. One result is that it is no longer meaningful to speak of the elites of industrial management, the elites of finance, and the elites of government and how they relate to each other. The elites have been merged in the new state-management.

This development requires a review of many of our understandings of the role of the federal government in relation to individual freedom in our society. For example, antitrust laws, and their enforcement by the executive branch of the government, have been designed to preserve individual freedom by limiting combinations and preventing conspiracies in the economic realm. The laws have been enforced with varying intensity, but have pressed in particular on the largest firms by restraining them in their growth relative to smaller firms in the same industry.

These laws exempted government because government, in particular its executive branch, was seen as acting for the nation as a whole. With the new development of the state-management, the government-management is now acting for the extension of its own managerial power.

It is worth recalling that Eisenhower warned against the acquisition of unwarranted influence by the military-industrial complex, *"whether sought or unsought."* One of the controlling features of the new industrial management is that, like other managements, it may be expected to act for the acquisition of additional influence; such behavior is normal for all managements.

DEVELOPMENT OF THE STATE-MANAGEMENT CONCEPT

From 1965 to 1969, several developments converged to compel attention to the operations and efforts of a top industrial-management in the Department of Defense. There seemed to be no militarily rational explanation for certain major military policies: the persistent pile-up of strategic overkill power, and the continuation and expansion of the war in Vietnam. The pile-up of nuclear overkill power (by 1968, 4,200 nuclear warheads in the largest missiles and planes, as compared to 156 Soviet cities of over 100,000 population) made no military sense whatsoever. It only made sense as a way of continuing far-flung mining and industrial productions and the expansion of the military organization. At the same time, the war in Vietnam was conducted at very high cost and without traceable offsetting returns. This, again, made no sense in terms of many conventional theories of the role of government and the relation of government to business.

Some critical comments in response to the ideas expressed in my book *Our Depleted Society,* published in 1965, included a skeptical view about its central thesis. The thesis is that priority given to military production and allied work was responsible for a shortage of skilled manpower in many other classes of work in the society. This thesis was not plausible to many people, because of their estimate that the United States is indefinitely rich, indefinitely productive. The development from 1965 to 1969, nevertheless, has supported the thesis of a depletion process with great force. Some people were also skeptical of the idea that priority given to the Pentagon could conceivably produce such a wide-ranging set of depletion effects in society. Has there been a plot to produce such a result? If so, who are the plotters? If not a plot, then is all this a result of the "military-industrial complex"? But the complex has no office, no defined executive; who is in charge?

At the same time it appeared that the Department of Defense was uninterested in and opposed to serious planning for conversion from a military to a civilian economy. This policy orientation was confirmed in my discussion with the Secretary of Defense and with members of his staff in the spring of 1965. The same policy was reflected in the report of the *Committee on the Economic Impact of Defense and Disarmament,* of July 1965. The Committee report recommended a continuation of a fragmented, uncoordinated, and altogether inadequate set of federal activities which might be relevant to problems of conversion from military to civilian industry. What was bad for the country, nevertheless, was helpful to somebody. Otherwise, how could one explain the firmness with which the problem was dismissed by the top officers of the Department of Defense? It later became clear to me that these men were protecting their management of the biggest industrial empire in the land. But recognizing this fact first required knowing about the existence and characteristics of the top management itself.

In 1961, at Columbia University, I began a series of studies on industrial conversion. These produced a considerable volume of data on the internal managerial characteristics of military-industry contractors. All this information converged on the estimation that the management criteria and decision processes of the military-industrial firm were markedly different from management operation of the ordinary civilian-industrial enterprise. It also became clear that the operation of the military-industrial enterprise was not managerially autonomous, for all these firms were required to function within the framework of rules set for them by their principal customer.

The studies at Columbia in 1965–1966 inquired into the details of decision-making in military-industrial firms working with the Department of Defense. These analyses explored the elaborately detailed regulations formulated in Washington, covering every major aspect of the managing of an industrial enterprise.

The next step was to inquire into the nature of the organization in the Department of Defense which produced this system of regulations. At this point, I could draw on prior studies that I had done on the operations and costs of industrial administration and, especially, on the organization and operation of central administrative offices of large multiplant firms.

The information that I gathered on organization in the Department of Defense fitted closely with the information that had been accumulated on the style of organization and operation of central administrative offices of major industrial firms. And so, apart from the fact that the names of the government administrative bodies were different from those of private organizations and that this new organization was located in a government office, it was quite clear that, on functional grounds, the groups operating under the office of the Secretary of Defense were a true central-administrative office performing the principal management functions characteristic of such offices elsewhere in American industry. This finding was the crucial clue to discovering the general characteristics of the new state-industrial-management, the creation and operation of which marks an essential alteration of American economy, government and society.

CHARACTERISTICS OF THE STATE-MANAGEMENT

As in other major industrial managements, the state-management shows a propensity in problem-solving to select solutions that also serve to extend its decision-power. Furthermore, this selective preference is a built-in professional-occupational feature that operates with great regularity as a characteristic of people doing their jobs in management organizations. This may be illustrated by the policy preferences shown with respect to questions of the draft, overkill, and the gold reserve of the United States.

In considering the policy options that were selected, it is crucial to recall that the new industrial management is located in the Office of the Secretary of Defense, whose chief is the Secretary of Defense, and that he, in turn, is a Cabinet officer directly responsible to the President of the United States. Therefore, the basic policy decisions of the new state-industrial-management are also the decisions of the principal political officers of the federal government.

During the last years, many proposals have been offered for coping with the elimination of discrimination in the military draft. From the wide array of possibilities in this field, Robert McNamara put himself on record as preferring the idea of universal service. This policy would require every young man to give three years of national service, with military service being a major part of this three-year service period. Regardless of intention, this particular alternative, if implemented, would give the Secretary of Defense and his associates control over three years of the lives of about 10 million young Americans. This policy preference, if implemented, would make available to the top military-political officers of the United States a pool of several million young men to be deployed at home or abroad in accordance with their policy orientations at the moment. The effect of this policy preference is greatly to extend the decision-power of the state-management over additional millions of man-years.

For several years, there has been a growing awareness of the irrationality of piling up nuclear overkill power. The United States armed forces can now deliver more than six tons of TNT for each person on our planet. Obviously, no one is about to discover how to destroy people or communities more than once. Furthermore, no one has found, or is likely to find, ways of converting this destructive-overkill power into a defensive shield. Nevertheless, the spending of as much as $22 billion a year for maintaining, enlarging, and operating the strategic overkill force continues. This military irrationality, particularly when practiced by a Secretary of Defense who proclaimed "cost effectiveness" principles, defies explanation by ordinary criteria.

Many policy options are conceivable: stop production of further overkill weaponry; stop production and also retire some significant parts of the available overkill stockpile; stop production and retire some of these weapons as part of an international agreement, with accompanying inspection; or, continue the research and development and production pile-up of further overkill power. The last option was preferred. This makes sense if we see the Secretary of Defense— functionally—as the Chairman of the Board of Directors of a state-management that accumulates decision-power as a priority end-in-view. For then the additional billions for overkill are sensible expenditures. These billions maintain control over a great network of subsidiary firms with millions of employees. And so, what is patently preposterous by the test of military rationality is altogether rational by the criteria of service to the decision-power requirements of the new state-management.

The declining gold reserves of the federal treasury, and the problems it portends for the value of the dollar at home and abroad, are a further illustration of the power extending propensity of the new management. For several years, the annual reports of the Secretary of Defense to the House Armed Services Committee have disclosed the critical importance of military expenditures abroad as a dominant factor in the nation's payments deficit. The United States Treasury had $24 billion in gold in 1950; by 1968 the Treasury gold reserve had diminished to $10 billion. At the same time, claims in the form of dollars and other paper redeemable in gold, held abroad, amounted to more than twice the gold reserve held by the federal treasury. This development has threatened a crisis in the international value of the dollar and, by implication, a crisis of the value of currency at home. Inescapably, a decline in the value of the dollar relative to other currencies would affect every piece of paper with the dollar sign on it. Accordingly, the Secretary of Defense has given considerable attention to the role of military expenditures abroad in the balance of payments. In 1967, for example, the net adverse balance of military expenditures was $2.3 billion; this accounted for the lion's share of the nation's adverse balance of payments that year.

Since 1961, the federal government has been closely aware of the crisis potential that is implicit in the continuing adverse balance of payments of the United States, with a parallel loss of gold reserves and a threatened collapse in the relative value of the dollar. Among the various alternatives that could be utilized for correcting this chronic condition, however, there has been sustained avoidance of change in the cold war pattern of basing American international relations mainly on military power. Foreign policies that relied less on a military component would necessarily include a reduction in the size of armed forces and reductions in the military-industrial enterprise directed from the Department of Defense. As a result, pressure from the state-management has been to cope with the problem of balance of payments by a program of international arms sales, promoted by the Department of Defense itself. The state-management pretends thereby to help the international balance-of-payments position of the United States, but does so by the method that is uniquely suited to the maintenance and extension of its decision-power: an enlargement of military-industrial activity at home and abroad.

In connection with the value of dollar balance-of-payments gold problem of the United States, it is critically important to remember that private finance and private industry would be seriously affected by a collapse in the value of the dollar. Private industry and finance are involved in long-term investments and commitments, which include assumptions about a currency of reasonable value. These assumptions, however, are not essential for the managers of the new state-machine. Private managers must recoup invested money as a prime method for securing capital for further investment. This requirement does not apply to the new state-management. Its capital and operating funds do not depend on a currency of stable value, but rather on the proportion of the GNP given to it each year by the Congress of the United States.

Therefore, the managers of the state-management have a special view of the gold reserve problem, the balance-of-payments issue, and the significance of the value of the dollar—rather different from the attitude that is natural to productive economic organizations of every sort. The managers of the Pentagon hold firmly to their viewpoint and argue that their preferred approaches to the nation's balance-of-payments problem are also in the larger interest of the nation. They hold that maintaining and enlarging the military-industrial base of the United States is part of the economic growth at home and contributes to the military establishments of "free world" nations, while also linking these nations to United States sources of supply. The Department of Defense management extends control over the dependent military establishments because of their necessary reliance on American sources of supply to maintain and operate new weaponry produced in this country.

In the present case, the drive for improvement of their standing as managers requires them to maintain and enlarge the military-industry and military organizations of the United States; that is precisely what the state-management has done. From 1960 to 1970, the budget of the Department of Defense has been enlarged by 80 percent—from $45 to $83 billion. All large managerial organizations, whether private or governmental, carry on planning and calculate choices among alternatives. When confronted with an array of different ways to solve a particular problem, members of a managerial team are impelled by their particular professional-occupational requirements to select those options that will maintain and extend the decision-power of the managerial group, and improve their own professional standing in the managerial hierarchy. This sort of selective preference by managers is operative in industrial management whether private or public.

An enterprise is private when its top decision-making group is not located in a government office. For this analysis of the Pentagon, what is crucial is whether the top decision-making group is a true management. A management is defined by the performance of a set of definable functions which give management its common character, whether the enterprise is private or public. A management accumulates capital for making investments. Management decides what to produce, how to carry on production, how much to produce, and where to dispose of the product at the acceptable price. It is the performance of these functions by the new organizations in the industrial directorate of the Department of Defense which defines it as a bona fide industrial management. In addition, the operating characteristics of this new management are comparable to those of other industrial managements. The special characteristics of the state-management are associated with its location in the government and its control over military production.

While the industrial-management in the Department of Defense actually owns only a minority part of the industrial capital that is used for military production, it exercises elaborate control over the use of *all* resources in thousands of enterprises. This differentiation between ownership and control is the classic one of the modern industrial corporation. Ever since Berle and Means did their classic study on *The Modern Corporation and Private Property,* it is well understood that the top managers of an industrial corporation do not necessarily wield property rights over the assets used in production, but do control the use of these assets. The differentiation between ownership and control is a central feature of the new state-management.

The Pentagon management also displays the other characteristic features of corporate organization. Management decision-making usually includes a hierarchical organization of the administration group and built-in pressures for expanding the decision-making sphere of the management. Hierarchical organization means the separation of decision-making on production matters from the performance of the work itself, and the investment of final decision-power in the men at the top of the management organization. This sort of organization structure is visible in the Pentagon's organization charts and in the key role played by the Secretary of Defense and his closest aides in controlling the enlargement of nuclear and conventional forces from 1961 to 1969.

Success of management is ordinarily shown by growth in decision-power, measured by size of investment, number of employees, volume of sales, or quantity of goods produced. Such criteria indicate a true competitive gain only when they reflect a differential increase as against other management; thus, what is critical in defining the importance of a management at any one moment is not simply the absolute quantity of sales, but more importantly, the proportion of an industry's activity controlled by the management. Similarly, an increase in the volume of sales or the size of investment or the number of employees is significant only in terms of a proportional increase. In a military organization, for example, if everyone is promoted at the same time by one grade, then no one has been promoted. Similarly, promotion in a hierarchical organization must be relative promotion, and a gain in managerial position must be a relative gain. If we are competitors, then your gain must include my relative loss or you have not gained. This idea of relative gain in managerial position applies not only within a single managerial-hierarchical organization, but also applies *among* managerial organizations.

Within and among managements, the controlling criterion of managerial success is, therefore, competitive gain in decision-making position. From 1960 to 1970, the Defense Department budget rose from $45 to $83 billion, with industrial procurement roughly 50 percent of these amounts. No other management, private or public, has enjoyed such growth. The military-managerial machine is in a class by itself.

I have emphasized here the idea of enlarging decision-power as the occupational imperative, the operative end-in-view of modern corporate management—as against the more traditional idea that profit-making is the avowed central purpose of management. Profit-making, as a step in the recoupment of invested money, has diminished in importance as an independent measure of managerial performance. This stems from the fact that modern industrial operations increasingly involve classes of "fixed" or "regulated" costs, which are subject to substantial managerial control during a given accounting period. For example, a management must decide how it assigns the cost, year by year, of a new factory or a road that it has constructed. There is nothing in the nature of the factory that determines whether its capital investment shall be allocated to the costs of operations in one year, two years, or twenty years, or varied each year according to degree of use. This decision is an entirely arbitrary one, subject to the convenience of the management, within the limits allowed by the tax authorities. Since such assignment of costs is managerially controlled and has substantial effect on the size of profits that remain after costs, profits *per se* have a lessened importance as an autonomous indicator of managerial success. Moreover, there is accumulating evidence that some industrial costs, notably the costs of administration and of selling operations, are enlarged even where that involves reduction in the size of profits that would otherwise be available in a given accounting period. Such reductions in profit are ordinarily made and justified in the name of long-term maintenance or extension of the relative decision-power of the management and its enterprise.

One of the characteristic processes in industrial managements during the twentieth century has been an elaboration in the scope and intensity of managerial controlling. This has been accompanied by growing management costs and a growing ratio of managerial to production employees. All this has meant higher costs and, necessarily, diminished profits. But the choice of options in industrial management has systematically been toward enlarging the scope and intensity of managerial control, rather than toward management methods which would minimize costs and thereby enlarge profits or allow a reduction in prices. The state-management has also been piling on managerial controls, obviously giving priority to the consequent growth in its decision-power, as against possible economies that might be effected in its own central offices or in the operation of subsidiary enterprises of the Pentagon empire.

All this is no mere theoretical exercise for understanding the operation of the state-management. This organization skips over the customary processes of industrial capitalism for enlarging control via an intervening mechanism of investing and recouping money with a gain-profit, then reinvesting more money and, thereby, adding to decision-power. Instead, the state-management, drawing on its unique capital resource—an annual portion of the nation's product—applies this directly to increasing either the scope or the intensity of its decision-power. The usual processes of marketing products and recouping capital are leapfrogged by the state-management.

One of the characteristic features of private industrial management has been a sustained pressure to minimize costs in production. In modern industry, this effort is institutionalized by making it the special province of industrial engineers, cost accountants and others. The state-management, as I will show in Chapter 2, includes various professional groups that are identified as acting to control costs. But that does not necessarily produce cost-minimization. For cost control can be focused mainly on controlling the people in various occupations.

The Pentagon record—before, during, and after Robert McNamara —includes obvious cost excesses. Before McNamara, average prices on major weapons systems were 3.2 times their initial cost estimates.

Under McNamara, the famous F-111 airplane was costing $12.7 million per plane by December, 1969, as compared to one first cost estimate of $3.9 million—or 3.25 times the initial estimate. Such performance under the well-advertised regime of the state-management's "cost effectiveness" programs was characteristic of this era as well (see Chapter 7). This pattern of cost excesses during the rule of "cost effectiveness" is explicable, not as aberrant behavior, but as a pattern that is normal to the state-management. The state-management's control system (Chapter 2) includes monitoring for so-called cost overruns as a regular function. Payment for the cost overruns by the Pentagon has been the functional equivalent of a grant of capital from a central office to a division of its firm, serving to enlarge the assets of the larger enterprise.

Owing to the basic difference between private industrial management and the state-management with respect to the role of conversion of capital through the market place, there is a parallel, distinguishing interest in the stability and instability of industrial operations. Stability means operating within predictable and acceptable limits of variation in output. For private industrial management, this is a highly desirable condition, because this makes possible predictability in the ongoing processes of conversion of money from investment funds to products sold on the market place and to new capital funds fur further investment. Where costs, prices, and the value of the dollar in purchasing power are highly unstable, the investment-recoupment process of capital for private management is rendered extremely difficult to operate—it is put "out of control." These limiting conditions are not operative for the administrators of the state-management, for they deal directly with the conversion of capital funds into decision-orders on industrial operations. Also, their products need not be designed to be salable at a price producing a profit which they may accumulate for further investment. Their investment funds have been constantly acquired in the name of defense from a willing Congress and nation. Accordingly, instability in costs, prices, and profits are no major constraint for the managers of the state machine. And so, when military outlays at home and abroad become the traceable cause of danger to the value of the dollar relative to other currencies, it is not a source for alarm among the Pentagon managers. Some measures are taken to slow down the outflow of Treasury gold, but no major policy changes are introduced.

SCOPE OF OPERATIONS OF THE STATE-MANAGEMENT

Since its formal organization after 1960 under Robert McNamara, the new state-industrial management has focused attention on military production, its organization and control. At the same time, many Americans, seeing the array of managerial and technical talent deployed in the state-management, have suggested that the same group could apply its talents to organize almost anything—housing, public health, and so forth. Some individuals in the state-management may very well choose to change their employment. Indeed, there has been a sustained turnover, especially in some of the more senior posts of the state-management. Such flexibility does not apply, however, to the organization as an institution. Military organization and military production have special value as a base for the power-extending operations of industrial management.

For a management seeking to enlarge its operations, the military sphere offers the unequaled opportunity to obtain virtually unlimited quantities of fresh capital from the Congress of the United States. This is so because of the "defense" use of this money; the name, Department of Defense, is itself helpful. (Would Congress and the public be equally compliant with a War Department?) Thereby, the state industrial management has an unmatched opportunity for extending its decision-power. This is illustrated in the case of the draft. There are alternative ways of organizing military operations with varying numbers of men being required. There are also alternative ways of obtaining the services of a given number of men. The draft is the one way which not only secures the required number of men, but also guarantees decision-power by the military managers over a fixed proportion of the young people of the society at any given time. This extension of decision power, unprecedented in peacetime in American history, was made possible by the promise of the state-management to perform the service of defending the United States, a promise which cannot be fulfilled.

An important collateral feature of the military emphasis in the operation of the state machine is the substantially "untouchable" character of the entire military organization. Many people might otherwise want to be concerned with and have informed opinions about the operation of the largest organization in the nation. But they are constrained from doing this by the technological mystique that has been built up around military activity. The idea is that only persons with advanced technical training and access to secret information have the capability really to understand what is going on in this sphere. At the same time, because of the promise to defend the United States, the entire military establishment, including the affairs of the state-management, have been given a "sacred cow" quality. The Chamber of Commerce of the United States, for example, has a national committee which reviews budgets of various government departments and operations and makes recommendations, including those designed to achieve economies. The budget of the Department of Defense, which now comprises more than half the administrative budget of the United States, is excluded from this evaluation. This committee does not even make an effort to inquire into the operations of this Department. For all these reasons, the new management in the Department of Defense has an opportunity for extension of decision-power over defense-linked industry that is unequaled by any other management, public or private.

As a rule, industrial managements enlarge their decision-power by supplying a public with products that are acceptably serviceable in accordance with their understood purpose. In the case of the state-management in the Department of Defense, these ordinary tests of serviceability of performance are not operative. Scrapping old weapons and organizations, and multi-billion-dollar spending for the development, design, production, and purchase of new weapons of every kind —all this is independent of the particular military or political serviceability of the new weapons systems. Thus, the famous F–111 airplane project, for example: it was assigned to General Dynamics, which produced a defective plane at $12.7 million per unit compared with the anticipated cost of $3.9 million.

The presumed function of the Department, as the name implies, is that of a Department of Defense—hence, the service to be performed is that of shielding the United States from outside physical attack. However since several countries have acquired nuclear weapons in quantity, defense—in the ordinarily understood sense of that word—is no longer possible. Instead, the United States is engaged in an operation called deterrence—an attempt to forestall a society-destroying war by sustained threat of nuclear counterattack. In September, 1967, Secretary of Defense McNamara discussed the nature of the relationship between the United States and its principal military rival, the Soviet Union:

> The blunt fact is then, that neither the United States nor the Soviet Union can attack the other without being destroyed in retaliation; nor can either of us obtain a first-strike capability in the foreseeable future. (From address to United Press International, San Francisco, September 18, 1967)

Deterrence is not defense. Deterrence is not a shield. Deterrence is an experiment in applied psychology. There is no scientific basis from which to forecast the probability of the success or failure of this experiment. Just imagine the difference in the public and Congressional attitudes with respect to lavish granting of funds if the name were not Department of Defense but Department of Deterrence. In many public addresses and reports, McNamara elaborated on ideas like "deterrence" or "assured destruction capability." At no point did he, or the President of the United States, say plainly to the American people that the nation could no longer be defended. The pre-nuclear promise of defense has sustained reality only in the title of the Department.

Instead of defense, the managers of the Department sell weapons-improvement programs to Congress and to the public. It is constantly implied that as you improve the parts, you improve the whole. Thus, weapons-systems programs are formulated and sold to the appropriate committees of the Congress and to the public on the promise that they are, in each instance, better than what had existed before. The M-16 rifle is thereby better than the M-1 rifle, because it fires more than 10 times as many shots per minute. Minuteman-3 is better than Minuteman-1, since it can carry a larger nuclear explosive and presumably have a greater capability for penetrating conceivable defensive systems.

In nuclear as well as conventional weapons, technical improvement reaches a limit called overkill—meaning that, try though they may, even the United States state-management is unlikely to be able to kill more than once. Thus, technical improvement in the overkill range is militarily meaningless, but absolutely vital for sustaining the rule of the state-management over its military-industry empire. That is given first priority, in the name of defense. Thereby the budget of the Department of Defense in 1968–1969 almost equaled the peak spending of World War II.

Veteran chiefs of the Air Force, for example, announced that a few weeks of bombing of North Vietnam would produce termination of the war in that area by surrender of the Viet Cong and the North Vietnamese, or peace negotiations. This result was not achieved after many months of intensive bombing during which the daily tonnage of explosives dropped in Vietnam was in excess of the daily tonnage of explosives dropped over Nazi-controlled Europe during the Second World War. Evidently, military rationality has not been the controlling consideration in decisions on the budgeting of research, development, and production of new bomber fleets. The rationality that compels this is rather the serviceability of these programs for maintaining or extending the decision-power of the state-management.

There is another result of the acquisition of nuclear weapons in quantity. The prospect of escalation from conventional to nuclear war makes it unfeasible for the major powers to attempt to win political victories against each other by the use of conventional weapons, because there is no way to exclude the possibility that a military conflict started with conventional weapons may escalate to the nuclear, hence society-destroying level. However, such limits of usefulness of military power do not restrain the process of selling "defense," which is used to justify obsolescence of particular weapons in the name of improvements in weapon performance.

Military industry has major attractiveness as an arena for extension of decision-power insofar as it is mainly non-competitive, in the marketing sense, with existing industries. Thus, the aerospace, electronics, and ordnance industries have developed primarily into suppliers of the military establishment. Hence, these new industries, and the managements that operate them, do not compete in the same markets as managements in already established civilian industries. The managers of the state machine appear as competitors of civilian industrial management only when the scale of operations reaches the point of intensity where a rationing of crucial and limited resources, such as technical talent, is required. At that point, the military industry managers utilize the political powers of the federal government and its unequaled capital supply to enforce rationing of critical resources—either by outbidding in the areas of price, wages, and salaries, or by formal rationing (classifying some civilian industries as "non-essential") giving priority to military industry. Civilian industries, even such vital ones as machine tools, have been deprived of the services of young engineers as a result of not being classified "essential" by the Department of Defense.

The importance of these considerations for the managers of the military-industrial establishment is also confirmed indirectly by the unwillingness of the state-management to plan for non-military utilization of the manpower and industrial resources which they control. Both the Kennedy and the Johnson administrations were firmly resistant to efforts to establish a National Economic Conversion Commission. Under both John F. Kennedy and Lyndon B. Johnson, the policy was to leave these matters in the hands of the military-industry managers, who were already in charge. It is also noteworthy that the industrial planners for new weapons-systems collaborate with the military chieftains in preparing and advocating new weapons, even though the evidence of field use indicates that the weapons simply do not serve their declared purposes.

Among many sophisticated Americans there is at least a suspicion of the limited capability of the Department of Defense to implement its official defense function. Nevertheless, there is widespread support for the managers of the Department of Defense, and especially for its industrial activity. Americans have believed that "cost-effectiveness" has ruled in military decisions—because McNamara and his aides said so. The growth of weapons orders has been supported on the assumption that this produces new economic growth, with the further mythology that this economic growth does not deplete anything else— that the United States can have both guns and butter.

Military planners and educated men in American society have generally been reluctant to confront the meaning of the concentration of

energy release of nuclear weapons and its consequences for the meaning of warfare. It is now feasible, with ordinary nuclear weapons, to
release at one time and at one place energy equivalent to the sum of
explosives used during World War II in the entire European theater of
operations. There is no present or conceivable shield against such
concentrated explosive force. The word "defense" has come to have an
increasingly ceremonial, rather than military, significance. None of
this is altered by adding to or altering the characteristics of "offensive"
and "defensive" missile systems. The search for military and strategic
advantages through extensive sub-optimizing (improving subsystems
and single weapons) is thus an exercise in futility. The sum of particular weaponry changes cannot produce either "defense" or military
superiority in any ordinary meaning of these words. "Improvement"
of overkill has no military value or human meaning. (The same reasoning applies, of course, to the U.S.S.R.)

MYTHOLOGY THAT SUPPORTS THE
STATE-MANAGEMENT

The size of the United States Gross National Product, approaching
$900 billion for 1969, makes it difficult to absorb the fact that while
the nation is rich, it is not indefinitely rich. An important part of the
nation's productive resources are being used for growth that is parasitic
rather than productive. Parasitic growth refers to products which are
not part of the current level of living and cannot be used for further
production. Productive growth refers to products that are part of the
current level of living, or that can be used for further production. The
activities of producing for and operating the military establishment
fall in the category of parasitic growth. This holds despite the fact that
the people who do the work are paid wages and salaries, and that
these are used, in turn, to supply their own level of living. The crucial
point is that the product of the military-serving workers, technicians,
and managers is a product that does not enter the market place, is not
bought back, and cannot be used for current level of living or for
future production. This economic differentiation is independent of the
worth which may be assigned to military activity for other reasons.
With $900 billion per year, a military budget of $83 billion appears

as less than 10 percent of the GNP. Such arithmetic, however, conceals the fact that the lion's share of the nation's research and development manpower is used for military purposes, that this manpower is present in finite supply even in a rich society, and that this imposes severe constraints on what can be done in the many spheres of civilian life that require the services of this class of skilled manpower. The long-standing military priority for skilled manpower, financial and other resources was the final constraint on the ability of the Johnson administration to implement its "Great Society" programs. Many of the programs looked fine on paper. The preambles to the various laws of the Johnson administration's legislative program read as admirable descriptions of conditions in American society and as statements of intent. Only one thing was lacking: the commitment of men and money to make the work possible. This commitment was restrained by the fact that priority was given to military and related work.

This is not to say that the effects from giving priority to the military cannot be surmounted. This could be done in two ways: first, the drastic regrouping, under central control, of civilian production and other resources; or, second, changing the whole national priorities schedule away from military emphasis. Regrouping of industrial resources could mean, for example, the arbitrary conversion of two of the three major automobile firms, allowing the auto market to be supplied by the remaining firm. Thereby, an enormous block of industrial resources, manpower, and so forth, would be made available for other uses. This is technically conceivable, but it is not socially conceivable as long as the country wishes to have something other than a rigorously state-controlled economy and society. A garrison society, in which the state is empowered to dispose of resources at will, would be able to make this sort of regrouping. But such a regrouping of industrial resources under state control has not been acceptable to the American people except in a war crisis. Within the present political-economic framework, fresh resources for productive economic growth could only be made available by a basic change in national priorities. In detail, that would mean utilizing the federal public-responsibility budget of the nation for other than military priority purposes, which would necessarily involve a major reduction in the decision-power of the state-management. This is why the managers and apologists for the state-management are vigorous in maintaining the mythology of unlimited wealth, unlimited growth, and the absence of a priorities problem in American society.

The American people and the Congress have accepted decision-making by the state-management in the belief that it possesses critical expertise, not only in military matters, but also in the management of industry and the economy. In its 1966 Report, the Joint Economic Committee of the Congress declared:

> Let no one, at home or abroad, doubt the ability of the United States to support, if need be, simultaneous programs of military defense of freedom and economic and social progress for our people, or (2) our capacity and preference to live and grow economically without the stimulus of government spending on defense or a competitive arms race.

Here the Committee affirmed that government spending for military purposes is an economic stimulus and that the country can afford guns and butter at the same time. This assurance among the members of the Joint Economic Committee of Congress reflects repeated assertions in a similar vein made by the President and by the Secretary of Defense, the two senior executives of the state-management. Accordingly, in the presentation of the federal budget, the accompanying analyses of economic growth characteristically show no differentiation between parasitic and productive growth.

Against this background, the mayors of principal American cities have formulated varying estimates of the capital investment needed to bring material conditions of life up to a reasonable standard. In 1966, the mayor of Detroit, Jerome P. Cavanaugh, estimated that $242 billion would be required to solve the plight of the cities. The chief officers and ideologists of the state-management respond to such proposals in two ways. First, they say, there is no reason why such money could not be made available, if the nation only had the will to do it. Second, they say, there is no reason why this cannot be done while maintaining military priority in the federal government's budget, the largest pool of tax funds in the land. In a similar vein, many editors have written during the last years on the theme that "Cities Cannot Wait" (for example, *The New York Times,* August 22, 1966). But these writers show no readiness to come to grips with the military budget and the scale of the military organization and management in the federal government, both of which preempt the money, men, and materials needed to establish decent conditions in many areas of civilian life. In a memorable address at the University of Connecticut, Senator Fulbright stated the contradiction:

> There is a kind of madness in the facile assumption that we can raise the many billions of dollars necessary to rebuild our schools and cities and public transport and eliminate the pollution of air and water while also spending tens of billions to finance an open-ended war in Asia.

Even in the wealthiest economy, war expenditures change from economic stimulus to economic damage: first, when the military activity preempts production resources to a degree that limits the ability of the society to supply necessities such as shelter; second, when the military spending causes rapid price inflation, thereby depressing the level of living of all who live on limited incomes; and third, when price inflation disrupts the process of civilian capital investment which requires capability for predicting the worth of a nation's currency.

During the last years, there has been more than a beginning of an understanding that the nation does, in fact, have a priorities problem. But there has been hardly a beginning in preparing for the conversion of resources from military to civilian use. The official economic advisors of the federal government have repeatedly counseled that if there is sufficient advance planning, and the will in Washington to establish a clear set of priorities, then a transition from war to peace activity can be made without great upheaval (*The New York Times,* April 14, 1968). The point is precisely that until now, there has been no advance planning or a will in Washington to establish peace-time priorities, and the lack of will in this realm contrasts sharply with the clear will and the openhanded dedication of resources to the requirements of the state-managerial machine.

Many lines of evidence contribute to the conclusion that both recognition and denial of a national priorities problem cuts across conventional political lines. Support of the state-management and its functioning in the name of defense is independent not only of party, but also of personalities. The Kennedy administration was formally Democratic, but the architect of the present military machine, and its operating chief from 1961 to 1968, was a Republican, Robert McNamara. Support for the plans and the budgets of the state-management have come from both major parties in the Congress. At the same time, there has been a fair amount of turnover in the persons holding key posts at the top of the state-management.

Indeed, the very openness of operations of the state machine is one of its great sources of strength. Thus, no conspiracy, in the ordinary sense of the word, was required to get the American people to accept the myth of the missile gap and the subsequent major capital outlays for an overkill nuclear war program. The American people were sold on the myth and thought they were buying defense. Nor is a conspiracy required to secure fresh capital funds of unprecedented size for further expansion of the state-management. This is agreed to by a Congress and a public that has been taught to believe that all this activity is for defense and that it stimulates the economy of a society that can enjoy both guns and butter. In all of this, the controlling factor is not a political party or a single political theory, not a personality, not a conspiracy: the existence and normal operation of the Pentagon's management-institution dominates and gives continuity of direction.

The government of the United States now includes a self-expanding war machine that uses military power for diverse political operations and is based upon an industrial management that has priority claims to virtually unlimited capital funds from the federal budget. The state-management is economically parasitic, hence exploitative, in its relation to American society at home. The military-political operations of the Pentagon chieftains abroad, following the pattern of the Vietnam wars program, are parasitic there as well. To the older pattern of exploitative imperialism abroad, there is now added an institutional network that is parasitic at home. This combination is the new imperialism.

2

How the State-Management Controls Its Empire

In large American corporations, "decentralization" is the characteristic form of organization. This includes a number of divisions (subfirms) with their own managements, all finally governed by a central management office. The essential difference between the central management and the local management is this: the management of the divisions (the sub-firms) governs the detailed operations of the subfirms, and the top management sets rules that apply to all the subunits. Compliance with central management policy is policed by special administrative units established in the central administrative office. The result is that a central office can set policy for an indefinitely large number of sub-units. In the experience of private firms, no limit to size has been found beyond which, for example, the cost of administration rises in disproportion to the size of the firm. This helps to explain how it is possible that a central administrative office can control the affairs of 20,000 subsidiary firms. And that is the number of nominally private, industrial firms involved in contract relationships with the new management in the Department of Defense.

IDENTIFYING A MANAGEMENT

The structure and the declared purposes of the Defense Supply Agency and its sub-agencies do not suffice to identify these organizations as a true management. The identity as management is established by the critical test of whether or not they perform certain functions. Management decides on the nature of the product and the quantity to be produced, how production shall be carried out, and which persons shall be responsible for doing it; management decides on prices and profits and on delivery of the product. The persons or organization that decide on these matters is the management, whatever else the group may call itself. An organization may have the announced purposes of buying or selling, or designing or researching, or being a Department of Defense, but the critical factor is whether or not it performs the management functions. It is, therefore, essential to review a sampling of the ways by which the new organization in the Department of Defense exercises the controlling voice over each of the principal spheres of decision-making that comprise industrial managing.

In accordance with this pattern, the new management of the Department of Defense sets broad policy lines within which the subsidiary firms must operate. The top management also operates a national network for enforcing compliance with the policy rules which it lays down. This operation of policy making and policing is carried out by 15,000 men who arrange the terms of agreement (contract) by which a formally private firm comes within the orbit of control of this new, government central office. Approximately 40,000 men are involved in administering the terms of these agreements, that is, in ensuring compliance with policies defined by the top management.

The relationship between the Department of Defense and the so-called contractor firms has sometimes been described as the relation between buyer and seller. It is true that there is buying and selling. However, the buying-selling relationship hardly begins to cover the conditions under which the subsidiary firms must operate. The overriding fact is that the selling firms sell to one customer. Moreover, this customer is not replaceable, that is, there is no diverse market of other customers—other Departments of Defense—to whom the supplier firms might sell their products. Apart from the existence of one customer and the obvious leverage that this gives to him, there is also the fact that this "customer" has organized himself for controlling, in depth, the affairs of the supplying firms. This intervention operates over the whole range of decision-factors that customarily relate the central office of a multi-division firm, as in Ford, General Electric, and others, to the several divisions of that firm.

As a result of these controls, the relation between buyer and seller becomes a relationship between top management and subsidiary management. Again, I recall to the reader that the decisive factor here is not ownership but control. And so, while the Department of Defense top management actually has property rights in only a minority of the assets used by the subsidiary enterprises, the new state-management exercises final control over their activities.

The system of rules formulated by the central office of the Pentagon management is contained in several manuals, the most important of which is *The Armed Services Procurement Regulations (ASPR)*. This manual is issued in loose-leaf form and is equivalent, in size, to about four volumes. (The *ASPR* is purchasable from the United States Government Printing Office; the cited regulations can be verified to the satisfaction of any reader.) A second volume to which I will refer repeatedly in this discussion is *The Defense Procurement Handbook*. This manual is published by the Department of Defense "for use in training and for providing basic information about procurement to all personnel concerned of the Army, the Navy, the Air Force and the Defense Supply Agency." This volume has special interest for this analysis because it is a basic textbook, instructing new members of the central management on the nature of their duties and responsibilities.

The formal name of the new state-management's industrial arm is The Defense Supply Agency (DSA), formally located under the Office of the Secretary of Defense in the Department of Defense. The DSA was established in 1962 and consolidated organizations that had operated separately, under the jurisdiction of the several armed services. Thus, the DSA assumed the supply and service functions previously assigned to the following separate organizations:

1. The Armed Forces Supply Support Center.
2. Military Subsistence Supply Agency
3. The Clothing and Textile Supply Agency
4. The Medical Supply Agency
5. The Petroleum Supply Agency
6. The General Supply Agency
7. The Industrial Supply Agency
8. The Automotive Supply Agency
9. The Construction Supply Agency
10. The Military Traffic Management Agency.

Under the new consolidation, several million items that are used in common by all branches of the armed services are purchased, controlled, inventoried, and distributed by a worldwide network of warehouses and transportation units controlled by the DSA.

The DSA includes two altogether new organizations that have special importance for the present analysis: the Defense Contract Audit Agency and the Defense Contract Administration Services (DCAS). The DCAS was established in 1963 for the purpose of providing all military departments and defense agencies with consolidated administration services under a central manager. This means that while negotiation for the purchase of special material for the separate military services is handled by the procurement officers of the separate services, the purchasing contract, once formalized, is turned over to DCAS. The Administrative Contracting Officer operating under DCAS has assigned responsibilities, defined by the *ASPR*. The following is reproduced directly from four pages of the 1968 edition of *ASPR* and portrays the scope of the contract administration's function:

28 June 1968, Rev. 29   122.1

Procurement Responsibility and Authority

1–406   Contract Administration Functions. When a contract is assigned for administration, functions which have been determined to be the responsibility of the contract administration component will automatically be performed by that component, and a delegation or assignment letter is unnecessary. However, if special instructions pertaining to administration of a particular contract are to apply, they should be contained in a letter accompanying the contract when it is assigned for administration. Each contract assigned by a purchasing office to a contract administration component for administration shall contain or be accompanied by all procuring agency instructions or directives which are incorporated in such contract by reference. Functions listed below are the responsibility of, and, except as provided in 20–703.3, shall be performed by, contract administration offices. This paragraph constitutes the authority of the contract administration office designated in accordance with Section XX, Part 7 of this Regulation, to perform contract administration functions to the extent applicable, in accordance with this Regulation and the provisions of contracts assigned for administration as follows:

(i) review contractor's compensation structure;

(ii) review the contractor's insurance plans;

(iii) review and approve or disapprove contractor's requests for payments under the progress payments clause;

(iv) determine the allowability of costs suspended or disapproved on a DCAA Form 1 when a written appeal has been received from the contractor, direct the suspension or disapproval of any costs when there is reason to believe that they should be suspended or disapproved, and approve final vouchers;

(v) negotiate provisional, interim billing, and final overhead rates when the contract contains the clause in 3–704, except when negotiation responsibility is placed elsewhere in accordance with Departmental procedures;

(vi) negotiate understandings consistent with agreements negotiated under 15–107 applicable to treatment of costs under contracts currently assigned for administration;

(vii) negotiate prices and execute supplemental agreements for spare parts and other items selected through provisioning procedures;

(viii) review and evaluate contractor's proposals in accordance with 3–801.3(b) and furnish comments and recommendations to the procuring contracting officer when negotiation will be accomplished by the procuring contracting officer;

(ix) when authorized by the purchasing office, negotiate or

negotiate and execute supplemental agreements incorporating contractor proposals resulting from change orders issued under the Changes clause (Prior to completion of negotiations and issuance of the supplemental agreement, any delivery schedule change shall be coordinated with the purchasing office.);

(x) manage special bank accounts;

(xi) assure timely notification by the contractor of any anticipated overrun or underrun of the estimated cost under cost-type contracts;

(xii) review, approve or disapprove and maintain surveillance of the contractor's procurement system;

(xiii) consent to the placement of subcontracts;

(xiv) monitor contractor's financial condition and advise the procuring contracting officer when contract performance is jeopardized thereby;

(xv) when authorized by the purchasing office, negotiate prices and execute priced exhibits for unpriced orders issued by the procuring contracting officer under basic ordering agreements;

(xvi) issue tax exemption certificates;

(xvii) conduct post-award orientation conferences;

(xviii) issue work requests under maintenance, overhaul and modification contracts;

(xix) negotiate and execute contractual documents for settlement of partial and complete contract terminations for convenience, except as otherwise prescribed by Section VIII;

(xx) perform necessary screening, redistribution and disposal of contractor inventory;

(xxi) perform property administration;

(xxii) prepare findings of fact and issue decisions under the Disputes clause on matters on which the contract administration office has the authority to take definitive action;

(xxiii) assure processing and execution of duty-free entry certificates;

(xxiv) in facilities contracts—

(A) evaluate contractor's requests for facilities and changes to existing facilities, and provide the procuring contracting officer with appropriate recommendations thereon;

(B) assure required screening of facility items before acquisition by contractor;

(C) approve use of facilities on a noninterference basis in accordance with paragraph (b) of the clause in 7–702.12;

(D) assure payment of any rental due; and

(E) assure reporting of items no longer needed for defense production;

(xxv) perform production support, surveillance, and status reporting, including timely reporting of potential and actual slippages in contract schedules;

(xxvi) perform pre-award surveys;

(xxvii) perform industrial readiness and mobilization production planning field surveys and schedule negotiations;

(xxviii) monitor compliance with labor and industrial relations matters under the contract, apprising the procuring contracting officer of actual or potential labor disputes, and removing material from strikebound contractor's plants upon instructions from the procuring contracting officer;

(xxix) perform traffic management services including issuance and control of Government bills of lading and other transportation documentation;

(xxx) review the adequacy of the contractor's traffic operations;

(xxxi) review and evaluate preservation, packaging and packing;

(xxxii) provide surveillance of contractor design, development, and production engineering efforts;

(xxxiii) review engineering studies, design, and proposals, and make recommendations to the system/project manager or purchasing office;

(xxxiv) evaluate and monitor contractor engineering efforts and expenditures in accordance with contract terms;

(xxxv) conduct surveillance of contractor engineering practices with regard to subcontractors;

(xxxvi) review, on a continuing basis, contractor test plans and directives for compliance with contract terms; compare milestone; progress, and cost against contract requirements;

(xxxvii) assist in classification of waivers and deviations;

(xxxviii) evaluate the adequacy of contractor engineering data control systems, including assurance that systems provide for timely incorporation of changes in data being acquired;

(xxxix) monitor contractor value engineering programs;

(xl) review cost reduction proposals, and submit comments regarding effect of proposed changes on the engineering requirements of the contract;

(xli) evaluate and perform surveillance of contractor configuration management systems and procedures;

(xlii) perform surveillance of contractor engineering change systems; review Class I engineering change proposals, and comment on engineering feasibility and need; assist in price analysis of engineering changes; review Class II engineering changes to insure proper classification;

(xliii) evaluate the contractor management, planning, scheduling, and allocation of engineering resources;

(xliv) evaluate and monitor contractor reliability and maintainability programs;

(xlv) review and evaluate for technical adequacy the logistic support, maintenance, and modification programs accomplished by the contractor;

(xlvi) make appropriate comments to purchasing offices on any inadequacies noted in specifications;

(xlvii) perform procurement quality assurance;

(xlviii) maintain surveillance of flight operations;

(xlix) assure contractor compliance with applicable safety requirements;

(l) assure contractor's compliance with small business and labor surplus area mandatory subcontracting program, conducting, on an as-required basis, small business and labor surplus area set-aside surveillance, and providing advice to small business and labor surplus area concerns;

(li) administer the Department of Defense Industrial Security Program (This function shall be performed by the Defense Supply Agency on behalf of all Departments.);

(lii) make payments on assigned contracts (but see 20–706);

(liii) assign and perform supporting administration; and

(liv) assure timely submission of required reports.

Procurement functions not designated as contract administration functions shall remain the responsibility of the purchasing office.

This enumeration of the formally designated responsibilities of the administrative contracting officer indicates that his scope extends to every facet of the supplying firms' operations. For example, the ability to review and approve a contractor's wage and salary schedules, and to determine the allowability and allocability of costs, gives him pervasive authority over every aspect of the operation of the sub-enterprise. Where the regulations, as in item XXXV, state that the administrative contracting officer shall "conduct surveillance of . . . engineering practices with regard to subcontractors," this means that the representative of the new state-management may review and recommend changes in the design and operation of the subsidiary firms' relationships with its supplier firms.

The headquarters of DCAS is located in Alexandria, Virginia, and operates through eleven regional offices in the United States. Below the regional offices are district, area, and, finally, plant offices, the latter being the base for representatives of DCAS at the offices of principal military-industrial firms. Through this network, the buyer-seller and contractor relationship has been converted into a relationship of top management to subsidiary management.

The regional offices of DCAS are impressive operations. (See the descriptive material in the Appendix.) The New York regional office, for example, employed 3,606 persons as of January, 1968. By contrast, the central office of the Standard Oil Company (New Jersey), one of the largest private firms in the world, employs a staff of 3,000. Included in this staff are contract administrators, contract termination specialists, plant clearance specialists, quality assurance personnel (including quality assurance engineers), production specialists, industrial engineers, systems engineers, auditors, financial analysts, lawyers, negotiators, transportation specialists, data specialists, and packaging specialists. Under the New York regional office are three district offices and numerous plant offices.

In order to give the national top management an independent check on the operations of subsidiary managements, a Defense Contract Audit Agency was established under the Defense Supply Agency. The Defense Contract Audit Agency has been a primary instrument of the top management for ensuring detailed compliance with regulations. The functions of all parts of DSA and of the procurement officers in the separate services is helped by a cost- and economic-information system that is operated in every department in the Department of Defense. This is a centralized collection of data on prices, contract terms, characteristics of contracting firms, and the like. It should be noted that the scope of the industrial managing function of the Department of Defense extends to managing industrial purchases on behalf of the National Aeronautics and Space Administration (NASA). That organization uses the industrial management apparatus under the Department of Defense for a large part of its industrial procurement. The network of national, regional, and local organization under the Department of Defense is an important factor in transforming the nominal privacy of the contracting firm into an actual submanagement position.

The top management in DSA has encouraged the subfirms to appoint "program managers" within their management, with the duty of managing all phases of a military procurement contract, and with general authorization to direct departments or divisions of a subfirm to take actions for securing program objectives. This is a special form of organization that is interposed into the ordinary enterprise organization. The program-manager scheme is an extension of the Department of Defense top management into every facet of the enterprise. In another way, the use of this form of organization reflects the instability of operations of the military-industrial enterprise. A product equals a program, but products are being constantly changed. Therefore, the program organization for researching, designing, developing, and producing these products must also be modified. It is characteristic of military products that they are not produced for inventory by the manufacturing firm, but rather are produced in precise quantities according to directions of the military top management.

The central regulations codified in *ASPR* are issued jointly by the military departments. However, each department separately issues its own regulations to implement the general rules of *ASPR*. These separate rules "provide additional policy and procedural guidance within the framework of *ASPR* policy." Thus, if an *ASPR* regulation indicates that a contract administration officer has the authority to review an aspect of operations of the supplying firm, then the subsidiary regulations can specify the conditions under which this is to be done and precisely what constitutes an appropriate examination, as well as criteria of compliance. Thus, there are possibilities for variation in procedure and implementation within the framework of basic common rules. This again is characteristic of the central office-controlled multi-division firm.

STATE-MANAGEMENT'S POLICIES FOR SUB-FIRMS (CONTRACTORS)

The product to be produced by subsidiary firms may originate with designs from the Department of Defense or from one or more subsidiary contracting enterprises. What is critical is that the Department of Defense makes the final decision as to the specification of the product. In this connection, the manufacturing enterprise which accepts the contract is in a special relationship, for there is only one permissible customer for this product. This is enforced by various security regulations, as well as by the way in which these relationships are understood by the manufacturing firm and the Department of Defense. Therefore, the main commodity which submanagement sells to top management is not so much a specific product, as its competence to perform operations in accordance with specifications given by the top management.

This relationship is made concrete by the review of production facilities carried out under the direction of the top management prior to contracting and even subcontracting. The authority of the top Pentagon managers to decide on product details is specified in sections 1 and 7 of *ASPR.* This is further underscored by the specific power of the top management to review the design of military products and to order changes in design (*ASPR* 7-103.2). At all times, the specifications and the drawings of the products in question are open to review by the Contract Administration Officer (*ASPR* 7-602.2).

Characteristically, changes in product design must be made through procedures that include consultation between the top Pentagon managers and the contract-performing enterprise. There is no ambiguity, however, as to who has final decision power. It is the contracting officer who can order unilateral changes in drawings, in design, and in specifications. Power to order changes in the nature of the product has become a critically important matter in the design of military products and has led to the development of a subdiscipline for managing engineering changes called "configuration management." The policy manuals issued by the various military services to define procedures on changes in specifications cover more than one thousand pages.

An adjunct to the final right of the top government-management to change products specified in the contract is the right to terminate or alter contracts with respect to the quantity of product to be produced. This right of the government to breach contracts establishes the government as more than simply a purchaser. Insofar as the government, in respect to military products, is the single purchaser, the ability to breach contracts gives the Pentagon control over production by the contractor industrial enterprise.

Control over the quantity of goods to be produced is, by formal regulation, in the hands of the government managers (*ASPR* 1-325, *ASPR* 7-103.4). This control over quantity extends to changing quantities to be produced after contracts have been signed. For example, the major contract for producing the F-111 multi-purpose airplane involved 1,700 aircraft for the Army and the Navy. This number was progressively reduced as a result of changes in military requirements, changed decisions by the Navy as to the adequacy of its version of the plane, and changes in prospective foreign sales. Another aspect of quantity-of-product decisions is the control over making or buying parts of the principal product. Under the terms of formal regulations (*ASPR* 3-902), the top Pentagon management can decide what parts of the product to be finally delivered ought to be produced by the prime contractor or purchased elsewhere.

Obtaining capital and deciding how to use it is a critical part of the decision-process of industrial management. The state-industrial managers have wide discretionary power with respect to the provision and the use of both fixed and working capital. Fixed capital includes land, buildings, and major production equipment. Working capital is the fund from which wages, salaries, raw materials, and similar purchases are made.

Under the *ASPR,* the top management is able to furnish all types of fixed capital, in kind, to a contractor, to be used subject to regulations of the government. From 1957 to 1961, thirteen major contractors made use of $1.5 billion of government property as against $1.4 billion of privately owned fixed capital. In 1965, the Depart-

Large Air Force Contractors with More than 50 Percent Government Facilities (1960)

CONTRACTOR	LOCATION	TOTAL INVESTMENT ($ MILLIONS)	PERCENT GOVERNMENT OF TOTAL
Helicopter Division, Bell	Fort Worth, Texas	18.7	51.9
Wichita Division, Boeing	Wichita, Kansas	126.6	98.1
Arma Division, Bosch	Garden City, N.Y.	9.9	59.6
Douglas Aircraft	Tulsa, Oklahoma	66.8	99.9
Astronautics Division, General Dynamics	San Diego, Calif.	63.5	61.3
Convair Division, General Dynamics	Fort Worth, Texas	99.5	100.0
General Electric	Cincinnati, Ohio	166.1	54.1
AC Spark Plug Division, General Motors	Milwaukee, Wisc.	41.3	55.0
Hayes Aircraft	Birmingham, Ala.	7.3	75.3
Tucson Division, Hughes Aircraft	Tucson, Arizona	31.3	90.4
Kearfott	Clifton, N.J.	0.8	100.0
Marietta Division, Lockheed	Marietta, Georgia	92.3	85.3
Norair Division, Northrop	Hawthorne, Calif.	42.8	67.8
Raytheon	Waltham, Mass.	19.6	62.8
Ryan Aeronautical	San Diego, Calif.	7.0	50.0

SOURCE: Special Subcommittee on Procurement Practices of the Department of Defense, Committee on Armed Services, United States Congress, *Hearings Pursuant to Section 4 Public Law 86–89, 86th Congress, 2nd Session, 1960, pp. 603–604.*

ment of Defense spent $56 million for plant and equipment that was placed at the disposal of sub-managements. In 1967, $330 million was expended for these purposes. As a by-product of public hearings held in 1960, the Armed Services Committee of the House of Representatives produced a list of fifteen large Air Force contractors operating with more than 50 percent government equipment and facilities.

Various arguments have been offered to justify this large-scale provision of fixed capital by the government to private firms. The government, it is said, is asking for special work, which may not continue beyond the period of the particular contract. Therefore, there would be no incentive for a private firm to invest in heavy equipment which may not be useful to it once the particular work has been completed. The government, on the other hand, could conceivably transfer the equipment to other users. Also, it has been pointed out that when the facilities are purchased and made available by the government, this is done with public investment money and there is no interest paid on it. Therefore, there is no interest payment to be reimbursed to the subfirm by the government.

The consequences of large-scale supplying of machinery and buildings by the Pentagon extend in several directions. The private capital market is bypassed, and a major source of revenue for private bankers is curtailed. Also, the firms receiving this equipment do not have autonomous decision-power with respect to its use. Independently of the reasons offered in justification of this practice, the effect of a large-scale control of fixed capital by the government places definite constraints on a nominally private sub-management. Since the assets are government-owned, they cannot be used as security for loans from private banks. Once the managers of a military-serving enterprise become dependent on government as a source of fixed capital, the involvement becomes self-extending. There are the risks to the sub-management owing to the limited market for the product; at the same time, the government top managers stand prepared to furnish additional capital, when justified, for use in producing their products. Once a firm is involved in this relationship with the government top managers, it is further constrained in the use of these facilities for non-governmental purposes (*ASPR* 7-702.12; 7-702.23; 13-000; and 13-405). Formally, charges must be levied for non-governmental, commercial use of government-owned, fixed capital facilities. But in view of the larger interest which the Pentagon top management has in assuring an industrial base, there is a real question as to what is "non-governmental." Once a particular submanagement has the capability which the state-management wishes to have available for its purposes, then activity which contributes toward maintaining or enhancing that capability is arguably in the government's interest. This is a fundamental consideration that serves to confound attempts to define what constitutes private use of government-furnished facilities, and charges for such use.

The regulations formulated by the government top managers give elaborate guidance for providing working capital in various forms. The government regulations stipulate a preference for private financing. But once the bow is made in this direction, the regulations elaborate many ways by which working capital is made available to government sub-managers. The preferred form of working capital is clearly the progress payment. The government-serving management submits evidence of expenditures and activity on behalf of the government order. In 1967, $4.7 billion was paid by the Department of Defense in progress payments to its sub-managements.

Progress payments vary in form according to the type of contract involved. Thus, under fixed-price contracts, the top management issues checks on the basis of invoices and vouchers. Under cost reimbursement contracts, monthly payments are made following an audit. For the most part, progress payments consist of periodic payments based upon evidence of a given proportion of work completed. The comparison of work-performed to work-estimated may then be audited by the Defense Contract Administrator before the progress payment is approved.

The Pentagon top management has prescribed general limits to progress payments. They may not exceed 70 percent of total costs or 85 percent of direct labor and material cost (an additional 5 percent being allowed on contracts with small business). Beyond these amounts, progress payments may still be made, but these are termed "unusual" progress payments and require special approval. These "unusual" progress payments have become a regular part of the relationship between the top Pentagon managers and their submanagements, and the regulations under which they are made have produced this interesting feature: the payments "usually cover future contracts with the same contractor." In other words, provision can be made for paying well in excess of 70 percent or 85 percent of costs already incurred. These "payments" are made by the government top managers without any interest charge.

Working capital may also be provided in the form of advance payments: this is money made available to a contractor by the top management at the time the contract is formalized, that is in advance of the expenditure to be made and in advance of evidence of completion of the contracted work. Loans and guarantees of loans can also be made available to sub-managements. These have been known to be granted in order to bolster an enterprise in financial difficulties owing to some aspect of its civilian business (*The Wall Street Journal,* December 23, 1966). Clearly, the Pentagon's top managers have evolved an elaborate network of regulations and practices by which they provide fixed and working capital to sub-managements under their control, thereby penetrating deeply into the decision-processes of the subordinate managements.

Whether these effects were intended or not, it is necessarily of crucial importance to see how the government top managers understand their capital-supplying function, and how their view of the matter necessarily involves them in elaborate control over subordinate firms. The following are extracts from Section 4 of the *Defense Procurement Handbook* on "Payments and Contract Financing," defining the state-management's policy orientation for the instruction of its own administrative staff.

> The contractor must have sound finances to perform the contract successfully. Therefore, the government is concerned about finances throughout the course of the procurement. At the pre-award phase it analyzes the contractor's financial condition to determine whether he is "responsible" as ASPR 1-903 defines the term . . .
>
> Since the government desires to increase its base of supply, it often provides financial assistance to its vendors. Thus pre-award financial analysis serves a second purpose: it helps determine the type and amount of financial assistance needed for the procurement. A realistic appraisal of these needs before award helps avoid

strain on working capital as the contractor progresses with the work.

Throughout, the contractor is expected to use private financing. There are various forms of assistance the government may also provide. To promote private financing, for example, the government permits the contractor to assign his claim for payment. It may also guarantee his private loans in suitable cases. To reduce the need for such financing the government makes intermediate payments of two kinds: partial payments on fixed-price contracts, and interim payments on cost-reimbursement contracts. These increase the contractor's cash inflow from the contract; thus, they reduce the amount of working capital he must obtain from other sources.

The government may also provide direct contract financing in appropriate instances. Customarily progress payments are used most often. Unusual progress payments and advance payments are also available. All three may be used in any combination that is needed if justified by the financing regulations (*ASPR* Appendix E). Contract financing, too, may materially increase the contractor's cash inflow. Thus the government and the contractor have considerable flexibility in assuring adequate working capital for the procurement.

Early payment may have the effect of reducing the contractor's incentive to perform. So the government includes terms in the contract to protect its investment in the work. These include the various withholding provisions that permit amounts to be set aside until specified performance is completed. Included, too, are the various security terms which give the government preferred rights in property. But the government doesn't rely exclusively on these rights; it monitors performance as work progresses in order to anticipate financial problems. It then promotes remedial action with the contractor. This is far preferable to both sides and provides sure protection of the government's investment in most cases . . .

Thus, financial administration of a procurement is composed of three elements. The first is financial analysis, which determines financial "responsibility" and the need for financial assistance. The second is the actual providing of authorized assistance to insure adequate funds. The third is the monitoring performance to protect the government's investment. All three are important in obtaining the objectives of the procurement.

Clearly, the top industrial management in the Pentagon is at once a provider of capital to its submanagements and an elaborate controller of these submanagements—in the name of ensuring efficient use of these capital funds.

Who Shall Do the Work? The first step in deciding how industrial work shall be done is to decide who shall do it. From the standpoint of the state-management, this means the choice of the submanagement that will be responsible for the performance of production. The regulations (*ASPR* 1-903) define the procedure for determining what the top management terms "responsibility": that is, a management with predictable competence for performing the requisite work while complying with top-management rules. For this choice of submanagement, a comprehensive financial analysis is customarily carried out. This analysis is similar to what an investment banker does when deciding whether to underwrite securities, or like what a management does when deciding whether to merge with, or seek control over, another firm. The nature of the pre-contract award surveys are detailed in *ASPR* Appendix K. The selection of a subsidiary management also includes the selection of "systems" managements. These are management teams which, in turn, must perform the task of selecting sub-managers. The so-called systems management is the one given responsibility for a large military program—such as a major missile. Since no single firm can perform all major aspects of a large military program, the systems management, in turn, selects submanagements, each of them to be responsible for major aspects of the work.

Characteristically, so-called prime contractors do not necessarily perform all of the work within their own facilities. Thus, about 50 percent of the value of the final product is work performed by various subcontractors. The top managers of the Pentagon stipulate the procedures for the selection of and relations with subcontractors (*ASPR* 3-900). The purpose of these regulations is to guarantee that prime contractors will adequately supervise the work of subcontractors. The federal top managers reserve the right to review and decide upon the placement of individual subcontracts.

State-management staff are directed to make these decisions on the basis of specific considerations set forth in the *Defense Procurement Handbook* (XI-9).

The following are the decision rules to be applied by contract administrators:

1. The consistency of the subcontract with the contractor's approved make-or-buy program, if any (*ASPR* 3-902).
2. The responsibility of the prospective subcontractor (*ASPR* 1-906).
3. The reasonableness of the subcontract price. This is determined by (a) the presence of adequate price competition among potential subcontractors, or (b) price and cost analysis (*ASPR* 1-303; 3-807.3).
4. The existence of certificates of current pricing data and/or a requirement that they be submitted with change order estimates. This consideration applies (with certain exceptions) if the contractor intends to award (a) a cost-reimbursement, incentive, or redeterminable-type subcontract; (b) a fixed-price type subcontract in excess of $100,000; or (c) any subcontract in which the modification will exceed $100,000 (*ASPR* 3-807.3; 3-807.4; 7-104.42).
5. Subcontract provisions for adequate protection and care of government property that will come into the subcontractor's control (*ASPR* 13-104.2).
6. Appropriate reduction in subcontract cost for no-charge use of government industrial facilities (*ASPR* 13-407).
7. Suitable implementation of other government requirements—Small Business and Labor Surplus Area Programs, patent rights, contract types, security requirements, Buy American Act, Davis-Bacon Act, and so forth.

In principle, a prime contractor's management is not necessarily free to subcontract. The decision on whether to subcontract is limited by the relations preferred by the state managers (*ASPR* 1-707; 1-808).

As the central office in the Pentagon develops a relationship with an industrial submanagement, its investment in the operation of that management takes many forms. Government-supplied capital is often used in the facilities operated by the submanagement. The management of the contractor becomes experienced in dealing with the top management of the Pentagon. A network of contract negotiators and administrators is built up on both sides—a major professional convenience for all concerned. Furthermore, the top management in the Pentagon tries to maintain and promote the financial and other competence of major submanagements. As a result, the financial condition at one moment does not necessarily determine the decisions of the top management.

The top management may act to restore financial "responsibility" which has been damaged because of bad decisions in various commercial markets. Such practices have been noted in the relation of the Pentagon top managers to the Douglas Aircraft Company (*The Wall Street Journal,* December 23, 1966). A similar relationship was involved in the granting of the F-111 (TFX) airplane contract to the General Dynamics Company as against the other bidding firm, the Boeing Company. In 1963, when the selection of General Dynamics was announced, it was noted that the Boeing Company had, in fact, given considerable evidence of being the technically more advanced contractor and had been a significantly lower bidder on the first run of twenty-three airplanes. A Washington reporter, Clark R. Mollenhoff, has explored the circumstances of this contract award in his volume *The Pentagon.* He reports there that:

> General Dynamics, deeply in debt, had a vital interest in the multi-billion-dollar TFX warplane contract. With that TFX contract, General Dynamics could recover from the shattering financial loss by the Convair airplane division. If General Dynamics failed to win the award of the TFX contract, the huge defense complex faced the possibility of more serious trouble.

The Convair Division of General Dynamics had lost about $400 million in an effort to build a commercial four-engine jet. The awarding of the F-111 contract to this firm had the effect of ensuring its continued availability in the family of industrial managements working for the Pentagon.

Just as the top managers of the Pentagon specify rules for the selection of managements, they also stipulate rules for disqualifying them. Thus a so-called Joint Consolidated List is regularly formulated and circulated, listing contractors who, owing to violations of various rules, are to be excluded by the Defense Supply Agency and by the various services from procurement during a stipulated period.

Deciding how to produce. Once the Pentagon top management has decided that a given product is to be produced and has selected the likely management team for this work, it then enters into a contract-definition arrangement with the prospective industrial contractor. During this period, the submanagement is paid a fee for executing an elaborate planning operation for review by the Pentagon. As reported to me by an engineering manager of a major military contractor, this planning operation, called Contract Definition, includes the following principal elements:

(1) Project management structure, and management and engineering personnel: The submanagement is required to define not only the structure of responsibility, but to designate the persons who will be in the managing positions for the prospective military industrial work. This includes a detailed presentation and justification of the professional capability of principal project managers.

(2) Work-breakdown structure: This requires a fairly detailed specification of the main sections of work to be performed and how they are to be organized.

(3) PERT network critical checkpoints: The Program Evaluation and Review Technique is a formal scheduling method for enabling a management to control, in detail, the progress of interrelated work. The *ASPR* regulations require the preparation of such schedules for many contracts, thereby allowing the top Pentagon managers to monitor work performance of the submanagement.

(4) PERT-cost: This is a schedule of work to be done, arranged not according to time but according to the cost elements involved.

(5) Management, cost control, and reporting techniques: This is a summary statement of the principal cost-control devices to be used in the performance of the work. This enables the top management to decide, in advance, whether there will be adequate monitoring capability on its side.

(6) Make-or-buy plans: The blueprint in this sphere allows the top management to determine whether the submanagement is being realistic about the work it can perform. It also requires the submanagement to specify the contractors who may be brought into the performance of the work.

The state-management also writes regulations on production operations. From the standpoint of the marketing view of government as a buyer, with private industry as a seller, it is reasonable to understand that quality-control considerations are important. The buyer wishes to verify the nature of the goods that he has contracted to purchase. The following is an authoritative account of how the quality-control function has evolved in the Department of Defense:

> Several years ago the sole method used by the government in determining the contractor's compliance to the contract requirements was to perform product inspection. This inspection was either concurrent with the contractor's inspection, or independent of the contractor's inspection. The inspection was generally performed on a sampling basis and mostly on the finished product. In recent years it has been determined by the Department of Defense that this was not the optimum method of determining contract compliance.
>
> The thinking within DOD [Department of Defense] today supports the theory that if the contractor's quality management performs their function properly and efficiently, the product should turn out to be in compliance with contract requirements. Therefore, the government representative does not spend all of his time performing product inspection. He is now interested in quality organizational charts, responsibilities of various quality personnel, capability of quality personnel, adequacy of quality procedures and controls, and compliance to quality procedures. This evolution of the government representatives' functions has been reflected in his job title. At first he was called a Quality Inspector, then he was called a Quality Control Representative. Today, his title is Quality Assurance Representative.

The nature of the quality-control effort by the Pentagon top management has clearly altered from control of the quality of product to control of the quality of management in performing its supervisory function. The direction of development in controls is toward deep penetration into the detailed affairs of industrial production operations. When the Pentagon management undertakes to judge the "adequacy of quality procedures and controls," this automatically involves checking on the detailed production processes within the sub-enterprise.

The quality-control management practices of the Department of Defense now include the obligation of submanagements to comply with the program requirements specified in a standard military specification (MIL-Q-9858A). This regulation on quality-control requirements includes a specified program of action to assure that all work affecting quality—including such things as purchasing, handling, machining, assembling, fabricating, processing, inspecting, testing, modifying, and installing—is prescribed in clear and completely documented instructions by the submanagement. The documentation of these specifications is stipulated in order to help the central management staff check performance according to the detailed instructions.

The scope of the quality program requirements contained in MIL-Q-9858A is indicated by the topics included in the statement of requirements. These include: organization of quality-control management; initial quality planning; work instruction; records; corrective action; costs related to quality; drawings, documentation, and changes; measuring and testing equipment; production tooling used as a medium of inspection; use of contractor's inspection equipment; advanced metrology requirements; responsibility for control of purchases; purchasing data; manufacturing control over materials; production processing and fabrication; completed item inspection and testing; handling, storage, and delivery; nonconforming material; statistical quality control and analysis; and government inspection at contractor or vendor facilities.

About 9,000 men employed by the Defense Contract Administration Services are engaged in checking compliance with these regulations among military contractors in the nation. In addition to the general quality requirements, the Department of Defense has also prepared tens of thousands of specific equipment specifications. These are included in contracts in order to define the supplies being procured. Included in these specifications are details concerning inspections and tests that the contractor must perform. Characteristically, in formal contracts with submanagements, the Department of Defense further stipulates other procedures concerning: methods of processing and incorporating engineering changes; acceptable techniques for performing various environmental tests; general standards of workmanship; acceptable methods of verifying equipment reliability; requirements for using standard and special parts wherever possible; applicability and method of applying sampling procedures; and requirements for maintaining and calibrating inspection and test equipment. There is little ambiguity in the meaning of these specifications.

They require compliance by the submanagement in a host of production procedures. Compliance is controlled by DCAS. In the realm of the manufacturing process, very little is outside of control and surveillance by the top-management staff.

An industrial management makes decisions about *hiring, deploying, and paying* its employees. The top management in the Pentagon intervenes, in depth, in each of these areas of decision-making in the operation of its submanagements. In the name of national security requirements, the Pentagon requires each submanagement to formulate the procedures for checking on the political security of all personnel and to provide appropriate facilities for such operations. The selection of key managerial and technical personnel is regulated by the Pentagon management in the pre-contract evaluation of the prospective submanagement. A management and technical personnel "audit" is an essential part of contract negotiations procedures. Thereby, the top management is able to raise questions as to the adequacy of the key persons to be responsible for directing work on its behalf.

The payment of wages, in accordance with both minimum and average wage levels, is stipulated as an area for supervision (*ASPR* 12-601). The Pentagon top managers have a stake in assuring some uniformity in wage levels throughout the country. The principal unions of blue-collar and white-collar employees in military industries are organized nationally; therefore, changes in a particular enterprise are bound to be mirrored elsewhere in the country. I am advised that in contract negotiations between unions and military industry managements, when the point is reached where the local management and the local union come to terms, it often becomes necessary to bring the prospective agreement to the Pentagon central management for their approval. After all, it is they who pay the bill.

The regulation of overtime work is an example of the depth of penetration into decision-making by the Pentagon managers into the local military-industrial enterprise. The right of the Pentagon managers to intervene in the performance of overtime work is stipulated in regulations that are binding on every contractor (*ASPR* 12-102.3). Working overtime normally involves paying a premium price to the men so engaged. Thus time-and-a-half and even double- and triple-time wages are involved, depending on when the overtime work is performed. Overtime work is ordinarily required in an enterprise as a way of compensating for unpredictable events. Delay in the arrival of raw materials, breakdowns in machine parts, unusual labor shortages or absenteeism in sections of the plant—all of these may require overtime work in order to put work back on schedule. Also, overtime may be a regular feature of some operations, where a systematic miscalculation has been made in planning. Clearly, the working of overtime reflects on management procedures, and it is a response to the level of competence of management and engineering planning, and operational efficiency throughout an enterprise. As the Pentagon managers undertake responsibility for approving overtime work, they necessarily become involved in calculating the justification for overtime work. According to regulations, the justification must relate the costs of doing this work in terms of the benefits to be obtained. In many industrial situations, such a decision requires in-depth regulation and surveillance of operations of the enterprise. It has become normal for the field agents of the Pentagon management to review requests for overtime, prior to the performance of such work.

Another major aspect of intervention in personnel relations is the requirement that a contractor notify the top management of actual or potential labor disputes. This is tantamount to an invitation to participate, even if indirectly at first, in negotiations between the sub-management and the representatives of the work force.

Integration of operations, involving the great division of labor in a modern industrial plant, requires the systematic organization of work by means of various industrial engineering methods. The selection and use of these methods is regulated by the Pentagon top management (*ASPR* 1-1700). During the last years, they have been responsible for pressing the introduction of Program Evaluation and Review Technique (PERT) methods among industrial contractors. Apart from the worth of this technique in any particular case, there is always one benefit implicit in the introduction of this technique, and that is an increase in the ability of top management—or a management not on the scene—to exercise a detailed check over the conduct of operations.

Safety regulation is another sphere over which detailed control is exercised. The design of work tasks and the selection of industrial equipment involve a host of considerations, including the effects on safety of employees. The Pentagon management has stipulated that industrial contractors must conform with a set of formal safety regulations (*ASPR* 7-600).

When the government purchases standardized goods produced by many firms and bought by many parties, then a market price exists which can be readily agreed to as a benchmark for *setting prices.* However, a major part of military purchases involve goods that have no general market. In this case, the preferred method of setting a price is on the basis of cost. This approach, however, involves the government top managers in elaborate surveillance of cost categories and costing procedures in the subenterprises. The point of view of the Pentagon top managers on this question is stated in the *Defense Procurement Handbook* (p. XA2B).

A large percentage of Government procurement dollars is spent on limited-source or sole-source procurements for which no overall standards for comparison exist. For example, a contractor may have exclusive patent rights or special production techniques or other advantages. In these situations, ASPR 3-807.2 requires detailed analysis of the cost estimate as a usually necessary substitute for price competition. Cost analysis—properly conducted in the light of the contractor's situation and with a comprehensive knowledge of his particular industry—should enable the contracting officer to arrive at a price that is fair and reasonable: that is, a price that will provide a competent contractor with reasonable remuneration for the effective application of his technical, financial, and production resources to the timely delivery of the specified goods and services.

In order to implement its general policy of price-setting on the basis of cost analysis, *The Defense Procurement Handbook* devotes sixty pages to detailed instructions, establishing criteria for the diagnosis of costs in military manufacturing enterprises. (This follows the general policy defined in *ASPR* 3-807.2.) The procedures specified for cost analysis extend even to the use of particular industrial engineering techniques in estimating time required to perform work. Thus, the technique of Methods Time Measurement (MTM) is proposed as the planning device for estimating work time and labor costs.

A significant change in the location and the extent of control over cost and price estimation resulted from the Truth in Negotiation Law (P.L. 87-653), passed by the Congress in September, 1962. This law requires contractors to certify cost data submitted in contract negotiations as "accurate, complete and current." Hence, it is no longer simply the duty of the Pentagon's representative to make sure that the contracts he negotiates comply with the *Armed Services Procurement Regulations.* Under the Truth in Negotiation Law, a residual responsibility remains with the contractor, and the producing firm can be called to account under both civil and criminal liability should there be significant variance between the requirements of the *ASPR* and contractor behavior. This means that the contractor is no longer in an assured position once a contract has been negotiated and signed. Thereafter, he may be subjected to strict audit, including a determination of the accuracy of his cost data and methods used in compiling such data. Under the Truth in Negotiation Law, the contractor is open to formal procedures for repayment of a difference between cost incurred and costs that might have been incurred had methods preferred by the Pentagon top managers actually been employed.

Another major effect of the Truth in Negotiation Law is to bring the nominally private firm managers under the jurisdiction of the General Accounting Office (GAO), since the law permits the GAO to examine the costs and operations of the contracting firms. This also applies to the performance of the subcontractors. All this is probably a deterrent to grossly improper behavior. The wider effect is likely to make submanagements serving the Pentagon give careful attention to the policies and procedures by which their cost data are prepared. The examination of books, documents, papers, and other records of the contractor or subcontractor may be made up to as much as three years after final payment has been received on work performed for the Department of Defense.

It has long been recognized that control over *research and development*—its extent and detailed direction—is a crucial ingredient of industrial decision-making. Competence in research and development is a key factor in assuring the decision-power of a particular management. This is altogether reasonable, since modern industrial firms often operate in technologically-based industries. Hence, the critical ability to stay in the forefront of the "state of the art" is determined by competence in performance in the area of research and development. H. L. Nieburg, in his careful study *In the Name of Science,* has demonstrated the crucial effect of control over research and development in determining the relative position of submanagements in the military-industry field. Research and development, owing to its intrinsically "unplanned" nature, is characteristically difficult to "control." On June 7, 1962, the Department of Defense issued Instruction 3200.6 which defined research and development progression and divided it into the following categories: research, exploratory development, advance development, engineering development, management support, and operational system development. On the basis of this formulation, the top management in the Department of Defense attempted to define a series of functional groupings which its regional offices could use for controlling the progression of weapons development from early research to production stages. With this kind of control, it is theoretically possible for top management to order the curtailment of a program, even after some stages have been completed. Indeed, this has been announced as a major justification for the division of research and development into segments that can be phased into the production cycle.

With such refinement of managerial decisions, the detailed surveillance and control over the various stages of this cycle, from the very beginning to the final production of weapons, is facilitated. The use of such techniques can be justified under the following conditions: where there is research and production on great numbers of diverse weapons systems; where performance of the work is left to functionally separated managements, some oriented to commercial rather than to Pentagon goals; where it is deemed essential to apply central decision-control over operations that are geographically dispersed; where some means is required for controlling a large number of weapons-development proposals from numerous managements, each striving for enlargement of their own decision-power via new work on new weapons. While such considerations can be used to justify the introduction of central control over research and development, the effect of all this serves, independently of intention, to give the central management in the Pentagon in-depth control over the operation of thousands of industrial firms.

The *profitability* of operations in military-industry firms is not only a derived effect of cost estimating procedures; profit is also directly calculated and controlled under surveillance by the Washington top managers. Central control over the capital supply of military-contracting firms has a major effect on the profitability of their operations. The contrast is seen in profit as a percentage of sales, as against profit as a percentage of the net worth of the enterprise.

Independent investigators have come to similar conclusions: military-industry firms tend to have a lower ratio of profits to sales, as compared to civilian manufacturing firms, but a higher ratio of profits as a proportion of net worth. The reason for this is that a substantial proportion of the capital invested in military-industry work is not owned by stockholders of the local firm, but by the central management in Washington. Dr. John J. Kennedy (at Ohio State University) reported that, in 1959, profit as a percent of sales for defense firms was 2.6 percent, compared with 6.4 percent for non-defense firms. For the same enterprises, profit as a percentage of invested capital was 12.4 percent for the defense firms and 12.1 percent for the non-defense firms. The costs of a group of major military-industry firms were diagnosed by Murray L. Weidenbaum of Washington University for 1962–1965. He reported profits on sales for the defense firms as 2.6 percent and for a sample of average industrial firms as 4.6 percent. The same sample of defense firms showed a return on net worth of 17.5 percent, while the commercially-oriented firms showed a return on net worth of 10.6 percent.

Although these profit results are the consequence of many factors, they are traceably connected to the detailed regulations by which the Pentagon managers determine adequacy of profit to be paid to their submanagements (*ASPR* 3-808.1). The procedures preferred by procurement officers and contract administrators for determining profit levels primarily involve a calculation of cost components, to which various profit rates are assigned. The profit calculations have certain unique features. For example, the Pentagon management's representatives are empowered to order reimbursement of state and local taxes on profits to military contracting firms (*ASPR* 12-205.41). Studies performed by the federal government's General Accounting Office found $500 million of waste in military industrial contracts during the period May, 1963 to May, 1964. Since these studies were done on a sample representing 5 percent of Department of Defense and NASA payments, it is reasonable to infer that there was approximately $10 billion of questionable charges to the government during that one-year period, taking the population of military and space contractors as a whole.

How did such an extravaganza of contractor costs and profits make sense in terms of the avowed intentions of McNamara to purchase at minimum cost? How did it make sense in terms of the establishment and operation of an elaborate cost-surveillance system? The existence of procedures to set costs and profits does not necessarily mean that the procedure will result in low estimates of costs or profits. In fact, the contrary has been the case. The Pentagon top managers see to it that substantial profits accrue to their subsidiary managers—enough to assure financial health and growth of the subenterprises—for that financial health builds the firm, thereby enlarging the domestic part of the state-management's empire.

In May, 1969, it emerged that the state-management had known for some time that the 120 C-5A intercontinental jet transports would involve a bill of $5.2 billion, instead of the announced $3.1 billion. Announcement of this massive cost overrun was said to have been withheld from the public to protect the value of Lockheed's stock. It is also worth examining the case of the F-111 (TFX) airplane, because that particular aircraft program was controlled directly by the Office of the Secretary of Defense. Thus, the handling of this largest single contract for military aircraft will be a good indicator of what criteria take precedence in the management priorities of the Pentagon.

The original calculated cost of the F-111 program was $4.9 billion. By 1968, the cost of a 1,700-plane program would have been $14.6 billion, on the basis of official testimony to the Senate Armed Services Committee reporting cost per plane to be $8.6 million. This implied a cost overrun of $9.7 billion by 1968, against the original 1963 estimate. At that time, it was clear to me and to others that something of this sort would happen. The 1962 studies of Peck and Scherer disclosed that, on the average, final prices on large military systems had been 3.2 times initial cost estimates. In fact, in 1963 I circulated a memorandum to members of the Congress and to Washington news-men, predicting that the cost of this contract would rise to between $10 to $14 billion. This estimate was based upon previous cost performances under major military contracts and on fragmentary information on prices quoted to potential Australian buyers of the F-111 plane. For this analysis, it is essential that the significance of the profit category—and its magnitude—in terms of the major objectives of the Pentagon top managers be understood.

In the relations of the state-management chiefs to their submanagements, the rate of profit is not a reward for risk-taking, but rather a way of controlling submanagement (contractor) performance. Therefore, what is actually a bonus to the submanagement is called "profit," in accordance with the fiction of the privacy of the contractor management and the autonomy of the contractor's operations. Profit regulation is also justified by the Pentagon managers as an incentive to contractor performance. But this implies the dubious assumption that dividends to stockholders or bonus payments to management have a traceable incentive effect on the performance of the blue-collar and white-collar work forces engaged in the work itself.

No conventional rationale justifies or explains either the existence of a profit category or the escalation of costs and profits under Pentagon top-management control. The profit category must be understood here as another form of payment by the federal managers to their submanagements. This is exactly the way in which it is discussed in the *Defense Procurement Handbook*—as a regulated (cost) way of controlling contractor performance (p. 63). From this standpoint, profit is a payment to submanagement for something, that is, for accepting and complying with decisions made by the top managers in the Office of the Secretary of Defense.

People accustomed to thinking about the activities of managers and firms in terms of a free-market economy are often aroused at apparently large military-industry profits. But these practices do not produce a similar reaction from the government top managers, because they have different priorities. Their major end-in-view is not the minimization of cost for particular military goods, but rather the maintenance and enlargement of the entire military-industrial empire and their control over it.

Shipment of industrial goods, once produced, is an essential management function. For sub-firms serving the Pentagon top management, transport of finished goods is subject to control by the administrative contracting officer who is empowered, unilaterally, to alter method of shipment, packing of goods, and place of delivery.

POLICING COMPLIANCE WITH TOP MANAGEMENT POLICIES

The decision-making powers of the Pentagon top management, as stipulated in the *ASPR,* and in a virtual library of subsidiary regulations thereto, become operational by means of an elaborate policing process exercised over subsidiary managements. The policing function is performed by Administrative Contract Officers, organized in a national network under DCAS. The intensity of their direct surveillance ranges from resident administrators on the premises of the larger submanagements, to periodic visits, to occasional sampling inspections for contractors on smaller projects.

Running parallel to the system of direct surveillance is an elaborate network of documented reporting. For example, the prime contractor of the Titan-III missile system submitted, biweekly, reports on 2,500 key events, indicating time-and-cost progress. This sort of elaborate reporting is facilitated by the application of PERT time-and-cost scheduling. In 1962, independent studies disclosed that the management of one major contractor submitted 1,411 reports to the central office controllers.

Detailed reporting of this sort is part of the normal operation of the "progress information and evaluation" systems requirements of the *ASPR,* administered by DCAS. The Pentagon's regulations specify preferred internal cost systems for the guidance of submanagements (*ASPR* 3-800). Department of Defense Form No. 375 is the basic form required for reporting on the progress of manufacturing production by military contractors. *The Defense Procurement Handbook,* the basic manual for Administrative Contract Officers, recommends the following types of regular reports in order to implement the requirements of progress information and evaluation systems: production schedules; monthly progress reports (DOD Form 375); material

Reports Submitted by One Contractor to the Government in One Year, by Functional Area

Engineering 396
Manufacturing Controls 94
Manufacturing Engineering 45
Factory 16
Controller 150
Materials 133
Quality Control 30
Customer Service 512
Facilities 35

TOTAL 1,411

SOURCE: John Joseph Kennedy, *Description and Analysis of the Organization of the Firm in the Defense Weapon Contract Industry,* (Ph.D. dissertation, Ohio State University), University Microfilms, Ann Arbor, Mich., 1962, p. 102.

inspection and receiving reports (DOD Form 250); progress reports according to the specialized requirements of particular military services; status reports on research and development work—including the number and names of key personnel, facilities used, direction of the work, experiments being conducted, and the latest work done; financial management reports (DOD Form 1097); reports on cost incurred on contract (DOD Form 1177). In addition, Administrative Contract Officers, in fulfilling the control requirement of top management, are directed to conduct progress evaluation conferences and reviews and to superintend the installation and operation of special scheduling and cost control systems, as required.

In large industrial firms, the extension of the scope and intensity of decision-making by the central administrative office is normal, an intrinsic feature of this type of organization. This extension process has been taking place in the management of military industry in the new central administrative office established within the Department of Defense. That this central office bears such titles as Defense Supply Agency, Defense Contract Administration Services, or Defense Audit Administration—rather than Central Office of the U.S. Military Establishment—is irrelevant. The critical fact is that the function of the central office is described by this last designation. Thus, it is not surprising that in major areas of management control, the trend has been toward increasing both the scope and the intensity of control by the central management over subsidiary managements. This is further revealed in the important sphere of quality control. The change from control over the characteristics of the finished product, to control over the management organization that carries out the quality-control function, is an extension of the scope of decision-making. An intensification of decision-making is also indicated by the formal regulations which make detailed production operations, as well as the equipment necessary to that production, into relevant parts of the quality assurance program.

The function of capital supply is another crucial aspect of decision-making that indicates extension of central managerial control. Among alternative possibilities for financing its industrial production, the Pentagon managers declare a preference for various forms of progress payments. This way of supplying capital involves intensive examination of records, and this, in turn, requires that the record-keeping systems themselves be controlled. Similarly, the requirements for record-keeping by submanagements have been greatly intensified by the specification that PERT be employed, not only for the scheduling of time but also for keeping track of cost.

The extension of the pattern of decision-making, by means of the creation of the new central office in the Department of Defense, is at variance with intentions stated at various points in the *Armed Service Procurement Regulations* and in the *Defense Procurement Handbook*. These policy volumes affirm a reliance on the private enterprise of the contractor for the fulfillment of the requirements of government work. In reality, however, private enterprise has been reinterpreted to mean the behavior of these persons (nominally private) acting within the framework of a reward-and-penalty system designed and operated by the new central office. The degree to which the submanagement meets the requirements set from above becomes the measure of his "enterprise."

Once this extension of decision-making has become a regular aspect of the operation of Pentagon top management, with no independent market competition in existence to act as a constraint, and with profit based upon arbitrary calculation of cost, then it follows that there will be fantastic cost and profit excesses (as noted). Indeed, the difference between high cost and high profit becomes blurred. Investments in research and development, which in the private commercial firm must come out of accumulated profits, are counted as costs in the arithmetic of the military-industrial subfirm and are paid for as such by the top management.

The case of the F-111 airplane is again noteworthy because the managerial details of this program were controlled directly by the top managers of the Pentagon. Once the designated contractor proved to be a disastrous performer—off schedule on the production of planes, planes built with as much as six tons of excess weight—there was no cutting of losses and shifting to another contractor for the production of the same sort of plane or of another type of aircraft. Either of these moves would have meant a major cutback in the scale of operations of the General Dynamics Company, which had become a major factor in the network of management and industrial resources operated under Department of Defense top management. Top management preferred to see its costs rise three times on an immense contract, rather than suffer a reduction in the scope of its industrial empire which a financial debacle of General Dynamics would have caused.

By means of this contract alone, a large part of the publicly heralded cost-effectiveness gains under McNamara's central office management of the Department of Defense was wiped out. The primary industrial effect of the control system over submanagements, as operated from the Department of Defense, is not to reduce costs but to extend control. The state-management extends the scope and intensity of its decision-power independently of the cost-minimization, marketing, or profit-gathering operations of a traditional market-oriented management.

Here is the summary of key functional contrasts between the military-industrial complex and the state-management. As a market, the complex set prices; the state-management, because it is a management, regulates cost, price, and profit, and can set priorities independent of price. The complex (market), to the extent that it contained elements of competition, could be entered by the autonomous decision of any firm; the state-management opens new divisions only after formal application and review. The complex made no investment decisions, but the state-management does. As a market, the complex did no direct decision-making on production. The state-management is heavily engaged as a production decision-maker. The complex was loosely organized; the state-management is highly organized, with formal allocation of powers. Formal evaluation of operations was no part of the complex, but is an integral element of the state-management's control system. The complex (market) did not plan, but the state-management does elaborate planning. Finally, the complex, as a market, had no built-in mechanism of expansion. The state-management is strongly shaped by the presence of the normal managerial-occupational imperative for success through differential enlargement of decision-power. Thereby, the state-management has a built-in engine for expansion of its power.

3

Extension of Control over Means of Production

In an industrial society, people depend for most of their goods and services on organized, specialized production. That is why decision-power over production affects many facets of life—by means of those things selected for, or omitted from, production, and by the design, quality, and price of those things produced. The very size of the production empire controlled by the Pentagon limits the sorts of goods that can be made available to society in general. The scope of the decision-power exercised by state-management through the Department of Defense is suggested merely by the size of its budget. For fiscal year 1970, this budget has, at this writing, been proposed at $83 billion —exceeding the Gross National Product of most of the nations of the earth. During 1968, the Pentagon bought $44 billion of goods and services, making that management the largest of its kind in the world.

The federal government takes about half of corporate profits for its use. More than half of these tax billions, in turn, are controlled by the state-management. Thereby, the state-management concentrates control over capital to a degree undreamed of by the economists of private financial and industrial capitalism. The state-management has pre-empted the leading role in the control of industrial capital, once held by the chiefs of private industry and finance.

In this chapter, I will delimit and explore several dimensions of the Department of Defense empire at home and abroad: the industrial network; manpower; control over research and development; and the worldwide sales system for military goods.

In 1950, that part of the federal budget allocated to military purposes was $12.9 billion, or 32.7 percent of the total federal budget. For the fiscal year 1969, the military budget was $81 billion, or 56 percent of the federal government's total budget of $146 billion. From 1961 to 1969, United States spending for military purposes amounted to $546 billion. Over that ten-year period, approximately 10 percent of the GNP has been devoted to military purposes. This is consistent with a reported top-level policy decision, made during the 1950s, that the government of the United States ought to be spending about 10 percent of its GNP for military and related purposes.

It is likely that the total outlay for military purposes exceeded the Defense Department budget. Many activities that serve the Pentagon are formally carried out by other government agencies: the Atomic Energy Commission; the National Aeronautics and Space Administration; the Central Intelligence Agency and other intelligence organizations; nominally civilian agencies like the Department of Commerce; parts of the Executive Office; and others.

Another way to measure the resources used for military purposes in the United States is to calculate the amount on a per capita basis; $439 per capita would equal the 1969 military budget.

As of June, 1969, property owned directly by the Department of Defense amounted to $202 billion. This included land, buildings, production equipment, offices, communications facilities, airports, and the value of purchased military equipment. By 1969, the Department of Defense owned twenty-nine million acres of land. The scope of resources controlled by the Department of Defense is further revealed in the size of the contracts awarded in a given fiscal year. Thus, for fiscal year 1967, $44.6 billion in contracts were awarded by the Department of Defense.

As one examines various financial statements—for example, the budgets proposed for 1967—one finds that this amount is not accounted for as being spent in that year. There is a difference between new spending authority voted as part of a budget and actual spending. In "The Fiscal Year 1969–1973 Defense Program and the 1969 Defense Budget," Robert McNamara listed the unspent balances at the end of each fiscal year. Thus, for the fiscal years 1967, 1968, and 1969, respectively, the unobligated balances planned for the end of those years amounted to $13, $11, and $11 billion.

The contracts awarded by the Department of Defense during fiscal year 1967 involved fifteen million purchasing actions. This bears directly on the size of the staff needed to administer this industrial empire.

Another aspect of the Department of Defense operations is the scale of the "post exchange" operation. In this auxiliary service function, the Department of Defense ranks as the third-largest retail distributor in the nation, exceeded in sales volume only by the Sears Roebuck Company, and the A&P Food Stores. The size of this "retailers" market (uniformed and civilian military personnel and families) is larger than the market created by the combined populations of Philadelphia, Boston, Detroit, Pittsburgh, Cleveland, San Francisco, and St. Louis.

The Department of Defense is also a major factor in housing construction. Thus, housing for military families involved expenditures in 1965, 1966, and 1967 of $1.8 billion. This exceeded total spending during the same period by the federal government for all other public housing.

The industrial contracting and base operations conducted by the Department of Defense have profound effects on the economic fortunes of particular regions in the United States. A recent study indicates that, during the period from 1952 to 1962, military outlays accounted for more than 20 percent of the total economic growth of states such as California and Mississippi. At the same time, the growth of some of the key east north central states, like Michigan, Wisconsin and Indiana, was severely curtailed by cuts in defense spending. This is owed to the fact that while taxes used for military purposes are collected as part of individual and corporate income taxes, and account for more than half of tax expenditures, there is no necessary relationship between tax receipts and tax expenditures for military purposes, state by state. This inequality, and the effects it has on economic development, have raised Congressional as well as other pressures, compelling the Department of Defense to give elaborate attention to its reports concerning *Military Prime Contract Awards by State and Region*. Thus, the Department of Defense publishes annual reports of the above title, specifying expenditures for major classes of military research and production by state and region.

It is noteworthy that during the Vietnam war the 5-year-force-structure budgeteers of the Department of Defense were unable to forecast any reduction in the budget of the Department of Defense following an end to that war. That is, owing to an accumulation of unfunded projects for new military systems and new hardware, the number of projects deferred by the Vietnam war military spending would not be reduced. The idea here is that even after the end of the Vietnam war, the reduction of $30 billion in annual outlays that it entails would be offset, and then some, by spending for new military systems.

Finally, in assessing the economic authority exercised by the Department of Defense, it is important to examine U.S. military spending on a standardized per-capita basis, compared with such outlays in other countries. Professor Emile Benoit of Columbia University has estimated the real cost per capita (measured in dollars of equivalent purchasing power) of military budgets in the principal countries of the world. The following enumeration speaks for itself.

Real Cost per Capita (1966)

United States	$322
U.S.S.R.	191
Germany (West German Federal Republic)	79
United Kingdom	105
France	94
Mainland China	9

Among a group of countries including Italy, Canada, India, Japan, Poland, Sweden, Czechoslovakia, Australia, Spain, Indonesia, The East German Democratic Republic, Yugoslavia, Brazil, and the Netherlands—the range is from $3 per capita in India to a high of $132 per capita in Sweden. On the whole, for this group of "secondary" powers, average outlay is $15 per capita. This compares with the U.S.-U.S.S.R. average outlay of $256 per capita. Clearly, the Department of Defense, with its outlay of $322 per capita, leads the world in military spending, with 67 percent more military spending than the U.S.S.R.

INDUSTRY

American industry contracted for $44.6 billion of work for the Department of Defense during the 1967 fiscal year. These activities were elaborately planned by the Joint Chiefs of Staff for each of the separate services and were finally translated into industry contracts by the Defense Supply Agency and related organizations. These activities within the Department of Defense actually represent only one part of the military planning effort in the United States. It is the "National Plan for Emergency Preparedness," published by the Office of Emergency Planning (in the Office of the President), which gives an outline of the planning to be done for the United States during and after major military operations.

Department of Defense spending for industrial and related purposes is only a part of the federal government's military activity. For example, during 1964, the budget of the Atomic Energy Commission was $2.7 billion, of which primarily military operations cost the AEC $2 billion, or 75 percent of its budget; the operations of NASA have also reflected a substantial military priority. Harold Brown, then Secretary of the Air Force, interpreting Russian motivation in the space race, said: "It is the same mixture that we ourselves have . . . I will put military goals reasonably high among them." H. L. Nieburg, in his volume *In the Name of Science,* noted that during the last year of the Kennedy administration, a special effort was made to identify projects of an Air Force character apparently being carried out under the formal administration of NASA. Said Nieburg: "During this period McNamara set out to identify Air Force projects in the vast maze of NASA's contracts and bring them under control." General Curtis LeMay (retired) stated on January 23, 1967, that he did not think that the United States is: ". . . in space for a peaceful purpose

. . . The Russians are not in space for peaceful purposes" either, he added. "They have a program that is militarily orientated. If we are going to keep peace in space we will have to have a police force out there." About 94 percent of NASA activity is oriented toward the Apollo, space race, moon race activity, as against research-oriented activity outside the earth's surface.

Pentagon control over industry is enhanced by the concentration of activity within particular firms. This is shown in the annual listing of "100 Principal Military Contractors According to the Net Value of Military Prime Contract Awards." In 1967, the 100 largest contractors accounted for some 65 percent of all military contracts awarded. The first 10 contractors on this list included: McDonnell-Douglas Corp., General Dynamics Corp., Lockheed Aircraft Corp., General Electric Company, United Aircraft Corp., Boeing Co., North American Aviation, American Telephone and Telegraph Co., General Motors, and finally, Ling-Temco-Vought. These ten firms accounted for 30 percent of total Department of Defense spending among industrial firms.

The relation of the Department of Defense to U.S. industry was strongly affected by the development of Systems Management Contracting during the 1950s and 1960s. This mode of contracting allows a particular firm to undertake over-all management direction of very large military industrial programs by means of the establishment of a sub-central office under Pentagon control. The Air Force inaugurated this sort of activity during the 1950s. By this means, the Air Force could quickly accumulate a far-flung network of industrial activities to serve its operations, in the absence of in-house research and in-house military arsenals of its own (which the Army had).

The Air Force came out of the Second World War as a major organization, but without the Army's sort of research and development capability. In order to inaugurate with speed many new military-industrial programs, the Air Force invented the device of designating private firms, or newly-created "non-profit" organizations, as managers over major-unit military programs. This illustrates the sustained use of negotiated contracts, as contrasted with competitive bidding. Over a period of two decades, negotiated contracts (as against advertised and competitively bid contracts) amounted to 86 percent of the

Pentagon total. It is also noteworthy that from 1948 to 1966, there has been no dramatic alteration in the proportion of military-industrial work negotiated.

Who controls military industry? What part of military-serving industry is private? The 100-largest military-industry firms are almost all privately-owned enterprises. But control must be differentiated from ownership. The managers of corporate industry do not own the resources of their firms, they only control them. The formally private military-industry firms operate on behalf of a monopoly customer, with no alternative customer in sight. This marketing dependency reinforces the direct managerial control system.

This market dependency is revealed by the following list of principal military contractors, showing their sales to the Department of Defense from 1961 to 1967, and the percent of total sales from each firm to the Department of Defense.

Prime Military Contracts Awards 1960–1967 to U.S. Companies, for Firms Totaling More than $1 Billion in This 7-year Period.
(In millions of dollars)

	7-YR. TOTAL	PERCENT OF TOTAL SALES
1. Lockheed Aircraft	10,619	88
2. General Dynamics	8,824	67
3. McDonnell-Douglas	7,681	75
4. Boeing Co.	7,183	54
5. General Electric	7,066	19
6. No. American-Rockwell	6,265	57
7. United Aircraft	5,311	57
8. American Tel. & Tel.	4,167	9
9. Martin-Marietta	3,682	62
10. Sperry-Rand	2,923	35
11. General Motors	2,818	2
12. Grumman Aircraft	2,492	67
13. General Tire	2,347	37
14. Raytheon	2,324	55
15. AVCO	2,295	75

(*Continued on next page*)

	7-YR. TOTAL	PERCENT OF TOTAL SALES
16. Hughes	2,200	u
17. Westinghouse Electric	2,177	13
18. Ford (Philco)	2,064	3
19. RCA	2,019	16
20. Bendix	1,915	42
21. Textron	1,798	36
22. Ling-Temco-Vought	1,744	70
23. Internat. Tel. & Tel.	1,650	19
24. I.B.M.	1,583	7
25. Raymond International *	1,568	u
26. Newport News Shipbuilding	1,520	90+
27. Northrop	1,434	61
28. Thiokol	1,301	96
29. Standard Oil of N.J.	1,277	2
30. Kaiser Industries	1,255	45
31. Honeywell	1,129	24
32. General Telephone	1,124	25
33. Collins Radio	1,105	65
34. Chrysler	1,091	4
35. Litton	1,085	25
36. Pan Am. World Air.	1,046	44
37. F.M.C.	1,045	21
38. Hercules	1,035	31

u—Unavailable.
* Includes Morrison-Knudsen, Brown & Root, and J. A. Jones Construction Co.
SOURCE: Dept. of Defense, Directorate for Statistical Services.

At the top of the list are the Lockheed, General Dynamics, McDonnell-Douglas, and General Electric companies. The first three are overwhelmingly Pentagon subfirms. General Electric, however, averaged only 19 percent of its sales to the military. Whereas the percentage of sales to the Department of Defense has been a minor part of the total activity of the firm, that activity is characteristically concentrated in separate divisions and facilities and is managed by separately designated managements. The 19 percent of General Electric's activity for the Department of Defense was not spread among the large number of General Electric divisions. Rather, certain divisions of General Electric specialized heavily or solely in military contract work.

The idea of the privacy of military-industrial managements is a form of well-cultivated fiction which conforms with the legal privacy-in-property right but not with the reality of the prime managerial control operating out of the Pentagon. An important instrument of Pentagon control is direct ownership of the key production facilities used by major military contractors. The following list of Pentagon-owned industrial production equipment (located in 1,900 companies) shows that 209,000 pieces of industrial production equipment, valued at $2.5 billion, were utilized by industrial contractors, as of November 30, 1967. The state-management controlling (and owning) this basic industrial equipment is clearly one of the largest, if not the largest, single management of metal-working operations in the world.

15 Largest Holders of Government-Owned Industrial Production Equipment, 1967

	NUMBER OF PIECES	COST
General Electric	9,011	$ 114,752,148
North American Aviation	8,924	105,636,333
AVCO	6,395	89,633,519
General Motors	6,014	83,979,781
General Dynamics	7,298	79,174,713
Lockheed	8,359	77,068,029
TRW	3,495	64,706,654
Douglas Air	4,777	57,837,398
ALCOA	457	47,505,011
Aerojet	3,666	46,119,900
Ling-Temco-Vought	2,964	42,047,137
United Air	2,141	37,115,005
Boeing	3,286	36,915,820
Curtis-Wright	2,173	36,661,534
Raytheon	4,329	32,896,692
Total for 1,900 (estimated) companies	209,598	$2,578,627,370

SOURCE: U.S. Congress, Joint Economic Committee, *Economy in Government Procurement and Property Management*, Washington, D.C., 1968

The state-management is an extensive user of automatic data-processing equipment. The U.S. government, with the Department of Defense having a lion's share of this activity, has been buying or leasing $3 billion worth of data-processing equipment each year. Studies of the aerospace industry disclose that the largest part of the heavy equipment of that industry has been financed by the federal government. Thus, the Department of Defense owns 36 percent of the large-capacity profile milling machines of the nation, and 58 percent of this class of equipment that is numerically (automatically) controlled.

By 1967, the submanagements working under the Pentagon had been supplied with $14.7 billion of government-owned property, as follows:

Government Property Held by Contractors
(*as of June 30, 1967*)
(*In billions of dollars*)

Industrial plant equipment (mostly metalworking equipment costing over $1,000)	$ 2.6
Other plant equipment costing less than $1,000 (furniture, office machines, etc.)	2.0
Materials, electronic gear, cloth, duck, sub-assemblies, parts, hardware items, etc.	4.7
Real property (buildings, plants, etc.)	2.4
Special tooling and test equipment	3.0
TOTAL	$14.7

SOURCE: Joint Economic Committee, Congress of the United States, Report of the Subcommittee on Economy in Government, *Economy in Government Procurement and Property Management,* Washington, D.C., April, 1968.

Typically, this property is intermixed with privately-owned material and gives the state-management major leverage over the submanagement.

There is no exact compilation of the number of firms involved in the industrial network controlled by the Pentagon. This is because thousands of prime contractors subcontract for work. In individual instances, it has been possible to trace out four layers and more of subcontractors. Thus, if 15 to 20 thousand firms are involved in prime contracts, then the total number of industrial and other firms engaged by the Department of Defense is a multiple of that by at least three times. For example: one version of an antiballistic missile system (Nike-X) was reckoned to cost about $5 billion (to be manufactured within five or six years). It is estimated that 15 thousand companies would produce hardware and support services for this system alone. For this project, the general system-integrator is the Bell Telephone Laboratories and the prime contractor for manufacturing the Western Electric Company. However, for the performance of this work, Western Electric would subcontract more than 60 percent of the new awards to some 3,000 companies in nearly every state of the union. Thus, major subcontracts during 1969 are scheduled to include $59 million to General Electric, $60 million to Raytheon, $55 million to McDonnell-Douglas, $35 million to Martin-Marietta, and $9 million each to RCA, Texas Instrument, and Motorola.

In its *Defense Industry Bulletin* (February, 1966), the Department of Defense gave an account of the layers of primary, secondary, and tertiary contractors on the C-141 project, a large Air Force jet freighter constructed by the Lockheed Corporation in its plants in Marietta, Georgia. The Department of Defense announced:

Major subcontractors and subsystem contracts on the Starlifter are shared by 33 companies over the U.S. Whatever the total of the employees of the subcontractors and vendors who draw their pay checks from funds derived from the C-141, it can be multiplied by 5 to give a truer picture of the number whose livelihood is affected by this defense program. This is because in the communities involved there are grocers, clothiers, furniture dealers, appliance dealers, etc. who feed, clothe, house and generally care for the needs of those who are working on a defense contract.

After receiving the prime contract on the air frame for the C-141 for the Air Force Systems Command Aeronautical Systems Division, Lockheed's plant in Georgia sublet the wing to the Avco Corporation in Nashville, Tenn. in competitive bidding. The wing includes a fuel pump. The Tenn. subcontractor in Avco obtained a fuel pump from Tesco in Bedford, Ohio. To build a fuel pump

Tesco needed, among other things, a switch and a cannon plug. The Ohio firm bought the switch from the Micro Devices Co. of Dayton, Ohio, and the cannon plug from a concern in Los Angeles. . . .

A tracing of the path of the defense dollar through the subcontracting and vending program involving other parts of the Starlifter would find it in virtually every state going from prime to major contractors into the third and fourth level, to vendors and subsuppliers ad infinitum. For example, Rohr Corp. of Chula Vista, Calif., largest C-141 subcontractor, sublets 49 percent of its contracts on engine nacelles. Companies receiving this 49 percent from Rohr, in turn, sublet 40 percent of their part to other firms. Rohr subcontracts at the time the study was made totaled $85.9 million. Since then additional billions are being negotiated for follow-on C-141s.

An important element in the state-management's control over industry is the Pentagon's ability to start new projects that sustain activity in its sub-firms. Thus, the Department of Defense, and Secretary of Defense McNamara himself, played a leading part in sponsoring the supersonic airplane project. This project, with an estimated cost of $4,500 million, would be a major new activity for firms that have supplied missile systems and major aircraft to the Department of Defense. The supersonic plane project has been pressed for several years despite the inability of the sponsors to cope with such problems as sonic boom and its destructive effects on structures, ships, and natural features of the earth's surface. In the midst of considerable doubt as to the commercial economics of the supersonic transport, this project was given top industrial priority, ranking it with military first-priority industrial work. All this smacks of self-interested sponsorship of crackpot technology, one of whose most marked effects is to provide a major new activity for a sector of the state-management's industrial empire.

The supersonic transport is one in a large series of projects sponsored by the state-management, the same management that has invested hundreds of billions of dollars in nuclear overkill systems without any rational or defined limit. In 1963, several colleagues and I called attention to the existence of massive overkill capacity in the U.S. armed forces—including an ability to destroy the population-industrial centers of the U.S.S.R. 1,250 times over (allowing 50 percent failure to deliver warheads). When you vary the assumption, you change the estimate of overkill. But these differences are meaningless: there is no significant difference in human terms between an overkill of 2, or 200, or 2,000. The existence of an overkill buildup was finally confirmed by the Department of Defense itself, but there was no response in terms of cutting off new money for these purposes. That would have meant cutting down the industrial empire. Clearly, it is always possible to develop a more accurate missile, a more powerful warhead, a more efficient fuel in power-weight ratio, and the like. As these "improvements" operate in the overkill range, these changes are without military meaning. However, as contributions toward maintaining the decision-power of the state-management, such "improvements" in military technology are obviously serviceable.

MANPOWER

Within the 1968 labor force in the United States of 74 million men and women, the Department of Defense controls the largest block of manpower under one management. The 10 percent of the labor force directly involved with the Department of Defense includes 1.2 million civilian employees of the Pentagon and 3.5 million men and women in uniform. In 1968, the Pentagon employed 1,384,744 civilians and 1,205,654 U.S. military personnel in foreign countries. The Pentagon had "real military property" in 2,257 "locations" in countries outside the U.S. These bases cost the U.S. $6.05 billion in capital outlay, and they cost about $4.8 billion a year to maintain and operate. A labor force of 3 million in the U.S. has been estimated by the Department of Labor as being directly involved in military industry. This estimate of numbers involved in military industrial work is probably an understatement of the number so engaged, because it is difficult to account for people in the network of multiple subcontracting characteristic of military-industry operations. Also, these estimates of persons acting for the Department of Defense do not account for the men and women in federal agencies such as the AEC, the CIA, NASA, and others, who are acting primarily on behalf of the military establishment. For example, by the end of fiscal year 1968, 270,000 people in industry, universities, and government installations were working for NASA. Another way of seeing the magnitude of operations of the state-management is to note that the California Institute of Technology, whose staff administers and conducts many research and development projects for the Pentagon, has been spending more federal tax dollars per year than is required for the operation of the entire legislative branch of the federal government.

A most important aspect of the manpower engaged by the Department of Defense is its occupational mix. On the whole, people engaged in defense industries are substantially more highly skilled as a group than those engaged in civilian industry or the rest of the economy as a whole. For example, of those engaged in defense work, about 16 percent were classed as professionals, compared with 13 percent in the labor force as a whole. Also, 21 percent in the military-industry force were skilled blue-collar workers, as compared with 13.4 percent in the overall labor force. The most striking aspect of concentration of skill on behalf of the Pentagon management is seen in the employment of scientists and engineers. In the aerospace companies in 1960, 106,000 scientists and engineers were employed—12 percent of the total employed in the United States that year. This number is scheduled to amount to 194,000, or 20 percent of the total industry labor force, by 1970. A further indication of the market pressure for the employment of scientists and engineers by the military defense industry is the number of column-inches of scientist and engineer employment advertising in a recent Sunday issue of *The New York Times:* 1,900 column-inches of advertising were published for scientist and engineer employment in aerospace industry—45 percent of the total professional employment advertising space. The federal government itself has been a major employer of engineers and scientists, with a total of 149,000 in 1966. Of these, 81,000—more than half—were employed by the Department of Defense and the Atomic Energy Commission.

The state-management is involved in varied relations with trade unions. Washington offices of the AFL-CIO and affiliated unions are often petitioners to the state-management for contract assignments, thereby supplementing the efforts of local managements. The state-management is able to use national unions in its efforts to sell the

Congress and the country on new military systems. Late in 1968, the Pentagon ran a set of briefings on the antiballistic missile system for the unions in the Building and Construction Trades Department and the Industrial Union Department, of the AFL-CIO. Shortly thereafter, the International Brotherhood of Electric Workers opened the pages of *The Electric Workers Journal* (March, 1969) to give a vivid exposition of the Sentinel system—its military and construction characteristics. The IBEW members were informed:

> . . . the construction phase at each site will average about 22 months [and that] at the peak of construction, the Corps of Engineers contractor will have between 900 and 1,375 construction workers on a single site, depending on which of two types of installations are involved.

The January, 1969, issue of *The Carpenter* conveyed the same good news to the members of the carpenters' union. In this way, the unions and their members are taught to view the state-management as the employer, apart from the identity of the submanagement (contractor) in charge at any given locality.

The role of the Pentagon as a controller of manpower has included rapid extension into areas ordinarily understood as the province of other departments and levels of governments. Soon after the Second World War, the Department of Defense desegregated manpower within its own forces, and thereafter pressed for desegregation of housing in areas surrounding military bases. Owing to the number of military bases and the large number of men involved, this immediately involved the Department of Defense in affecting housing policy over a wide civilian area. Ordinarily, one would understand the problem of enforcing compliance with the Constitution and with provisions of housing laws to be the problem of the relevant civilian agencies of government, not a responsibility of the DOD.

During 1968, the Pentagon started programs to develop new forms of building technology. These are to be applied directly to the construction of buildings on military bases. This entry of the Department of Defense into building technology, however, is also being done in the name of developing new technology for the housing industry.

The Pentagon operates a large medical service. But it is only recently that the Pentagon has set up formal programs for researching the design and the administration of hospital facilities. The state-management has declared that it is concerned with developing technology in this sphere and making it available for the rest of the society. With its unmatched budgets and easy access to more capital in the name of defense, the Department of Defense could even take a lead in this sphere of work, presumably the responsibility of the designated Department of Health, Education and Welfare.

Under Secretary of Defense McNamara, the Department started "Project 100,000." This was the project designation for a program to train for literacy and related skills the considerable number of young men who have been found by Selective Service testing to be unsuited for military duty, owing to inadequate education. Obviously the Department of Defense would benefit from being able to draw on a newly enlarged and more competent manpower pool. It is also clear that the Department of Defense is, therefore, entering into a sphere of activity, namely basic education, which until recently was the province of local governments in the United States.

During the last years, the state-management has also undertaken responsibility for employment levels in regional economic development in the United States by explicitly formulating criteria favoring preferential contract allocation to, and plant location in, economically underdeveloped areas. This pressure has carried over into the network of Pentagon contractors. By March, 1968, the Republic Aircraft Corporation proposed a program for revised construction of its F-105 plane. Part of its proposal included "a plan to hire, train, and motivate several thousand of the nation's hard-core unemployed as part of the subcontracting activity. More than 2,000 of these jobless will be hired and trained as production workers." In mid-1968, the Defense Department announced that it had hired more than 50,000 young men for summer work, about 70 percent of them from city slum and poverty areas. Civil police activities have lately been the subject for Defense Department development, in the name of helping to suppress domestic violence. The Pentagon has also sponsored Project Transition. This is a program to teach skills for civilian jobs to young men who are about to complete their military service. Occupational training is a traditional military function for military occupations. It is something new, however, for the Department of Defense to undertake responsibility for civilian occupational training on a large scale. Finally, these extensions of state-management control into extra-military functions by the Department of Defense have recently been formulated as policy. Secretary of Defense Clifford stated in October, 1968: ". . . some measure of social utility should be included in the award of industrial contracts." Defense Department regulations prohibit it from awarding a contract that involves paying a premium to relieve economic ills regardless "of the significant contributions such a contract might make to the hard-core unemployment problem and the total national interest." The Secretary of Defense said that "the time has come to re-examine this legislation." The editors of *Business Week* commented on this policy announcement, saying that "the Pentagon has the money and muscle to move in these areas which other government agencies may lack." The state-management, controlling the unmatched budgets and unobligated funds of the Department of Defense, is able to extend its decision-power into areas far removed from its formal and ostensible central defense mission.

RESEARCH AND DEVELOPMENT

More than one-half of the research money of the nation, and as much as two-thirds of the research and development, scientific and engineering talent are at work for the state-management. By the end of 1964, after three years of the Kennedy-Johnson administration, a Congressional Select Committee on Government Research, chaired by Representative Carl Elliott, reported that:

> . . . in the world of our probable future, our ability as a nation to compete will depend to a great extent on the efficacy of today's research into our grave social and economic problems. . . . In the sense of mission-oriented programs, we are spending greatly on defense, space, and nuclear missions and virtually nothing on the mission of securing our probable competitive future . . . apart from strictly economic problems many of our social problems have become very costly. In comparison to the dollars spent on the space program we can well afford some additional pennies for research into these and many other areas.

The committee further stated:

. . . it is critical that the government avoid policies or procedures which lead to inefficient deployment or stockpiling of trained personnel. Manpower cost is as important as fiscal cost in consideration of major programs. But this has not been a significant criterion in major program choices to date. The huge technical programs of NASA, DOD, and AEC have absorbed large numbers of engineers and scientists. Yet no one at the time of decision has reckoned their worth on these programs as opposed to their alternative use in teaching, private industry, or other government programs.

These judgments by a moderate Congressman from Alabama reflected an analysis of government sponsorship of research after a long period during which priority was given to the military uses of engineering and scientific manpower.

Ever since his famous farewell speech (Appendix B), the late General Eisenhower has been repeatedly quoted as calling attention to the "prospect of domination of the nation's scholars by federal employment, project allocations, and the power of money." Less attention has been given to the role he had played in initiating the "Military-Industrial-Complex" by institutionalizing control of the Department of Defense over industrial and university research and development activity in the nation. In a memorandum dated April 27, 1946, General Eisenhower outlined a general policy on scientific and technological resources as military assets and defined the desired relationship between the Department of Defense and research and development functions in the nation. The issuance of this policy memorandum (Appendix A for full text) was, effectively, the founding act of what the General (fifteen years later) termed the "Military-Industrial-Complex." Eisenhower announced in 1946:

> The future security of the nation demands that all those civilian resources which by conversion or redirection constitute our main support in time of emergency be associated closely with the activities of the Army in time of peace. . . . In order to ensure the full use of our national resources in an emergency, the following general policies will be put into effect:
>
> 1. The Army must have civilian assistance in military planning as well as for the production of weapons. Effective long-range military planning can only be done in the light of predicted devel-

opments in science, and technology. As further scientific achievements accelerate the tempo and expand the area of our operations, this interrelationship will become of even greater importance . . .

2. Scientists and industrialists must be given the greatest possible freedom to carry out their research . . .

3. The possibility of utilizing some of our industrial and technological resources as organic parts of our military structure in time of emergency should be carefully examined . . .

4. Within the Army we must separate responsibility for research and development from the functions of procurement, purchase, storage and distribution . . .

5. Officers of all arms and services must become fully aware of the advantages which the Army can derive from the close integration of civilian talent with military plans and developments . . .

In general, the more we can achieve the objectives indicated above with respect to the cultivation, support and direct use of outside resources, the more energy will we have left to devote to strictly military problems for which there are no outside facilities or which for special security reasons can only be handled by the military. In fact it is our responsibility deliberately to examine all outside resources as to adequacy, diversity and geographical distribution and to insure their full utilization as factors of security. It is our job to take the initiative to promote the development of new resources if our national security indicates the need. It is our duty to support broad research programs in educational institutions, in industry, and in whatever field might be of importance to the Army . . .

In the interest of cultivating to the utmost the integration of civilian and military resources and of securing the most effective unified direction of our research and development activities, this responsibility is being consolidated in a separate section on the highest War Department level . . . By developing the general policies outlined above under the leadership of the Director of Research and Development the Army will demonstrate the value it places upon science and technology and further the integration of civilian and military resources.

From 1946 to 1969, the military establishment has pursued the general policy line of the Eisenhower memorandum. More than one-half of the research and development technical talent of the nation has been deployed, directly and indirectly, in the service of the Pentagon. Single firms, nominally private, have become employers of enormous technical staffs. North American Aviation could boast in August, 1966: "Leonardo da Vinci advanced science in nearly every known field of his day. What would he have been able to do if he had been able to work with 16,000 scientists and engineers . . ." That is the number of scientists and engineers engaged in diverse fields under the direction of the North American Aviation management.

During 1967, the federal government supplied $15 billion, or 63 percent, of the nation's total research and development outlays of $24 billion. Within the federal sphere, the Department of Defense and the military supporting activities of the AEC and NASA have accounted for about 80 percent of the government total.

Government financing has supported the rapid growth of research activities in industry and in non-profit institutions. This was especially the case during the period from 1956 to 1963, when government spending for total research increased by 20 percent, or more, almost every year. After 1963, the rate of growth began to diminish. By 1965, with increased pressure on the budget from the Vietnam war, the growth of federal research outlays was sharply curtailed. Suddenly, research laboratories became highly vulnerable to federal budget decisions. Until recently, dependence on federal support for research was a central feature of the physical sciences and the engineering technologies. More recently, there have been proposals for drawing the social sciences into the orbit of government control by increasing support given to them.

In 1967, a Committee of the National Academy of Sciences advised the Department of Defense to increase its support for, and use of, research in the fields of the social and behavioral sciences. The National Academy study group argued that the Department of Defense "must now wage not only warfare but 'peacefare' as well," and that "pacification, assistance and the battle of ideas are major segments of the DOD responsibility. The social and behavioral sciences constitute the unique resource for support of these new requirements and must be vigorously pursued if our operations are to be effective." Thereby, the "Report of the Panel on Defense, Social and Behavioral Sciences" recommended that the Department of Defense enter into functions hitherto left to the Department of State. The Report even recommended techniques for spreading "publicity concerning the distinguished behavioral scientists who have long-term commitments to the DOD . . . as a way of reassuring younger scientists and improving our research image."

The Report advised the Department of Defense not to ask people to do research on counterinsurgency, guerrilla warfare, and so forth, but rather to improve techniques for attracting younger scientists to work on Department of Defense problems. They judged that "There is evidence that the long-term funding of research centers does produce young scientists who are more mission-oriented and receptive to opportunities in DOD research. However, there seems to be little planned effort on the part of DOD research management to recruit these young men. A planned program of recruiting at these centers and at appropriate graduate schools should be initiated." With sterling advice of this sort, we may expect the Department of Defense to enlarge its programs in the social and behavioral sciences.

New perspectives of the Pentagon in the social sciences were formulated in February, 1968, by Donald M. MacArthur, Deputy Director for Research and Engineering in the Department of Defense. He stated:

> Our tasks are getting larger and more demanding not only in the Defense Department but throughout the country and the world so we cannot rest upon last year achievements. We must tackle the old problems in new ways and many new problems in genuinely inventive ways. One task is easy, to see the problems: In our cities, in housing, in training people, in economic development, in controlling pollution, in creating new sources of food for expanding world populations . . . there should be simply no question about the Defense Department's commitment to employ the highest level of social and behavioral science expertise to solve many of our research and development problems.

Mr. MacArthur reported on the details of social and behavioral science research support from the Department of Defense during fiscal year 1966. Thirty-four million dollars was devoted to research in the following fields: human performance, manpower selection and training, human factors engineering, cultural and social factors, and policy planning studies. According to MacArthur, "The mission of the DOD encompasses broader responsibilities than those traditionally conceived. We must not only be prepared for armed conflict but contribute, for example, to military assistance and pacification. The social and behavioral sciences are a unique resource to meet these requirements."

So, notwithstanding the concern and even alarm among some social scientists after the Project Camelot scandal, the Department of Defense clearly plans to extend the scope of its research and planning operations in the political sphere.

In sum: the Department of Defense has built up a formidable national apparatus in research and development. This has grown to encompass the natural and the social sciences and their application to diverse technologies. The research establishments extend from those owned and operated by the state-management itself to industrial firms, to Pentagon-satellite "non-profit" research units, to laboratories in the universities. Throughout, the trend is not only to continue the traditional lines of work related to military problems, but to expand control into spheres hitherto considered to be civilian responsibilities.

INTERNATIONAL ARMS SALES

From 1949 to 1966, the government of the United States sold $16.1 billion in arms abroad and gave away $30.2 billion in additional arms and military equipment. This $46.3 billion in arms exports by the United States was arranged by the Department of Defense, excluding private sales not arranged through the Pentagon. The value of these arms exports is about $4 billion greater than the sum of all grants and loans made under the various economic assistance programs since the middle of 1948, including the Marshall Plan. From 1962 to 1968, arms sales alone amounted to $11.1 billion, and the sales goal up to 1975 is for $2 billion of armament sales each year. The Pentagon's plans also include military grants-in-aid, amounting to about $1 billion in military hardware each year. In all, the Department of Defense plans to export $3 billion worth of arms annually until 1975. The state-management in the Pentagon has become the world's leading supplier of armaments. This export trade helps to maintain and enlarge the military-industrial production network, while extending the scope of Pentagon control over "armed forces of customers," thereafter technically dependent nations.

In testimony to the House Committee on Foreign Affairs in 1964, Henry Kuss, in charge of International Logistics Negotiations, explained how the program has grown from an average of $300 million a year (1951 to 1960) to the $1 billion-per-year level by 1963. He stated:

> The increase in our military export orders follows the pattern of strong top executive actions which began with negotiations undertaken by Secretaries Dillon and Anderson in late 1960 to obtain German cooperation. It received its first major impetus from the successful conclusion of the Dillon, Ball, and Gilpatric initiatives in the Strauss/Gilpatric German offset agreement in 1961; and it reached its $1½ billion level through the Secretary of Defense's direction to promote sales and extend credit where necessary, and through the corollary actions of the Secretary of the Treasury and the President of the Eximbank [Export-Import Bank] to support the export efforts with new credit availability. Whether this level can be sustained depends to a great extent on a vigorous program by the Executive Branch and upon the continued availability of credit to enable us to compete with other nations selling around the world.

The role of the Pentagon managers in arranging and expanding international arms sales was confirmed by Senator Stuart Symington in July, 1967. The Senator, a Missouri Democrat and former Secretary of the Air Force, has been Chairman of the Senate Foreign Relations Subcommittee for Near Eastern and South Asian Affairs. After this group held hearings on international arms sales, a report was issued in which the Senator stated that ". . . There is evidence to suggest that the type and destination of American military equipment sold abroad is determined by middle-level officials in the Department of Defense, by private firms which either elude the restrictions, or are unable to get policy guidance from the administration, and by foreign governments which ignore or bypass the terms under which American weapons were provided to them." The evidence examined by this subcommittee disclosed that Pentagon managers participated in complex evasive maneuvers, by which the letter of the law was evaded, to make possible the sale of American arms to countries which had been, for political reasons, prohibited from purchasing such arms.

The sales organization, functioning under Henry Kuss in the Department of Defense, has taken on the character of a go-getting sales operation, with quotas assigned to the various regional arms salesmen. Why has this vigorous arms sales program been pressed forward by the Department of Defense?

The first consideration was the pressure on the Pentagon to act so as to recover dollars that had piled up abroad through American military spending. Since such dollars have been turned into claims on U.S. Treasury gold, and since the gold reserve of the Treasury has been dramatically depleted during the last two decades, the Pentagon was called upon to do its part in saving the value of the dollar. It participated, not by reducing the American military commitment abroad, but by enlarging it through the international sale of arms.

Nevertheless, the balance-of-payment effect has not been the controlling factor on these policies. A 1967 staff study on "Arms Sales and Foreign Policy" to the Senate Foreign Relations Committee noted that direct, traceable U.S. arms sales to developing countries have amounted to only 12 percent of the total from 1962 to 1966, and "If the United States were to lose its entire arms market in the underdeveloped world the impact on our overall balance-of-payments accounts would be small. Therefore, our justification for such sales must be based on the other considerations, such as influencing the development of the local military elites or helping a country resist the threat of external aggressions. Preventing the influx of military equipment of other nations, a sort of preemptive selling, has also been a strong U.S. motive in the underdeveloped areas of the world." Evidently, the controlling factor here has not been the balance-of-payment factor but rather the state-management's institutional imperative to enlarge the scope of its decision-power by "preemptive selling" in order to seize foreign markets.

This program of international arms sales is administered in close collaboration with officials of the State Department and Treasury. Weekly meetings are held between officers of these Departments to coordinate operations.

A second effect of the international sale of arms is to enlarge the Pentagon management's area of political control. From the middle of 1949 through mid-1965, 243,250 foreign officers and enlisted men took military training course at American bases in the United States and abroad.

In 1967, Eugene V. Rostow, Under Secretary of State for Political Affairs, expounded the political calculation involved in these arms sales. He told the House Banking and Currency Committee that U.S. policy was "not to sell arms [but rather to] help friendly developing countries reach their legitimate security needs while at the same time using our influence and managing our sales in such a way as to develop regional arms controls and to prevent excessive investment in military forces." The policy "is not working perfectly," he stated, "but it would be imprudent to stop trying [since] . . . we are not the only arms supplier." Mr. Rostow was here alluding to the international competition between the state-managements of major powers for extension of their decision-power through the manipulation of arms sales.

In various public statements, Mr. Kuss has aggressively justified the international arms sales program; for example, on the grounds that $9 billion in sales during a particular period would result in nearly $1 billion in profits to American industry, with about 1.2 million man-years of employment spread through the fifty states and the District of Columbia. Thus, Mr. Kuss identified the state-management in the Pentagon as a benefactor to the American economy.

Large-scale sale of arms abroad has been facilitated by a banking operation run by the state-management. In 1957, Congress made a credit fund of $383 million available to the Department of Defense. Since the law enabling the use of this fund required that only 25 percent of the extended credit be covered by the fund, the Department of Defense was able to extend $1,532 million in credits with this sum as a base. Another source of banking support for financing overseas arms sales was the Eximbank, 25 percent of whose extended loans during the fiscal years 1966 and 1967 were for arms purchases. Altogether, the Eximbank has financed more than $2.6 billion in arms purchases since 1963. Using the Eximbank operations, the Pentagon managers have subsidized the interest which foreign buyers have been charged for the money borrowed from the Eximbank to pay for arms purchases. The Pentagon management charged the recipients of these loans a lower interest rate for the money than it, in turn, had paid to the Eximbank for borrowing the money. An analysis of loans during the years 1966 and 1967 disclosed that in a series of cases involving as many as fourteen countries, the Pentagon managers charged the purchasing governments interest rates two or more percentage points below what it cost the U.S. Treasury to borrow money for comparable lengths of time in recent years. Not only has the Pentagon been using government banking operations to facilitate the arms sales, but also using the vast funds placed at its disposal by the Congress to subsidize these overseas sales.

In June, 1966, the Secretary of Defense himself intervened directly when a major arms-sales contract was threatened. The government of West Germany had at that time decided it would prefer to shift part of its contracted funds for the purchase of military equipment to industrial equipment purchases, the equipment to be used for West German economic aid in developing countries. The Pentagon management rejected the idea, and McNamara dealt firmly with the West German government, making it clear that the U.S. government was prepared to reduce forces in Germany should the West German government renege on its agreement to purchase U.S. arms.

The international arms sale operation is a many-sided activity. From the state-management's standpoint, this activity contributes substantially to the extension of its decision-power. The extended power operates in foreign countries as a type of political control by proxy. The proxy takes several forms: officers of foreign armies trained in the United States; dependence of foreign military forces on U.S. weapons, replacement parts, and so forth; the presence of U.S. military advisors among foreign armed forces. Since the state-management reaps certain cost benefits from some of the large-scale production of weapons in U.S. industry, the Pentagon is often able to compete against other nations' arms products in cost-price terms. This advantage is used to justify further arms sales and enlargement of the allied control functions. Thus, the extension of state-management controls becomes self-powered and self-justifying.

4

Extension of Control over the Universities and Research

The universities occupy a key role in industrial society. They are at the center of the network of activities and institutions producing new knowledge and educated men and women who wield knowledge of every sort. In 1966, according to the National Science Foundation, there were 242,800 scientists in the United States. About 36 percent worked in universities. Assuming an annual increase of 14,000, there would be 300,000 scientists working in the United States by 1970. As of 1966, the work of 43 percent of the nation's scientists was supported in whole or in part by the federal government.

The universities are primary centers for work in basic science as well as in many areas of technology. By 1968, about 6.9 million students attended American colleges and universities (2.2 million private, 4.7 million state), and these schools spent $13.2 billion ($1,900 per student). Federal funds for research and development in the universities grew from $813 million in 1963 to $1.3 billion by 1966-1967, an increase of 55 percent. This $1.3 billion, which includes the primary basic research sponsored by the federal government, amounts to less than 10 percent of the total research funding by the federal government. In terms of sources of federal research funds to universities, the Pentagon and allied agencies, Atomic Energy Commission (AEC) and National Aeronautics and Space Agency (NASA), together accounted for 46.5 percent of the total in 1967.

Other funds given to the universities by the federal government amounted to $2 billion in 1967. These federal funds supported teaching, construction of buildings, and the purchase of various facilities. In all of this federal support for education, the sciences dominated the field. The Office of the Secretary of Defense each year publishes a listing of the 500 principal contractors who perform research and development work. Included in this group is a list of non-profit institutions. These are led by the Massachusetts Institute of Technology (MIT), which received $119 million from the Pentagon in fiscal year 1968—27 percent of all the research spending by the state-management in American universities. This does not include funds received from NASA, the AEC, or other government agencies whose activities contribute to the military. While MIT clearly leads the field in the amount of money given it by the Pentagon, appreciable sums are given to many other universities as well: thus, Johns Hopkins, $57 million; the University of California, $17 million; Columbia University, $9 million; Stanford University, $6 million; the University of Michigan, $9 million; the University of Illinois, $8 million. These data disclose a considerable concentration of military-supported research in a handful of major universities.

As a result of long Pentagon support, guided by the Eisenhower memorandum of 1946, the universities became involved in wide-ranging, diverse activities on behalf of the Pentagon—from basic scientific research to development of weapons and social-control techniques. Certain of these activities have been publicly announced, including, for example, the operations of the Institute for Defense Analysis (IDA). This Institute, formally organized by a group of universities, was designed to do contract work, much of it classified in nature, for the Department of Defense. By successfully involving the universities in the formation and direction of this institution the

Pentagon produced a network of contacts that could tap the brains in the universities. The qualitative importance of this organization is not reflected in its budget, which is about $12 million per annum. However, this $12 million is concentrated on buying skilled brain-hours. As disclosed in its annual reports, IDA's work-range extends over the whole spectrum of military activity, from strategy in the use of intercontinental weapons, to problems of tactics and weaponry design in counter-guerrilla operations of various sorts.

The Department of Defense has sponsored a major aeronautical laboratory at Cornell University. During the period 1963–1966, researches in chemical and biological warfare were carried on in 38 universities under contract from the Pentagon. Owing to disclosures by faculty members of Michigan State University (*Ramparts,* April, 1966) we learn that ". . . The Michigan State professors performed at all levels. They advised on fingerprinting techniques, on bookkeeping, on governmental budgeting and on the very writing of South Vietnam's constitution. One was even instrumental in the choice of the President of South Vietnam. But in all this they never questioned U.S. foreign policy which had placed them there and which thereby they were supporting." Owing to initiatives by faculty members at the University of Pennsylvania (*Ramparts,* August, 1966), the public was informed about a course, Political Science 551, taught at that university. "Political Science 551 is a course for spies. Officially described in the University catalogue as 'Strategic Intelligence and National Policy,' Political Science 551 has been offered every semester for the last 10 years despite the fact that no responsible person on the campus seems to have a very clear understanding of why it is being taught." The syllabus for Political Science 551 shows the academic scope of the topics covered:

(1) Covert or clandestine intelligence activities at all levels in both peace and war. (2) Counterintelligence, from elementary security measures and loyalty investigations, to elaborate cover plans, ruses and deceptions; (3) Tactical low level or localized intelligence production including wartime and military combat intelligence; (4) Areas in the red end of the spectrum of international relations which are actually kinds of unconventional warfare but which are

frequently confused or connected with information gathering activities, and finally (5) National decision and policy making as based on adequate intelligence of problems associated with the resulting internal and external relationships, especially among civilian and military leaders.

An excellent collection of data on many aspects of the military's role in the universities was presented in a set of articles published by *Viet-Report* in January, 1968.

In 1967, the state-management's research arm (Directorate of Defense Research and Engineering) reviewed its relations with the universities and concluded that its activities were unduly concentrated in a few of the larger institutions. Furthermore, the Pentagon managers took note of the uneven development of the sciences and technologies. Smaller colleges and universities had been getting small shares or no funds at all from the main federal research-supporting agencies, those in the Department of Defense orbit. Accordingly, it was proposed that "new centers of excellence" be created under Project Themis.

In 1967–1968, Project Themis was started with $20 million and in fiscal 1969, this was raised to $30 million. Under Project Themis, 50 research contracts were awarded in the first year to that many institutions. These projects involved work under the following major categories: detection, surveillance, navigation and control; energy and power; information sciences; military vehicle technology; materials sciences; environmental sciences; medical sciences; and social and behavioral sciences. The topics appearing under the social and behavioral group are worth noting. They include:

Arizona State University—Human Performance in Isolation (Navy);

Kansas State University—Performance in Altered Environments (Air Force);

University of Kansas—Social and Behavioral Sciences (Advanced Research Projects Agency);

Texas Christian University—Human Pattern Perception (Army).

The state-management reaches out to universities in indirect ways as well. For example, military-industrial firms, especially the larger ones, have organized elaborate contacts with universities, notably those with technical schools. Thus, *American Machinist* (November 8, 1965) reports that:

> North American Aviation management alone serves on more than 30 college advisory boards, university engineering advisory councils and technology advisory committees in Ohio, West Virginia, Missouri, Texas, Oklahoma and California. The schools are doing their part too. Curriculums have been shaped to fit the new needs. There is a continual movement back and forth of professors to plants for lectures and employees to colleges and universities for more learning. Industry also has a program to bring teachers, counselors and students into the plants so that industry may say—"here is what we are doing—this is what we need."

By these means, the aerospace industry communicates the nature of the problems, technologies, and administrative fields which concern it, and expects various universities to produce persons with appropriate skills.

In several regions of the United States, universities have formed the nucleus for large aggregations of military research and production. Two of the most important of these are around Boston, along Route 128, and in Palo Alto, California, in the industrial park that adjoins Stanford University. At Stanford, as in Boston, there is crossing over between military-industrial and university posts. In some cases, members of the faculty initiate enterprises. More often, faculty members serve as consultants or officers—including board members—of military-industrial firms.

As a result of this sort of interlocking, it is inevitable that the understanding of what is important technically feeds back into the university classroom and laboratory. Thereby, the choices made from the array of options that always exist in fields of engineering technology are informed by the extramural activities of the faculty and the characteristics of the surrounding firms. These criteria of what is important are often validated in the student's eyes by the fact that the new industrial units are described as part of "space age industry," and the like. Furthermore, as is characteristic of heavily research-oriented military-industrial firms, they offer salaries significantly higher than those of civilian firms employing comparable staff. Furthermore, an important non-salary income is available to employees in these areas, in the form of a fine place to live. It is impressive to see the high level of public services in rich Palo Alto, and the beauty of the countryside around Stanford University and its industrial park, as well as the care that has been given to zoning the areas in terms of farming, commercial, industrial, university, residential and recreational activity.

While the largest part of federal government activity in universities has been oriented toward the natural sciences and allied technologies, as noted above, there has been increasing federal interest in the social sciences. Thus, by 1966, the federal government was giving American social scientists $25.3 million for foreign policy research, one-half of this coming from the Department of Defense. These varied modes of support from the Department of Defense, and allied agencies, have had significant impact on the character of American universities. On September 16, 1967, the Associated Press reported:

> The University of Minnesota is working on a government project so secret that not even the President of the University knows what it is. Neither do the Regents, who nevertheless approved continuation of the year-old project yesterday, after Vice President Lawrence R. London said the 'people working on it want it continued and the federal government believes it important for the defense effort.' Officials said that University President Malcolm Moose, who wrote speeches for former President Dwight D. Eisenhower, has not yet been cleared by the federal government to handle classified materials.

In this fashion, governance of the university is removed from the university itself; decisions concerning the nature of work to be done are made elsewhere, and state-management has extended its decision-power into the affairs of the university. Opportunities for the further extension of state-management control, directed primarily by the Pentagon, multiply where there are shortages of research and development funds in civilian agencies. Thus, from 1967 to 1969, the federal program for funding for universities was placed under considerable pressure. By February, 1968, it became apparent that the Department of Defense's research and development budget would increase by $600 million, while the AEC's research and development budget would grow by $429 million. These increases in military research budgets were paralleled by reductions (or failure to offset price inflation), in the research arms of civilian agencies of the federal government. Executive and Congressional preference for military research produced budget crises in many universities. For example, Columbia University announced on October 21, 1968: "Major cutbacks in grants from the National Science Foundation [NSF] will force Columbia to reduce funds for individual NSF projects by 25 to 30 percent during the current fiscal year."

The extension of state-management control into the universities has produced a secondary effect: the under-budgeting and under-staffing of teaching and research not receiving major government (read Pentagon) largesse. This phenomenon was cogently described, in 1965, in a report of the Congressional Committee on Government Operations on the "Conflicts between the Federal Research Program and the Nation's Goals for Higher Education." The committee stated at the very outset:

> Our federal research programs on the one hand and the nation's goals for higher education on the other are in increasing conflict. While both research and higher education share the common goals of extending scholarship, and developing the intellectual resources of the nation, the immediate interests of one are not necessarily those of the other.
>
> The first conflict is the present use of scarce manpower. Scientists and engineers are indispensible to research and development. They are also indispensible as teachers in the expanding higher education system. Since their numbers cannot be greatly increased over the short run, too much diversion into the one means deprivation of the other.
>
> The second is a conflict between present use of manpower resources and investment for future manpower resources . . . But research demands performance now; investment in trained manpower is necessarily of secondary concern. Education by its nature demands investment now, in training young people so that the nation can have the benefits of performance later. Short term research requirements may be satisfied by concentrating most of the science funds in a few excellent universities. But the long run effects of such concentration could be disastrous for other colleges and universities and hence ultimately for both research and higher education.

Precisely this pattern of concentration has been appearing in American universities. The federal research programs cited by the committee must be translated to mean the military research and development programs, since these have been getting the lion's share of all federal research budgets. From 1963 through 1967, the Pentagon, AEC, and NASA allocated $2.1 billion out of the total $5.4 billion federal research funds to universities.

Against this background, one notes preparation for further extension of the Department of Defense management control in the universities, in the recommendations of the Federal Council for Science and Technology. This Council proposed that closer ties be established between the federal agencies (undesignated) and the universities. The Council noted that highly desirable conditions have obtained in government laboratories closely tied to universities. They state:

> One senses a purpose, an alertness, an enthusiasm, a striving for excellence, a dedication, a feeling of accomplishment coupled with unlimited potential contribution, a vibrant participation at the advancing frontiers of science, an excitement, a sense of life, an involvement. This atmosphere, fostered by close association with the academic world—highly desirable and not easily attained—was seldom transmitted to the task force in laboratories lacking close university relationships. It seems clear that a close working relationship with the universities is a definite plus to a federal R&D laboratory.

The technical judgment of the council is probably valid. The consequences of this for university laboratories are also predictable, especially as the federal laboratories are mainly an arm of the most powerful industrial-management body in the land.

A proper assessment of the impact of Department of Defense management on university research is obtained not merely by examining what work is done, but by estimating what work is not done. What is the opportunity-cost of the Department of Defense control over the universities? Stated differently: What needs are not being met by universities? What lines of technology, for example, are not given emphasis because of project sponsorship by the state-management? In May, 1962, the Engineers Joint Council reported on "The Nation's Engineering Research Needs, 1965–1985." In 1970, this still reads as a major agenda of civilian technology opportunities foregone as a result of state-management research priorities. However, the more durable effect of Pentagon influence on the universities is owing to qualitative changes in the research environment made by the state management.

The Defense Documentation Center of the Defense Supply Agency functions to store and distribute scientific and technical reports to federal agencies, as well as to submanagements working for the Pentagon that are registered as eligible for this service. As research proceeds in various fields, subject to security and "classification" controls, knowledge of parts of a field are available only to those with access to the security-controlled data. Access to data is often an important economic weapon; in this case, it is controlled by the state-management.

The Department of Defense has had a major part in pressing the universities toward a change in their character. Clark Kerr, in his essay on "The Frantic Race to Remain Contemporary," stated that there are three changes taking place in the American university: growth, changing academic emphasis, and involvement in the life of the society. To Clark Kerr the latter has significance in that: "The university, in particular, has become in America, and in other nations as well, a prime instrument of national purpose. This is new. This is the essence of the transformation now engulfing our universities." The national purpose is operationally defined by the priorities governing the areas wherein public funds are applied. The fact that two-thirds of the national budget is being applied to military purposes gives an operational definition to the national purpose. Hence, the involvement of the universities may be more exactly stated as an engagement in existing military priorities. Thus, state-management has extended its rule even into those institutions where creation of new knowledge has heretofore been a primary value.

The successes of the state-management in turning the universities to its service, and away from their central purpose of teaching and producing new knowledge, has produced three main effects. The first is the limitation on resources for teaching and university-initiated research. A second effect of the state-management's success has been the rebellion by students against federal authority and its wars. On the Senate floor, December 13, 1967, Senator Fulbright diagnosed the connection, saying:

> "It seems more likely that the basic cause of the great trouble in our universities is the student's discovery of corruption in the one place, besides perhaps the churches, which might have been supposed to be immune from the corruptions of our age. Having seen their country's traditional values degraded in the effort to attribute moral purpose to an immoral war, having seen their country's leaders caught in inconsistencies which are politely referred to as a "credibility gap," they now see their universities—the last citadels of moral and intellectual integrity—lending themselves to ulterior and expedient ends, and betraying their own fundamental purpose, which, in James Bryce's words, is to "reflect the spirit of the times without yielding to it."

Finally, the effect of this invasion on the character of American society and its economy will endure long into the future, for persons trained in universities ultimately become key people in many facets of society. Therefore their capability becomes society's capability; the priorities they embrace become the priorities of many institutions. Similarly, the opportunities foregone during their education, and the knowledge foregone in their training, become knowledge and opportunities foregone by the entire society.

5

The Science-Fiction
of Defense and
Its Consequences

The responsibility for shielding the United States against external attack has been turned into a means by which the scope and intensity of decision-power of the state-management has been enlarged. Extension of control in this area has been pressed for relentlessly, although no technological method for shielding the United States, or any other nation, from a nuclear attack is foreseeable.

The Kennedy administration entered office after an electoral campaign that included a promise to remedy the missile gap. Allegedly, the United States faced the dangerous possibility of being defeated in a confrontation with, or under an attack by, a Soviet military force composed of intercontinental ballistics missiles (ICBMs) superior in number to our own. In February, 1961, after a month in office, Secretary of Defense McNamara announced that there was no missile gap. In his volume *A Thousand Days,* Arthur M. Schlesinger, Jr. reported that the Air Force had claimed the Soviet ICBM force then consisted of 600 to 800 missiles; the CIA had claimed 450; and the Navy, 200. The Navy estimate was judged closest to reality. Despite this estimate, orders were soon thereafter given to build up the U.S. ICBM force to an ability to deliver 1,710 nuclear warheads by 1969. This decision to increase sharply the U.S. supply of ICBMs triggered a new international nuclear arms competition. An examination of the Schlesinger and Sorensen books on the Kennedy administration, coupled with discussions with former White House staff members, disclosed those considerations which determined that decision.

Upon taking office, President Kennedy joined with the new Secretary of Defense in denying the Air Force a new heavy bomber fleet, having decided that intercontinental missiles were superior delivery vehicles. At the same time, this meant confronting the Air Force and its industrial allies, who were pressing for budgetary concessions. The White House settled this matter by granting money for building up the missile force. Also, having just concluded that an infusion of capital funds was needed in order to raise American economic activity to a higher level, the White House decided that an outlay of capital for missiles, as well as other military forces, was necessary. This particular form of economic stimulation was carried out through the period 1961–1963.

Further justification for the decision to build up our missile force was supplied by the new strategic theory that if the United States had a large and accurately directed missile force with which to strike at distant missiles on the ground, then it would be possible to wage and win an intercontinental nuclear war by aiming missiles at the missiles, rather than at the cities, of the opponent. It was argued that this would also induce an opponent not to direct his missiles at our cities. (This theory of "counterforce" prevailed until about 1968. *The Washington Post* of January 16, 1968, reported that by then this argument had been formally abandoned and our missiles were announced to be aimed at Soviet cities. The Soviet Union refused to play the U.S. nuclear war planners' game.)

By 1968, the strategic nuclear forces of the United States and the Soviet Union included enough matériel to destroy the main population and industrial centers of both nations. On the United States side, there were 1,710 intercontinental missiles based both on land and sea, plus 646 intercontinental bombers; a total of 4,206 nuclear warheads could be carried by intercontinental vehicles to the 156 Soviet cities that had populations of 100,000 or more.

In addition to the intercontinental missiles and bombers employed by the United States, there are the long-range aircraft that are deployed on U.S. aircraft carriers, U.S. air forces in Western Europe that could reach into the western part of the U.S.S.R., and shorter-range missiles in western Europe. The bombs or missiles that can be carried by these planes were not included in Defense Secretary Clifford's estimate of 4,206 nuclear warheads. Thus, taking the carrying capability of these planes and missiles into account would probably raise the figure by more than 100 percent, to a total of about 11,000 nuclear warheads deliverable to Soviet targets.

On the Soviet side, as of October, 1968, there were about 900 intercontinental missiles in place, plus approximately 75 long-range missiles mounted on Soviet submarines. The Soviets also had about 155 long-range bombers. All told, then, according to the Secretary of Defense, the Soviet Union had 1,200 nuclear warheads in long-range delivery vehicles that could be mounted against the 130 American cities with populations of 100,000 or over. (In order to round off the strategic picture, it is worth nothing that China has approximately 132 cities with a population of 100,000 or over.)

By any reasonable reckoning, the United States and the Soviet Union both have much more nuclear hardware than needed for the destruction of each other's main population and industrial centers. This multiple of necessary destructive capability demanded the invention of a new word to describe it, "overkill." The overkill capability on both sides is so great as to transform the basic nature of military power. At present, each of the great nuclear powers can destroy the other, and neither can prevent the other from so doing—and this holds no matter which one moves first. That is, the United States cannot be shielded from an externally based nuclear atack, nor can our nuclear weapons allow us to take over another nation so armed. Accordingly, the United States supports a Department of Defense which is unable to defend the nation from nuclear attack, an inability created by the application of nuclear technology to military purposes.

A revealing way to elucidate the change is to contrast our present condition with the circumstances surrounding the Battle of Britain in 1940. At that time, the Luftwaffe, using conventional explosives, launched a bombing attack against British cities. The British Royal Air Force won the Battle of Britain by knocking out about one in ten of the incoming bombers. Why did a 10 percent defensive success constitute a victory? Because one attacking bomber and its crew could, on the average, be used for ten trips, on each trip carrying a plane-load of high explosives. The damage that could be wrought by unloading 10 plane-loads of conventional high explosives on British cities was not sufficient to justify the loss of one bomber and its crew. When nuclear warheads replaced conventional explosives, this condition was fundamentally altered, for even if defensive forces could knock out 90 percent of an incoming nuclear attack force, the remaining 10 percent would alone be so destructive a force that the loss of all the other planes could be borne. Thus, a single aircraft carrying a number of nuclear bombs can destroy several metropolitan industrial centers. While hundreds of plane-loads of conventional explosives had to be used to destroy the city of Coventry, one plane with nuclear warheads could "Coventrize" several cities.

Nuclear weapons make the difference, owing to the unprecedented concentration of energy released at one time and in one place. One plane, or one missile, or one underwater mine, can carry explosive power equivalent to all the explosives released over Europe, during the Second World War. The consequence of this is that traditional concepts of defense—military superiority, military power, and military security—have been thoroughly undermined. Instead of promising defense, the Department of Defense now promises deterrence. That does not refer to the ability to shield a society from attack in a physical sense, but to a threat-to-retaliate system which, it is hoped, would constrain a potential opponent from making a first move. Such experiments in applied psychology are qualitatively different from physical systems with measurable shielding efficiency. For example, there is reasonable doubt as to whether a retaliatory response in kind to a nuclear attack is even rational. The survivors of a massive nuclear assault, if any, would need major outside help. Where would it come from if the largest industrial-population centers of the world were all destroyed?

A colleague once put the matter in the form of a story of two men in a desert. They quarrel, and one breaks the leg of the other, whereupon the injured man draws a gun to shoot his attacker. If he kills him, he satisfies his lust for vengeance, but loses any chance of getting out of the desert. Should he shoot? Since physical defense is no longer a useful concept among major nuclear powers, there is no longer any such thing as meaningful military superiority. An estimated ability to overkill—in multiples—does not denote superiority, since a capability to destroy a hundred or a thousand times over is neither militarily meaningful nor meaningful in any human terms.

These changes also limit the political uses of military power. At one time, whoever could exercise military superiority could exert political will. Thus, the industrial capability of the United States and other great countries during the Second World War was used to build military forces that could apply superior military power, thereby enabling the exercise of political will over a defeated opponent. In the relationship between major nuclear powers, this is no longer possible; there is no way of predicting the survival of anyone after a nuclear war who could or would be able to exercise political will. In this case, what is "victory," and what is "defeat?" Under circumstances of potential nuclear confrontation, the security of a society depends on the non-use of such weapons. Among nuclear powers, there is no longer a feasible way of using military power to achieve an end-result which in any meaningful way might be termed security.

On January 25, 1966, Secretary of Defense McNamara summarized the nuclear nature of the military, strategic confrontation between the United States and the Soviet Union.

> . . . Even if the Soviets in the 1970 period were to assign their entire available missile force to attacks on our strategic forces (reserving only refire missiles and bomber-delivered weapons for urban targets), our analysis shows that a very large proportion of our alert forces would still survive. And, of these surviving forces, a very large proportion could reliably deliver their payloads to their targets.
>
> The effective delivery of even one-fifth of the surviving weapons on Soviet cities would destroy about one-third of the total population and half of the industrial capacity of the Soviet Union. By doubling the number of delivered weapons, Soviet fatalities and

industrial capacity destroyed would be increased by considerably less than one-third. Beyond this point, further increments of weapons delivered would not appreciably change the results, because we would have to bring under attack smaller and smaller cities, each requiring one delivered weapon . . .

Such catastrophic calculations of nuclear war also apply to Europe and other continents. Another view of the consequences for the United States and the Soviet Union, derived from various types of nuclear exchanges, are presented in the following table, which the Secretary of Defense put before the Congress in 1966.

Costs of U.S. Damage Limiting Postures and Soviet Damage Potential

	Program Costs FY 1966–75			Soviet Damage Potential [a]	
	COST ATTRIB- UTED TO ASSURED DESTRUC- TION [b]	DAMAGE LIMITING INCRE- MENT	TOTAL U.S. POSTURE	SOVIET FIRST STRIKE	U.S. FIRST STRIKE
	(BILLIONS OF DOLLARS)			(MILLIONS OF U.S. FATALITIES)	
1970					
U.S.S.R. Expected Threat					
U.S. Approved Program				130–135	90–95
1975					
U.S.S.R. Threat I					
U.S. AD*Posture Plus					
Ltd Civil Defense	$22.4	$ 1.5	$23.9	130–135	90–105
U.S. AD Posture Plus					
Full Fallout Shelter	22.4	3.4	25.8	110–115	80–85
U.S. DL*Posture A	22.4	22.5	44.9	80–95	25–40
U.S. DL Posture B	22.4	30.1	52.5	50–80	20–30
U.S.S.R. Threat II					
U.S. DL Posture C	28.5	24.8	53.3	105–110	35–55
U.S. DL Posture D	28.5	32.3	60.8	75–100	25–40

The program costs shown on the table represent the value of the resources required for each of the alternative postures. The costs attributed to Assured Destruction represent the resources required to ensure that we can, in each case, deliver and detonate at least the minimum essential number of warheads over Soviet cities, even after a surprise Soviet attack. The costs for Damage Limitation represent the value of the additional resources required to achieve the various postures shown on the table. The last two columns of the table show the U.S. fatalities which would result under two alternative forms of nuclear war outbreak. In the Soviet first strike case, we assumed that the Soviets initiate nuclear war with a simultaneous attack against our cities and military targets, and with the weight of their attack directed at our cities. In the other case, we assume that the events leading up to the nuclear exchange develop in such way that the United States is able to strike at the Soviet offensive forces before they can be launched at our urban targets.

* AD is Assured Destruction; DL is Damage Limiting.
a Rounded to the nearest five million.
b The Assured Destruction posture designed against Threat I is more than just a minimal capability; it is designed to provide insurance against unexpected changes in the threat. In Postures C and D a larger strategic missile force is provided for Assured Destruction to counter the increased Soviet offensive threat and the much more extensive ABM defense. (Threat II requires about three times as much surviving, deliverable payload than Threat I, just to maintain our Assured Destruction capability.)

SOURCE: U.S. Department of Defense, *Statement of Secretary of Defense Robert S. McNamara before Subcommittee Number 2 of the House Armed Services Committee on the Fiscal Year 1967–71 Strategic Bomber Program,* January 25, 1966.

Many persons examining such a table read it as follows: they note the estimated difference in immediate U.S. fatalities between a Soviet first strike against U.S. cities, and a U.S. first strike against Soviet nuclear forces. Under the assumed conditions, these estimates suggest an apparently large difference in immediate U.S. fatalities were the United States to strike the Soviets first. In the first row of the table, there would be 130 to 135 million U.S. fatalities immediately upon a Soviet first strike, assuming the armament condition of 1970. However, if the United States were to strike the Soviet Union first, under assumed 1970 conditions, the immediate U.S. fatalities would be 90 to 95 million persons. On the face of it, this may be read as an argument for the United States to strike first, to "save" as many as 45 million lives. Hence, why not strike first? This nightmarish reasoning excludes from these estimates of immediate fatalities the following considerations: first, the population-destroying fires, epidemics, and so on, would leave little prospect of organized life within one year; and, second, each of these estimates is based upon *presumed* conditions which have no experimental base. There has been no observation of a nuclear war, so no one knows what in fact happens under these conditions. The photographs and subsequent observations of Hiroshima and Nagasaki certainly do show that a wasteland was created out of built-up city areas. In 1962, estimates on the consequences of major nuclear attacks, even with major civil defense systems in place, suggest that there is no workable way for eliminating society-destroying factors following a major nuclear exchange.

Furthermore, such tables do not refer to the consequences over a long period from contamination of water, contamination of the air and of the earth, the destruction of waste and sewage disposal systems, the failure of food supply, and the like. None of this adds up to defense. Instead, the Pentagon has become a vendor of "protection," wielding its fearsome estimates of nuclear war to scare Congress and the nation into ever-larger capital grants for the expansion of the state-management.

Apart from the main intercontinental strategic forces of the United States, tens of thousands of nuclear warheads are mounted in diverse delivery vehicles. These range from warheads that can be fired from cannons to nuclear explosives that can be carried by planes of various sizes, in torpedoes, in demolition kits, and so forth. In November, 1965, the Department of Defense announced that 5,000 atomic warheads were stored in Western Europe for tactical use by NATO and that a 20 percent increase in that number was then in the program.

A major change, made by the Pentagon in 1968, can multiply dramatically the number of deliverable nuclear warheads and improve their accuracy for striking intercontinental-range targets. A new technique called Multiple Independently-targetable Reentry Vehicles (MIRV) has been developed, which allows warheads to be packaged in multiples in a large missile, together with guidance systems that can direct each warhead on the missile's flight to particular and separate targets. Accordingly, from 5 to 10 directable warheads could then replace the single warheads that are now mounted in the present Minuteman and Polaris missiles.

In addition to the armament now in place, the Department of Defense has under review major new weapons programs which include the following: an 8,000-mile-an-hour intercontinental bomber with unprecedented range and carrying capability; plans for an altogether new intercontinental missile of unprecedented size; plans for air-to-ground missiles that would multiply the striking power of presently available intercontinental aircraft; as well as a $4-billion airborne radar system for protection and defense against incoming aircraft (the Soviet Union has 155 big bombers).

The Department of Defense has been moving along the research–design–planning–production cycle toward an antiballistic missile (ABM) system. Alternative ABM plans have been proposed, ranging from "thin" systems around some Minuteman missile bases or a few cities to "thick" systems for full continental coverage. The "thin" systems are designed allegedly to be a defense against a possible Chinese missile threat during the 1970's. The so-called "thick" ABM system would be designed to serve as a presumed shield against Soviet missile attack.

Those cities selected to be the future sites of the Sentinel ABMs for the "thin" or anti-Chinese missile system are: New York City; Albany, Georgia; Chicago, Illinois; Dallas, Texas; Grand Forks Air Force Base, North Dakota; Oahu Island, Hawaii; Salt Lake City, Utah; Seattle, Washington; Boston, Massachusetts; and Detroit, Michigan. An outlay of about six billion dollars is planned for the construction of this "thin" system, for which about three thousand companies will be engaged for the development and construction of components.

Conditions within the aerospace and military electronics industries shed light on the timing of the proposals for the ABM buildup. In 1961–1962, emphasis was on development of strategic forces. By 1966, these ICBM delivery systems had been substantially constructed. This appears in the change in the composition of the Department of Defense budget. Thus, strategic forces in 1962 received $11.2 billion. By 1966, spending for these purposes had diminished to $6.8 billion, or from 37 to 17 percent of all military spending. Apparently, both the research and the industrial production requirements relative to strategic delivery systems had diminished by 1966–1967. The

Minuteman system of 1,000 missiles in hardened sites was completed, and the Polaris submarine fleet was almost completed. Therefore, the introduction of the new ABM system ("thick" or "thin"), apart from its military merits or demerits, would have the effect of opening up a vast new market for 3,000 U.S. firms, while maintaining the scope and intensity of the decision-making power of the central management within the Pentagon.

Public justification for the concept of the ABM system is that in the event of a Soviet-American nuclear war, the system would be responsible for reducing by a calculated number the lives that would be lost. Thus, the Department of Defense has calculated that 130 million Americans could be killed in a Russian-launched surprise nuclear attack in the foreseeable future. If, however, an ABM system were built around fifty metropolitan areas, then immediate deaths in the United States would be cut to 60 million. This estimated difference between *immediate* fatalities in a possible nuclear war leads the Pentagon to the conclusion that 70 million American lives could be "saved" by an ABM system. This reasoning, which takes no account of the destructive consequences for society of *any* major nuclear exchange, is offered as proof of the necessity to go ahead with ABM systems. In Congressional hearings on the fiscal year 1968 Pentagon budget, Dr. John Foster, Director of Defense Research and Engineering, testified: ". . . it is quite likely that dozens or hundreds of these [Soviet ICBMs] that we hope to intercept will get through. They will get through because of errors, malfunctions and so on. In that event of course, we would suffer even greater damage." In an interview with *Life* magazine, during 1968, Secretary of Defense McNamara said that: ". . . I do not believe that a very limited ABM deployment is a step-up in a strategic arms race between the U.S. and the Soviet Union. Our deployment isn't designed to protect the cities of America against a Soviet strategic attack, and thus it in no way threatens the Soviet ability to deter an American attack."

The beliefs expressed in this statement were not necessarily shared by the rest of the Pentagon management. Thus, in hearings before the Senate Armed Services Committee on the fiscal year 1969 Pentagon budget, Dr. Foster was asked by Senator Symington if ". . . the [Sentinel] is not to protect us from the Soviets. Are you saying that actually it is the first step that we could take in protection against the Soviets?" Dr. Foster responded: "The statement that was made by Mr. McNamara, and concurred in by General Wheeler, was that this deployment is consistent with a first phase of a deployment against the Soviet Union. I don't recommend the latter because I don't know how to build a system that would do the job. I support Secretary McNamara's position but General Wheeler who disagrees with him believes this should be just the first step and he supports it." Evidently, the important members of the Joint Chiefs of Staff backed the limited ABM system as merely a step toward a major ABM system they wished to direct against the Soviet ICBM force, even though it would not "do the job."

What would be the cost of the antiballistic missile system? Although various press reports have suggested that the so-called "thin" system would involve an outlay of about $3 billion, Congressman Robert L. Leggett, Democrat of California and member of the House Committee on Armed Services, stated (in a report on July 5, 1968) that the supposed "thin" system would in fact cost about $6 billion. Some elaboration of the likely cost of the "thin" system was given by Dr. Charles Herzfeld when testifying on the budget of the Advanced Research Project Agency in March, 1967. He stated: "I think one could do reasonably well with $10 billion, maybe $12 billion, or $14 billion." Evidently, there is probable multiplication of cost by a factor of at least 2 that should be allowed for in judging the cost estimates prepared by the Pentagon.

The significance of the ABM, apart from sponsorship by the state-management, rests on the consequences of its construction and use: could it work? what effects would it have on the prospects for nuclear war? Dr. Herbert F. York, former Director of Defense Research and Engineering, told the Senate Committee on Foreign Relations, in March, 1969:

> Any active defense system such as the ABM, must sit in readiness for two or four or eight years and then fire at the precisely correct second following a warning time of only a few minutes. This warning time is so short that systems designers usually attempt to eliminate human decision-makers, even at low command levels, from the decision-making system. Further, the precision needed for the

firing time is so fine that machines must be used to choose the precise instant of firing no matter how the decision to fire is made. In the case of offensive missiles the situation is different in an essential way: although maintaining readiness throughout a long, indefinite period is necessary, the moment of firing is not so precisely controlled in general and hence human decision-makers, including even those at high levels, can be permitted to play a part in the decision-making process. Thus the trigger of any ABM, unlike the trigger of the ICBMs and Polarises, must be continuously sensitive and ready, in short a "hair" trigger for indefinitely long periods of time. On the other hand, it is obvious that we cannot afford to have an ABM fire by mistake or in response to a false alarm, and indeed the Army has recently gone to some pains to assure residents of areas near proposed Sentinel sites that it has imposed design requirements which will insure against the accidental launching of the missile and the subsequent detonation of the nuclear warhead it carries. These two requirements, a "hair" trigger so that it can cope with a surprise attack and a "stiff" trigger so that it will never go off accidentally are, I believe, contradictory requirements. This problem exists only in the real world and not on the test range; on the test range there need be no such concern about accidental misfires, the interceptions do not involve the use of nuclear weapons and the day, if not the second, of the mock attack is known. Another essential (but again difficult to quantify) difference between the real world and the test range lies in the fact that the deployed defensive equipment will, normally, never have been fully exercised and even the supposedly identical test range equipment will never have been tested against the precise target or targets that the deployed equipment would ultimately have to face. In the case of other defense systems which have worked after a fashion, practice using the actual deployed equipment against real targets has been possible and has been a major element in increasing their effectiveness. Thus, the Soviet SAMs in North Vietnam work as well as they do because both the equipment designers and the operating crews have had plenty of opportunities to practice against U.S. targets equipped with real counter-measures and employing real tactics.

For these and similar reasons, as well as because of the technical problems detailed for you last week, I continue to have the gravest doubts as to the capability of any ABM system I have heard of, whether or not the problem has been defined into being "easy" and whether or not it "works" on a test range. I am not here talking about some percentage failure inherent in the mathematical distribution of miss distances, nor statistically predictable failures in system components, but rather about catastrophic failure in which at the moment of truth either nothing happens at all, or all interceptions fail.

Would either a "thin" or "thick" antiballistic missile system actually serve the United States as a competent shield against nuclear attack? Technical judgment contends the answer is no. Dr. Ralph Lapp, on the team of the (World War II) Manhattan Project, and an analyst of nuclear military matters, estimated in January, 1967, that ". . . An anti-missile system might become the equivalent of France's World War II Maginot Line. . . . The Germans simply went around it. An enemy could go around an antiballistic system too. For example, he could patrol eight or ten submarines 100 or 200 miles off the West Coast of the United States. Each submarine could be equipped with dirty nuclear missiles each equivalent to one billion tons of TNT, which could be exploded in the atmosphere at that point. There would be no way to avoid the radioactive fallout which would coat most of the United States with lethal radioactivity and contaminate crops for decades to come." Dr. Lapp indicated that the Communist Chinese have submarines that could be used in this manner.

He also suggested that it would be an error to assume that the Russians or the Chinese need necessarily develop their nuclear capabilities along American lines. There are more ways to deliver nuclear warheads than by the intercontinental missiles and long-range bombers in which the United States and Soviet Union specialize. These would include planes with a short range which could be launched from small ships or from the decks of submarines. A German V-1 vehicle, driven by a primitive ram-jet type of motor, could also be used; these could be launched from submarines or freighters, 100 or 200 miles from enemy territory, at pre-set altitudes so as to evade coastal defense radar. There is nothing in known defense systems to prevent a determined attacker from bringing large nuclear warheads into a harbor in the bottom of a ship. Nuclear warheads could also be placed in a harbor as underwater mines. There is no technology available to prevent a determined attacker from placing nuclear warheads under water in international waters and rigging them to a remote-control trigger.

Such devices are within the realm of known technology, some

involving rather less technical sophistication than the array of known devices that could be attached to ICBMs to disrupt the shielding operation of any ABM system. Incoming missiles could be multiplied in number, some to contain warheads, some to contain devices designed primarily to confuse the radars of the ABM system. Radar-confusing devices would be multiplied by launching multiple warheads from single missiles, some with dummy warheads. Evasion and confusion could also be effected by exploding some warheads at high altitudes, thus drawing the defensive systems away from those warheads on their way in. These possibilities, and the likelihood of the development of additional deceptive devices, generate grave doubts as to the efficacy of any ABM system. Finally, even if an ABM system were to be 90 percent efficient (which is not predictable), that in itself would not necessarily constitute a significant defense for a continental area during nuclear exchange.

There is some evidence that the Soviets have been having a debate parallel to that going on in the United States. Some Soviet generals (Associated Press, February 21, 1967) announced that an ABM system would be competent to shield the Soviet Union. Two days later, the First Deputy Defense Minister of the Soviet Union announced that antimissile defense systems could not prevent all enemy rockets from reaching their targets. He stated: ". . . unfortunately there are no means yet that would guarantee the complete security of our cities and most important objectives from the blows of the enemy's weapons of mass destruction." These contrasting Soviet views parallel American differences of opinion.

During the April, 1969, Senate hearings on the proposed ABM, supporters could not produce a single independent witness of high technical competence who favored the construction of this system. The advocates were, understandably enough, the officers and staffs of the state-management, since the ABM was an unprecedented bid for the further extension of their managerial control over American economy and society, as witnessed by the capital investment the system would require.

A full-scale ABM system would cost about $50 billion. However, experience with major Department of Defense weapons programs indicates that final costs are characteristically three times the initial estimates. Therefore, the final cost of a complex system of this type, based on the performances of its predecessors, would not be $50 billion but $150 billion. To this must be added the cost of constructing a related system of civil defense shelters. The ABM system requires the explosion of nuclear warheads overhead, some of them, hopefully, far from U.S. cities, but many of them to be exploded nearby or directly overhead.

In 1962, Professor John E. Ullmann calculated the cost of building a shelter system designed to give occupants limited protection against the effects of nuclear weapons. Under 1968 cost conditions it would take about $500 billion to shelter a population of 200 million. The combined estimated cost of ABM equipment plus civilian shelters would total $650 billion.

No single project of this magnitude, military or other, has ever been known in the United States or any other society. The cost of the ABM would amount to almost half the value of all "structures in place" on the surface of the United States, and more than one and one-half times the value of all producers' goods used in American production, of every sort. If a so-called shield of this sort were to be constructed within a period of time short enough to allow the system to be militarily meaningful, say five years, an annual expenditure of $130 billion would be required. This would mean almost doubling the federal budget and, therefore, taxes.

Such a program could only be carried out within the framework of a garrison economy and a garrison society. Entire industries would have to be turned away from their civilian functions so as to take on military work. Finite resources, especially labor, would have to be closely controlled, and complete economic controls (price, wage, salary, profit) would be required to restrain the massive inflationary pressure of so much unproductive work, that is, work paid for but not representing purchasable goods. Civilian production of every sort would have to be curtailed and so would much of military production. The outputs of entire industries would have to be totally preempted —for example, those supplying construction materials of every sort. Furthermore, the production capacities of several basic industries would probably fall short of requirements, even if completely allocated to the new military programs.

Military-technical considerations compel attention to the likelihood that new weapons-systems, adding to the already enormous stockpiles of overkill, can only diminish the security of all. For no additions to any weapons-systems among the nuclear powers can alter the condition of equal vulnerability. As the United States moves ahead with programs for MIRV systems, and the Soviet Union does the same, the likelihood is that both sides will multiply the targetable warheads that each can deploy, while finding themselves in no way at any greater advantage than before the new weapons-systems were deployed. The MIRV system can be used to multiply deliverable nuclear warheads by as much as 5 to 10 times. As we contemplate the meaning of 4,000 to 6,000 or more city-destroying warheads in U.S. hands, with a comparable number in Soviet hands, we cannot avoid the realization that this can only produce a heightened sense of fear and insecurity on all sides.

None of this would be altered by attempts to use nuclear weapons for a so-called tactical, rather than a strategic, war. An international commission reported to the Secretary-General of the United Nations in 1967 on the destruction and disruption that would be caused by a tactical nuclear war in Europe. This commission found that the results from the use of smaller nuclear weapons would not differ in a meaningful fashion from the results of the use of powerful nuclear explosions. The commission concluded:

> . . . With 400 weapons, which is not an unreasonably large number if both sides used nuclear weapons in a battle zone, the physical damage caused would correspond to something like six times that caused by all the bombing of World War II—and all sustained in a few days rather than a few years . . .
>
> It is clear enough that the destruction and disruption which would result from so-called tactical nuclear warfare would hardly differ from the effects of strategic war in the area concerned [and] . . . the concept of escalation from tactical to strategic nuclear war could have no possible meaning in an area within which field warfare was being waged by nuclear weapons. . . . [*The New York Times,* October 25, 1967.]

While the great nuclear powers proceed with their arms race, smaller countries become more competent to produce their own nuclear weapons. Also, as the raw material required for atomic explosives becomes more widely available—owing to the large number of nuclear reactors in operation—there is a possibility that a black market in nuclear explosive materials might appear. The U.S. Atomic Energy Commission, concerned about possible black marketeering, named a special commission to inquire into the question of maintaining effective control over the increasing stock of weapons-grade material available in the United States and elsewhere.

Although the further development of the nuclear arms race offers no prospect of military advantage to any side, it does offer the Pentagon a chance for the further aggrandizement of its prerogatives. New programs for nuclear weapons, offensive and defensive, would require military budgets of an unprecedented size, together with mobilization of manpower and other resources to a degree hitherto unknown.

BACTERIOLOGICAL WARFARE

While public attention has been focused on nuclear weapons and their delivery systems, recent research gives promise of producing the poor man's atom bomb. For one thing, atomic bombs are becoming easier to build. In a review article dated October 25, 1966, *New York Times* science reporter Walter Sullivan pointed out: "It is cheaper today for a non-nuclear power to make an atomic bomb than ever before and it is getting easier each year. No major secret stands in the way of manufacturing a crude weapon. Secrecy remains a factor chiefly in the design of weapons of high yield that will fit into the bomb bay of an aircraft or the nose of a missile."

This means that many countries, probably with India leading the list, now have the access to fissionable material, the necessary funds, and the technical know-how for building atomic weapons. Although these weapons may be judged primitive by standards of yield-to-weight ratio and complexity of delivery system, still even the crudest atomic weapon gives a concentration of energy release that not even a great mass of conventional weapons can give. Further, Sullivan stated, "Indian officials have said privately that if such a decision were made, a crude bomb could be produced in 18 months at a cost of from $10 million to $20 million. American specialists believe that 3 years at a cost of $50 million is more realistic. For a country lacking India's plutonium production capacity the estimate is that it would cost a few hundred million dollars more to build the necessary reactors." These sums are not large compared either to the original cost of building atomic weapons in the United States or to the size of the current military budgets of the major countries of the world.

All of this casts the role of bacteriological and chemical weapons into high relief, as weapons that can be produced at a relatively low cost utilizing basic research already recorded in the literature. The major problems in the use of bacteriological and chemical materials as weapons lie in the area of the design of delivery systems and the allied problem of protecting one's own population, or forces, from such weapons when they are used. The U.S. Department of Health, Education, and Welfare defines biological warfare as: "The intentional use of living organisms or their toxic products to cause death, disability or damage in man, animals or plants. The target is man, either by causing his sickness or death, or through limitation of his food supplies or other agricultural resources."

After the Kennedy administration entered office in 1961, it undertook a major expansion of the research and development budget for chemical and biological warfare (CBW). Thus, in fiscal year 1961, the annual budget for CBW for the military services was $57 million. By 1964, this had been raised to $158 million and, by 1968, to more than $350 million. Details of the production of toxins and the devices for their delivery have not been made available to the public. Still, quite a bit is known about bacteriological and chemical weaponry, as well as the scale of resources applied to developing them. At Fort Detrick, Maryland, there is a Chemical Warfare Division covering 1,300 acres, with a set of laboratories and allied structures valued at $75 million. Situated there is: ". . . one of the world's largest animal farms. Its facilities for conducting research with pathogenic organisms are among the most advanced in the world." In 1967, Fort Detrick employed 120 men with Ph.D.s, 110 men with Master's degrees, 320 men with B.S.s, 14 M.D.s, and 34 other senior professionals, in addition to supporting technical staff. Only 15 percent of the work conducted there is published in non-classified scientific literature, because, as described in *Science* (January 13, 1967), ". . . much of the work inescapably has a special character, an inverted quality like that of medicine turned inside out. It consists in part, for example, of efforts to breed into pathogenic organisms precisely the characteristics—such as resistance to antibiotics—that medical researchers would like to see eradicated." It is in order to reach such goals that a program of basic and applied research is being pursued. The agenda of programs reads like that of a major meeting of a professional society of microbiologists and scientists in related fields. (See, for example, the publication from Fort Detrick entitled "Opportunities for Fundamental Research.")

Another major bacteriological and chemical warfare research center is the Dugway, Utah, Proving Ground, an area larger than the state of Rhode Island. Dugway is a principal station for field-testing chemical and biological munitions. During 1968, an accident at Dugway Proving Ground allowed a small quantity of lethal material to escape the boundary of the reservation, causing the death of 6,000 sheep in neighboring areas.

A review article in *Science* (January 20, 1967) reported:

. . . Biological munitions are produced at Pine Bluff Arsenal, a 15,000 acre installation outside Pine Bluff, Arkansas, which employs about 1,400 people. Pine Bluff also produces toxic-chemical munitions and riot-control munitions. Its job runs from manufacturing the agents to filling and assembling weapons. Research and development on chemical weapons, and some production and assembly of them, take place in a number of subunits of the Edgewood Arsenal, in Maryland. Various chemical munitions, reportedly including nerve gas, mustard gas, "incapacitants," and anticrop weapons, are produced at Rocky Mountain Arsenal in Denver. The U.S. also operates a major manufacturing plant—at an estimated annual cost of $3.5 million—in Newport, Indiana, where Sarin, a lethal nerve gas, is produced and loaded into rockets, land mines, and artillery shells. The plant is managed under contract by the Food Machinery Corporation, has 300 employees, and is reported to have been operating 24 hours daily since 1960. Additional chemicals were manufactured during the middle 1950's at another plant in Muscle Shoals, Alabama. A few years ago the Pentagon entered into contracts with about ten chemical companies for research and development on improved defoliants and desiccants; the chemical defoliants used in Vietnam are for the most part purchased commercially. . . .

The U.S. Army Field Manual 3–10 (*Employment of Chemical and Biological Agents*) states that biological weapons are noteworthy for their ability to ". . . accomplish their effects . . . with little or no physical destruction. This constitutes an advantage both in combat operation . . . and—from a longer range viewpoint—in post war rehabilitation, where overall rebuilding requirements would be reduced." That is, the charm of biological and chemical weaponry lies in the fact that all physical structures—streets, industrial plants, and so forth—are immune to their effects. Accordingly, while entire enemy populations may be destroyed, the physical goods and wealth among which they lived would presumably be left intact.

The above characterization of biological weapons in the U.S. Army Field Manual suggests a strategic use of CBW weapons. An independent view of the characteristics and effects of biological warfare weapons is summarized in the following tables on human diseases and infective agents for biological warfare and on animal diseases and infective agents for biological warfare. These data were compiled by Professor Martin M. Kaplan, microbiologist and epidemiologist, and were first published in the *Bulletin of the Atomic Scientists* in June, 1960.

The neat tabulations of these tables and the classification of effects as "strategic" or "tactical" conceals various nightmarish pathologic effects. For example (from *Science,* January 20, 1967):

. . . Rocky Mountain spotted fever is an acute infectious disease producing fever, joint and muscular pains, aversion to light, and sometimes delirium, coma, convulsions, tremors, muscular rigidity, and jaundice. Persistent effects may include deafness, impaired vision and anemia. Mortality in untreated cases averages about 20 percent but can run as high as 80 percent. Psittacosis, or parrot fever, causes acute pulmonary infection, chills, fever, sore throat, constipation, weakness, and, sometimes, delirium. Mortality in untreated cases is about 10 percent; death is more common among persons over 30. Coccidioidomycosis occurs as an acute, disabling disease resembling flu, and as a chronic, malignant infection that may involve any or all organs—including skin and bones—and produces abscesses. For the second form, mortality is about 50 percent. Botulism poisoning produces vomiting, constipation, thirst, weakness, headache, fever, dizziness, double vision, and

Table 1
Human Diseases and Infective Agents for BW

	STRATEGIC USE	TACTICAL USE	SPECIFIC PROTECTION AVAILABLE AGAINST PRESENTLY KNOWN STRAINS
A. *Bacterial Infections and Intoxications*			
* Anthrax	+	+	+ to ?
* Botulism	+	+	+ to ?
* Brucellosis	+	+	?
Cholera	−	+	?
Dysentery (Bacillary)	−	+	−
Erysipeloid	−	+	+
Diphtheria	−	+	+
* Glanders	+	+	−
Hemophilus influenza	+	+	−
Leptospirosis	+	+	? to −
Listeriosis	+	+	−
* Melioidosis	+	+	−
Meningococcal meningitis	+	+	+
Pertussis	−	+	+
* Plague (pneumonic)	+	+	+ to ?
Pneumococcal pneumonia	+	+	+
Streptococcosis (antibiotic resistant)	+	+	?
Staphylococcosis (antibiotic resistant and enterotoxin producing)	−	+	−
Trepanematoses	−	+	+
* Tuberculosis	−	+	?
* Tularemia	+	+	?
Typhoid and other salmonelloses and shigellosis	?	+	? to −
B. *Mycotic Infections*			
Blastomycosis	?	+	−
* Coccidioidomycosis	+	+	−
Cryptococcosis	?	+	−
Dermatomycoses (various)	−	+	−
Histoplasmosis	?	+	−
Nocardiosis	+	+	−

Table 1 (cont'd)

	STRATEGIC USE	TACTICAL USE	SPECIFIC PROTECTION AVAILABLE AGAINST PRESENTLY KNOWN STRAINS
C. *Viral and Rickettsial Diseases*			
* Adenoviruses (some strains)	+	+	?
* Anthropod-borne viruses (Eastern, Western, Venezuelan RSS, St. Louis, Japanese B, Rift Valley, Dengue, Yellow Fever, and others)	+	+	+ to − (I)
* B virus	+	+	−
* Coxsackie group (B)	+	+	−
Echo (some strains)	−	+	−
Infectious Hepatitis	−	?	−
* Influenza	+	+	+ to ?
Lymphocytic choriomeningitis	+	+	−
Mumps	−	?	+
Parainfluenza group	?	+	−
Poliomyelitis	?	+	+
Phlebotomus fever	−	+	− (I)
* Psittacosis	+	+	?
* Q Fever	+	+	? to −
Rabies	−	+	+ to ?
* Rocky Mountain Spotted Fever	+	+	?
Rubella and Rubeola	−	+	? to −
Scrub typhus	−	+	− (I)
Smallpox	−	+	+
* Typhus (epidemic)	+	+	+ to ? (I)
D. *Protozoal Infections*			
Bilharziasis	−	+	− to ? (I)
Dysentery (amoebic)	−	+	− to ?
Leishmaniasis	−	+	− (I)
Malaria	−	+	+ (I)
* Toxoplasmosis	+	+	−
Trypanosomiasis	−	+	? (I)

Key to symbols appears at end of Table 2.

SOURCE: Martin M. Kaplan, "Communicable Diseases and Epidemics," *Bulletin of the Atomic Scientists,* June 1960.

Table 2

Animal Diseases and Infective Agents for BW

	STRATEGIC USE	TACTICAL USE	SPECIFIC PROTECTION AVAILABLE AGAINST PRESENTLY KNOWN STRAINS
A. *Bacterial Infections and Intoxications*			
* Anthrax	+	+	+
* Blackleg and other clostridial diseases	+	+	+ to ?
* Brucellosis	+	+	+ to ?
* Botulism	+	+	?
Glanders	—	+	—
Leptospirosis	+	+	? to —
Listeriasis	—	+	—
Pasteurelloses	—	+	? to —
Salmonelloses	—	+	—
Streptococcal and staphylococcal (antibiotic resistant) infections	—	+	—
Swine erysipelas	—	+	+ to ?
* Tuberculosis	+	+	? to —
B. *Mycotic Infections*			
Aspergillosis	—	+	—
Blastomylosis	—	+	—
* Coccidioidomycosis	+	+	—
Cryptococcosis	?	+	—
Dermatomycoses (various)	—	+	—
Epizootic lymphangitis	—	+	—
Histoplasmosis	?	+	—
C. *Viral and Rickettsial Diseases*			
* African swine fever	—	+	—
* Arthropod-borne viruses (Eastern, Western, Venezuelan, Japanese B, loupingill, Rift Valley blue-tongue, African horse sickness)	+	+	+ to ? (I)
Borna Disease	—	+	—
Bovine mucosal complex	—	+	—
* Bovine pleuropneumonia	+	+	+ to ?
Chronic respiratory disease (poultry)	—	+	—

Table 2 (cont'd)

	STRATEGIC USE	TACTICAL USE	SPECIFIC PROTECTION AVAILABLE AGAINST PRESENTLY KNOWN STRAINS
Duck hepatitis	—	+	—
Equine infectious abortion	—	+	—
Equine influenza	—	+	—
* Foot and mouth disease	+	+	+ to ?
Fowl plague	—	+	+ to ?
Fowl pox	—	+	+
Heartwater	—	+	?
Infectious laryngotracheitis (fowl)	—	+	+
Infectious bronchitis (fowl)	—	+	?
Leukosis complex (fowl)	—	+	—
Lumpy skin disease	—	+	—
Newcastle disease	—	+	+
Psittacosis	—	+	—
Q Fever	—	+	? to —
* Rinderpest	+	+	+
* Sheepox	+	+	+
Swine fever (hog cholera)	+	+	+
Swine influenza	—	+	—
* Teschen disease	—	+	+ to ?
Rift Valley fever	—	+	+ to ?
* Vesicular exanthema	—	+	—
* Vesicular stomatitis	—	+	—
D. *Protozoal Diseases*			
Anaplasmosis	—	+	— (I)
Babesiasis	—	+	? to — (I)
Coccidiosis	—	+	—
Theileriasis	—	+	? to — (I)
Trypanosomiases	—	+	? to — (I)

+ = suitable.

— = unsuitable.

? = questionable, either because of the nature of the agent or insufficient knowledge.

* = especially suitable agent.

(I) = insecticide effective against usual carriers.

SOURCE: Martin M. Kaplan, "Communicable Diseases and Epidemics," *Bulletin of the Atomic Scientists,* June 1960.

dilation of the pupils. In the United States, death occurs in about 65 percent of the cases.

Particular diseases are not recommended for particular uses in unclassified Army publications, but the anticivilian character of biological weaponry is suggested: "While these agents might be employed against selected individuals, their main value appears to lie in producing mass casualties over large areas with resultant physical and psychological effects that could weaken or destroy the targets group's ability to wage war.

The characteristics of chemical-biological warfare agents given in the above tables are based upon open, non-secret publications, and this is necessarily an incomplete statement of the number of such agents and their probable destructive ability. Since the objective of the microbiologists and others working for the military services has been to heighten virulent characteristics in various strains of micro-organisms, the tables, based only upon the open literature, give an understated profile of the lethal quality of organisms that have been selectively bred for weapons purposes.

Bacteriological weapons have certain special fascinations for military planners wishing to prepare a variety of weapons for the "flexible response" strategy first formulated during the Kennedy administration. Biological weapons kill people, do not destroy property, and, unlike any other means of destruction, are self-multiplying. An opponent would be at a particular disadvantage because knowledge of the nature of BW weapons is possible only after their effects are being felt. Furthermore, these weapons are cheap, compact and, despite limitations imposed by temperature, sunlight, wind and humidity, can be widely dispersed by varied means. Dr. Milton Leitenberg wrote in *Scientist and Citizen* in 1967:

. . . Early discussions of BW made much of its suitability for covert introduction by saboteurs into the water and food supply of a city, into ventilating systems, or simply into the air. Recent emphasis has shifted to delivery by a more efficient means, dispersion by aerosols. As a Senate study of chemical, biological and radiological warfare pointed out, aerosols containing various BW agents would be suitable for dissemination over wide areas. This could be accomplished from the air by planes or drones (spray tanks or bombs) or by free balloons; from the ground by clouds or mist projected by generators located upwind from the target area, or by shells, rockets or missiles carrying BW warheads; and from the sea by clouds or mists launched from ships when inshore winds prevail. Rockets, missiles and shells could also be launched from shipboard. Floating mines, launched by ship or set adrift in ocean currents and set to detonate along coastal areas might also be used. The capability for anonymous delivery is retained by several of these newer delivery means, even by the modern airplane outfitted for aerial dissemination . . .

Nevertheless, biological warfare could put those who employ it in hazard. Just as any power releasing large amounts of radioactive materials into the atmosphere runs the risk of poisoning its own air supply, so in the case of BW there is a defined ". . . 'backfire' problem—the danger of infection to the user of a biological weapon or to a neutral. Infective microorganisms are living and self-propagating; thus BW has been called a 'human conflagration.' Given modern methods of developing the most virulent strains of particular microorganisms, the problem of how to prevent the spread of disease, rather than how to spread it, is probably the major concern . . ."

It is difficult to conjecture the exact scale of weaponry already prepared in the biological and chemical warfare field. One indication was obtained in August, 1968, when a panel of scientists and teachers, mostly from the University of Colorado, inquired into the safety problems associated with the operation of the Dugway Proving Grounds and the storage, near Denver, Colorado, of 100 steel tanks containing nerve gases. *The New York Times* reported on August 18, 1968: "Each cylinder contained enough nerve gas to kill one million people, the panel said." This suggests the existence of an overkill supply of bacteriological and chemical weapons parallel to the overkill stockpile of nuclear weapons.

Since atomic-nuclear weaponry had already made the traditional meaning of military superiority obsolete, the advent of the newer bacteriological and chemical weapons merely underscored that effect, although the implications of the two types of weapons systems are different. For example, biological weapons are likely to be more effective in countries where the population lives in concentrated areas, that is, in major industrial societies, and less effective in countries whose populations are dispersed in numerous small towns and villages.

At the same time, the development of bacteriological warfare technology puts an "equalizer" into the hands of small countries who might prefer to resort to it instead of trying to compete in the area of nuclear weaponry, which only relatively rich nations can afford to produce.

While nuclear and CBW weapons have tolled the bell for defense, the military managers and their ideologists are unable or unwilling to hear the knell. Instead, they indulge themselves and the nation in science fictions: first, that by "improving" weapons and having more of them, it will be possible to have "superior" powers; and second, that having large armed forces will deter an opponent. The combination of a quest for numerical and qualitative advantage, with the effort to deter an opponent by using a credible threat, brought the world near to destruction over the Cuban Missile Crisis of October, 1962.

THE CUBAN MISSILE CRISIS

In October, 1962, the governments of the United States and the Soviet Union, each with a considerable nuclear arsenal, were prepared to use their arsenals against each other's societies. The history of the American government's role in the crisis has been reported by Robert Kennedy and by journalists and political analysts. To this day, however, the literature of the Cuban Missile Crisis, and of the Kennedy administration, contains no diagnosis by the President, or any of his aides, as to what they thought led the Soviet Union to try to put missiles into Cuba in the first place. Sorensen's book on Kennedy lists some possible reasons for the Soviet move, but these speculations merely indicate that the White House never resolved this question. I believe that the Soviet move into Cuba was essentially a spasm, a fear-laden response to a series of United States military "successes."

There are substantive grounds for assuming that by August, 1962, the Soviet military and political chiefs knew that:

1. The U.S. government knew the exact location of Soviet land-based ICBMs.
2. The U.S. knew the major technological characteristics of Soviet missiles.
3. The U.S. knew the Soviet strategic plans for the use of its ICBMs.

4. The U.S. possessed both a quantity of missiles that was a multiple of Soviet ICBMs and an overwhelmingly larger general nuclear strategic force (including planes)—enough to make a nuclear "first-strike" a calculable proposition.

5. Within the U.S., there had been, in the spectrum of military policy literature, vocal representation of the "first-strike" position.

How did the Soviet Union know this? What plausible inferences could have been made by Soviet security chiefs about the significance of this analysis for their military position? And why Cuba?

The Soviets could know items 4 and 5 from the public press. As to the location of Soviet missiles: Until 1960, the United States was flying U-2 airplanes over the Soviet Union. These gave detailed photographs of new missile-sites. This provided the United States both with the number and the exact location coordinates of the Soviet ICBM system. By 1961, the U-2s were succeeded by Samos satellites. These satellites, operating at an altitude of about 125 miles, produced films that could differentiate objects three inches apart on the surface of the earth. And by this means, too, the government of the United States obtained continuing and accurate photographic evidence of Soviet missile sites.

As to items 2 and 3, one must take into account the effects of the successful military espionage operation of Colonel Oleg Penkovsky during a 16-month period terminating in August, 1962. Oleg Penkovsky was a colonel in Soviet Intelligence, a graduate of the Soviet missile school (ranking first in his class), and a member of the elite of Soviet society, having access to the highest level of military security information. According to the Soviet indictment, during the 16 months Penkovsky served as a Western intelligence agent, he delivered 5,000 frames of microfilm of Soviet top-security information and also (according to the account given in *The Penkovsky Papers*) conversed for many hours with Western agents during several trips to western Europe. The Penkovsky defection was publicly announced in the spring of 1963 and was elaborately reported in dispatches from Moscow, Washington, and elsewhere as a major rupture of the Soviet security system.

Owing to the nature of Penkovsky's position, it is entirely reasonable to infer that the information obtained by photographic means of

Soviet missiles and their location was now supplemented by abundant data on Soviet missile technology, and military doctrine concerning the use of ICBMs and other weapons.

Penkovsky was arrested in October, 1962, and had noted in his diary that he was under Soviet police surveillance from August, 1962 on. At some time between August and October, 1962, the Soviet high command had strong grounds for concluding that knowledge in the hands of Oleg Penkovsky was also in the hands of the United States government.

Soviet marshals trained in nuclear deterrence doctrine were probably impelled toward the conclusion that they no longer possessed a credible nuclear deterrent force. For the Penkovsky information in U.S. hands, added to prior U.S. knowledge, plus nuclear capability, meant that the U.S. had the means for conceivably destroying the main Soviet nuclear force. Under such conditions, nuclear strategic doctrine required restoration of a credible deterrent capability at all possible speed. This was almost obtained by the Soviet effort to place short and intermediate-range missiles in Cuba. The Cuban site was especially suited for such an endeavor, being 90 miles from the United States mainland and on the southern side, thus out of range of the main U.S. ICBM warning system located to the north (in anticipation of missile flights from the Soviet Union). Furthermore, secure control of missiles located on Cuban soil (possibly with warheads stored in Soviet submarines operating offshore) would have given the Soviet military an opportunity to deploy an impressive number of missiles close enough to the United States to be visible and credible, a threat to important U.S. metropolitan centers—thus restoring the credibility of the Soviet deterrent.

This theory of the missile crisis interprets Soviet military behavior in terms of modern nuclear strategy, accounting for each step they took and the timing of each step.

This viewpoint explains the Cuban missile crisis and the nuclear confrontation it brought as having been generated by a series of American military successes: first, in emplacing a large number of ICBMs, and second, in gathering military intelligence by means of the U-2 flights over the Soviet Union, as well as through Penkovsky's information. These successes seemed to diminish Soviet power. But a cornered major nuclear power is not left without alternatives. There are enough able men in each of the great states of the world to contrive fresh military and non-military moves when they judge their country to be in grave danger. This is what probably happened inside the U.S.S.R., and the attempt to place missiles in Cuba was one such move. The success of the American effort to gain numerical missile superiority and other military advantage was probably the trigger that initiated events that almost culminated in nuclear disaster.

The lesson for the 1970s is that every effort by the Pentagon to use U.S. technology for a further try at military superiority must be stopped, for if permitted it is likely that they would lead to nuclear war crises, with an end-of-the-world war not excluded. This is the dead end to which the state-management schemes for MIRV and ABM would lead us.

ANALYSIS

In the name of defense, the state-management based in the Pentagon has been deploying an increasing array of strategic weapons systems. Analysis of the characteristics of these systems does not reveal them to be serviceable shields for protecting the United States from external attack.

Military power, until the end of the Second World War, was an aggregation of men and matériel which could be used to successfully enforce the political will of a government. A major industrial society, therefore, had an advantage over smaller, or nonindustrial, societies. In this age of nuclear/bacteriological weaponry, this advantage has become minimal. Nations with a small industrial capacity are now able to develop weapons and means to deliver them, however primitive, which could strike deadly blows at even the largest, wealthiest, and most technologically advanced society. Therefore, if Pentagon management is allowed to continue to enhance its decision-power through the further construction of even more destructive devices, we are liable to move into an era of weapons even more frightful than those now existing. A catalog of such weaponry was made public by Nigel Calder in his volume *Unless Peace Comes*. The weapons described by such qualified persons as Dr. Gordon J. F. McDonald, former Vice-President of the Institute of Defense Analyses, include ones that can manipulate the forces of nature so as to produce catastrophes to order, including droughts, hurricanes, frosts, and tidal waves. Other possibilities include new types of chemical and biological weapons, as well as robot-operated and robot-controlled weapons of great lethal character.

Such technological capabilities would never remain unique to the United States, for knowledge of nature cannot be made the private preserve of any one nation. Further, there are no supermen who alone can understand nature. One of the myths in the United States during the late 1950s and early 1960s was that the Soviet Union had developed rockets of enormous size for their space journeys. Photographs and accompanying reports in *Time* (June 9, 1967) disclosed: "Instead of achieving a breakthrough in rocket technology believed by the West to have made the Gagarin flight possible, the Russians had simply strapped together enough smaller rocket engines to provide the necessary thrust." In a word, there had been no major development of enormous rockets for the Soviet space operations.

The tradition of military technology is permeated with the idea that suboptimization is the strategy basic to success, that is, that the military system as a whole is improved by an improvement in its parts. From this standpoint, the technical improvement of rifles, bullets, tanks, trucks, airplanes, bombs, guidance systems, etc., is desirable and regarded as appropriate in the expectation that the result will be greater military competence. This fundamental mode of thinking and acting has not been revised in light of the overkill condition created by the newer weapons. Instead, state-management has pressed the ideology of suboptimization into its service, using it as a guide for "advancing" on every military-technological front simultaneously.

One consequence of this quest for military superiority, fed by an $8 billion research and development budget, has been to lead the population to believe that defense and even military superiority in the nuclear age are indeed attainable (and admirable) goals. But this is untrue, and therefore the public has been led to believe in science fiction. The laws of nature cannot be preempted as the private property of any nation, and the wealth of this nation is not inexhaustible. Even if this wealth were unstintingly applied to military technology research, having technological leadership in all possible areas would not necessarily produce an ability to shield the United States from external attack. But the state-management has not only implied the reverse of this, they have convinced the American people to trust them with $1,000 billion of public capital since the Second World War in the name of supplying a defense for the United States.

One of the newer proposals, the one for MIRV, discloses the quality of their recommendations. There is no part of this technological innovation which cannot be duplicated by the Soviet Union. The program for researching, designing, and building these weapons will have the following consequences for the state-management: the scrapping of present missiles, including their frames, rocket engines, fuels, warheads, and guidance systems, together with the construction, assemblage and emplacement of entirely new elements of this sort; the whole massive accumulation of 1,700 intercontinental ballistic missiles, constructed between 1958 and 1968, will be declared technically obsolete, so that immense new capital outlays will be required for the construction of the newer version of ICBMs, to contain as many as 5 to 10 warheads per missile—or a total of 8,500 to 17,000 warheads. This is a nightmare, not defense.

These operations would in turn enlarge the scale of the state-management's operations, while leaving the United States no less vulnerable than it was before.

6

The Vietnam Wars
Program and
Its Consequences

"Vietnam, rather than being the exception, is the pattern for the future." This forecast was made by the editors of *Armed Forces Management,* a Washington-based military trade journal, in a July, 1966, editorial article. The editors wrote further: "Reasoning that poverty breeds violence, defense planners expect the incidence of conflict to increase in the future and be concentrated in the Southern Hemisphere —in Africa, along the littoral of the Asian subcontinent and in South America. While the United States eschews the role of global gendarme, it will help those nations which ask for its help. The prospects then are more American involvement in some of the most primitive areas of the world."

This prognosis by the editors of an unofficial military journal corresponds with the contingency-planning for future wars of intervention with United States participation. Secretary of Defense McNamara, in his statements to the Congress on budgets and defense programs (1966 and 1967), discussed prospects for internal wars in various parts of the world. The possibility of internal wars was considered for

Laos, Thailand, Burma, Indonesia, Iraq, Venezuela, Colombia, Bolivia, Guatemala, Uruguay, the Philippines, Nigeria, the Congo, Ghana, Uganda, and Burundi. The Secretary of Defense saw the prospect of civil wars in these and in other countries requiring, as in Vietnam, military intervention by the United States.

The military-political doctrine developed in and around the government of the United States from 1961 on justified U.S. intervention in internal wars in the name of the need to establish conditions of social stability. The reasoning was that stability is a precondition for economic development.

This perspective has been formulated as the doctrine of "flexible response," an enlargement of military options. Flexible response was the doctrine introduced in 1961, during the Kennedy administration, under which the Department of Defense was equipped with diverse military capability so as to allow military power to be used in varied situations. The increase of options also meant that this diversity of military power could be varied in intensity—escalated as required by particular military-political situations.

The identification in McNamara's annual reports of so many prospects for intervention bears out the prognosis that the United States government has developed a "counter-revolutionary reflex." Conor Cruise O'Brien pointed out in 1966: "In publicly assessing whether a given political revolution is or is not in the interests of the people concerned, the sole criterion now regularly and explicitly applied by the government of the United States is whether the Communists are associated with the revolution." Almost every population of any considerable size will contain a spectrum of persons with diverse political views, and there are bound to be some who are or could be arbitrarily designated as Communist. Thus, the State Department discovered 58 Communists in the Dominican Republic. Clearly, if the presence of 58 persons within a large political movement is accepted as a definition of its nature, as was the case in the Dominican Republic, then the doctrine of military intervention to block "Communist" takeovers has a wide range of potential application.

Many nationalist and anti-upper-class revolts in less developed countries have included guerrilla warfare. Such warfare was also part of Europe's military effort against the Second World War occupation forces; in Ireland the method was used against British rule. The history of guerrilla warfare indicates that three elements determine the success of this technique: first, the existence of a group of men prepared to make major personal sacrifices on behalf of a common cause; second, support for the guerrilla fighters by a population or part of a government; and, third, the ability of the guerrilla forces to look like the noncombatants surrounding them. Wherever these three conditions obtained, the history of guerrilla warfare shows that no available military technology has been able to overcome the guerrilla forces militarily, regardless of the military power or terror that was applied. This has been the case where guerrillas have operated in small countries as well as large countries, and against opponents with a relatively moderate tradition of using military power, as well as against opponents with a tradition of using military power as a terrorist weapon. Guerrilla techniques have been successful against opponents who have used simple military technology, as well as against opponents whose military techniques have been very elaborate.

The chiefs of the Pentagon were aware of these facts concerning guerrilla warfare in 1964 and 1965. Nevertheless, early in 1965, I made a point of visiting the Secretary of Defense to call his attention, directly, to the characteristics that make guerrilla warfare succeed, and to warn him of the prospect of a military "non-win" for U.S. forces in Vietnam, as a consequence of the "counter-insurgency" operations. It is, therefore, important to understand why such analyses and the evidence supporting them were disregarded. On one count, the Pentagon directorate were confident that they could invent new military and social technology that would overcome the advantages specific to a guerrilla army. But a second factor was also operative: a will to succeed against guerrilla warfare that was so strong as to compel the operators of the U.S. war of intervention to overlook the inherent advantages of the guerrilla fighters and to seek to overwhelm them either in terms of numbers or firepower or both. The Pentagon chiefs deceived themselves and the nation about United States military capability in Vietnam.

Militarily, the story of the Vietnam war is the story of an effort to overcome what was initially a guerrilla war by force of sheer firepower or by concentrating larger military forces in given locations. This latter was facilitated by the use of sophisticated transportation devices, such as helicopters.

Nevertheless, it is quite clear from the record of the Vietnam war, especially during the period 1963 to 1968, that the major effort by the government of the United States to overcome what was first a guerrilla war, and later became a combination of guerrilla fighting and fighting between conventional national forces, was not successful. It is reasonable to suppose that if the military operations in Vietnam were primarily of the latter sort, that is between conventional national forces, then the U.S. advantage in firepower, in military technology, and in general military sophistication might very well have made a military victory possible. But military victory was not possible, and it was not possible through this period despite a major U.S. effort because of the extent to which the South Vietnamese and North Vietnamese opponents were fighting a guerrilla war.

In 1965, in my volume *Our Depleted Society,* I cited the case of mortar attacks conducted against U.S. air bases. The military operations at that time, though small in scale and limited in number, gave the clue to the guerrilla form of the military-political method being used by the Vietcong. In 1964, various mortar attacks against U.S. bases clearly came from populated farm areas. Subsequent search operations by South Vietnamese and U.S. forces failed to disclose any trace of the mortars, the men who carried them, or the containers in which mortar shells were transported to the site. The disappearance of these men and their matériel in that area, without a trace, was possible only because the population was shielding them. It was physically impossible to move these weapons into that area, mount them, fire them, dismantle them and move away without being visible to a considerable number of local peasants. Evidently, the local peasants preferred to protect the guerrilla operators.

Exactly the same pattern has prevailed through many phases of military operations through 1968. Thus, rockets fired in substantial salvos into South Vietnamese cities required transportation to a distance of some six miles from the perimeter of major cities. Transported in several sections, they had to be mounted in place, and fired; the men who had done the work then withdrew. This has been done repeatedly and with military success, while there has been a notable failure to apprehend the men in the act of firing or withdrawing from the missile fire operation. Since this rocket firing is being done from only a few miles outside major South Vietnamese cities, in substantially populated areas, it can only be accounted for by the analysis of guerrilla warfare as stated above: that the fighting men take high personal risk, are befriended by the local population, and apparently melt into the local population, becoming undistinguishable from them in the eyes of American or South Vietnamese opponents. The lesson of these events, one set in 1964 and the other in 1968, should correct the bias many Americans have toward technically sophisticated and expensive ways of delivering military force. In the cases cited, mortars and short-range rockets, relatively simple and inexpensive devices, were used to accomplish the slaughter and destruction that could be otherwise administered either by fighter-bombers coming from some distance or by cannon. The use of these latter alternatives is of course relatively expensive, while the mortars and the rockets are rated rather low on scales of technological complexity and expense.

Since the 122-mm., three-part portable rocket used by the National Liberation Front (NLF) has a 41-pound warhead and a range of six and three-quarter miles, attacks with this weapon on cities could be stopped only by a cordon of troops along a perimeter about six and three-quarter miles from the city edge. For Saigon, this would require a force of 20,500 for guard duty alone—apart from the service troops for this many soldiers. Such a static defense around South Vietnamese cities would consume a great part of the field manpower of United States and South Vietnamese forces. As a result, the 1968 rocket attacks continued unchecked.

The essential point is this: guerrilla warfare is a military expression of a political movement supported by a major part of the South Vietnamese population. That is the crucial ingredient that made the NLF guerrilla component of the war undefeatable even by overwhelming U.S. military power.

The United States military operation in Vietnam acquired unheard-of dimensions in the effort to overcome the political support of the NLF by means of high-technology-applied destructive power. By 1969, U.S. forces had bombarded North and South Vietnam with 3 million tons of high explosives (80 percent in the South). This compares with 2 million tons of high explosives dropped during the Second World War in both the European and Pacific theaters of operations. American soldiers in Vietnam carried six times the firepower of G.I.'s in the Second World War, and U.S. forces spent about $400,000 per enemy killed (including 75 bombs and 150 artillery shells per corpse). U.S. forces spent $1.8 billion on heavy-construction programs in Vietnam, including about 1,500 separate projects: 6 new deep-water ports; 8 shallow-draft ports; 8 jet air bases; 80 auxiliary airfields; hundreds of miles of pipelines and roads; barracks for more than 600,000 men. At peak, the United States contractors operated enough earth-moving, construction, and concrete plants to dig the Suez Canal in 18 months and surface the New Jersey Turnpike every 30 days; a new "Pentagon West" houses the general staff; the Cam Ranh Bay harbor development cost $110 million and the allied depot was slated to be the largest in the world, with 3 million square feet of covered and open storage space.

Through September, 1969, American armed forces suffered 44,798 killed; the South Vietnamese military fatalities were 93,738. Also, through 1969, about 547,000 NLF and North Vietnamese soldiers were killed. At the same time, an unknown but very large number of civilians, probably many hundreds of thousands, were killed in South Vietnam. With this enormous carnage created by numerically superior U.S. and South Vietnamese armed forces, the Saigon correspondent of the London *Daily Telegraph* reported on November 2, 1968:

> The Government in Hanoi and the political arm of the Vietcong—the National Liberation Front—today administer over 1,800 of the 2,500 villages and over 8,000 of the 11,650 hamlets inside South Vietnam. Indeed, Saigon administers less than eight million of the total population of 17 million and of this eight million some four-and-a-half million are soldiers and civil servants paid by the state.

The nature of military operations in Vietnam is also indicated by the nature of many of the casualties. Thus, an officer returned from Vietnam has privately reported that fewer than 20 percent of the persons treated in United States armed forces hospitals have been battle casualties. In his estimate, the largest number were men suffering from tropical diseases, including forms of malaria difficult to treat and fungus diseases of various sorts. Americans in South Vietnam could hardly remain unaffected by the one in five South Vietnamese suffering from TB. The result has been that small but still significant numbers of Americans have contracted that disease.

In South Vietnam generally, there has been a surge in the incidence of epidemic disease of various sorts, as reported by the United Nations World Health Organization in its 1967 report on "Epidemiological Situation in Vietnam." The UN group reported:

> . . . Since 1962 the incidence of plague has risen in epidemic proportions in South Vietnam. . . . the threat of plague spreading from South Vietnam to other nations in the Pacific basin is causing grave concern among health and quarantine officials through the Western Pacific area. Cases of plague have been recognized in 27 of South Vietnam's 47 provinces and plague infection has also been found in rodents and fleas at a number of ports and airports including Saigon, Nha Trang, Cam Ranh, and Da Nang. During 11 months of 1967, there were more than 4,500 suspected cases of plague. The number of suspected cases was nearly double the number estimated for 1966 . . .

The rising rates of plague, cholera, and venereal diseases were cited as "outstandingly serious problems" in South Vietnam. Another disease which is on the upswing in the South is pneumonic plague, which has been reported in several areas of the country since June, 1966. Prior to that date, it had not been reported for more than 25 years. Other major health problems in the South include malaria and leprosy —even though incidences of those diseases have fallen in recent years. As mentioned above, tuberculosis was also identified as a major health problem in South Vietnam. "A prevalence survey . . . in 1962 showed that approximately 60 percent of the population was infected and 10 percent of children aged 10 years had x-ray evidence of clinically significant tuberculosis." Other communicable diseases reported in South Vietnam include all forms of dysentery, influenza, infectious hepatitis, scrub typhus, and human rabies, which exceeded 700 cases between 1964 and 1966.

These data suggest that one of the important by-products of sustained major military operations in South Vietnam has been a major destabilization of the ecology of the area, with the result that resistance to epidemic disease, which was at best marginal in large parts of the population, has been substantially reduced.

The character of military operations in South Vietnam is often best revealed by the visible effects of these operations. Bernard Fall wrote: "The one overwhelming fact about this situation which makes all considerations of ideology or politics pale, is the enormous might of American firepower." Operation Cedar Falls in the Iron Triangle, twenty miles northwest of Saigon, was fresh in his mind: "It looked like giant steel claws had raked the jungle." He spoke of the ground effect of fourteen consecutive B-52 raids which the Triangle had received during the operation. "But remember, when it was all over the Vietcong struck again and from the Iron Triangle. That is the real story of this war. The Americans can destroy but they cannot pacify. They may 'win' the war but it will be the victory of the graveyard."

Bernard Fall's description of the physical circumstances in the Iron Triangle area suggest a way in which the three conditions that lead to success in guerrilla warfare can, indeed, be overcome, and that is when the entire population and the physical space in which the population functions is destroyed. Under those conditions, there is no supporting population and there are no guerrillas either. Destruction on this scale is indeed feasible for the government of the United States, not only with conventional weapons applied with sufficient intensity, but surely with the further application of chemical, bacteriological, and nuclear weapons. The United States has been constrained against the use of these weapons to achieve a "final solution" in Vietnam by a combination of political and military factors, including the response that would follow from such acts inside the United States and elsewhere in the world. On the military grounds discussed in the previous chapter, it is plausible to infer that the security of the United States would indeed be diminished if a precedent were established for the use of population-destroying chemical and biological weapons in wars of this type.

Military operations in Vietnam have been conducted on a lavish scale. For example, the inflow of reports from intelligence sources is so large that the Defense Intelligence Agency reported on July 10, 1968, that unprocessed reports from Southeast Asia alone filled 517 linear feet of file drawer space at the Washington headquarters of this agency. Even if one allows for several teams of men working over these documents, it is clear that a backlog of this size corresponds to several months in work time, and several months is obviously a period in which very many things could happen, to which some of the data in the files would be germane.

While the Vietnam war was being pursued, the state-management was going ahead with major plans for pursuing similar types of military-political operations in other parts of the world. That is the significance of major Pentagon projects: for example the C-5A aircraft and Fast Deployment Logistics (FDL) vessels. Hanson Baldwin reported, on June 24, 1966: "In current thinking the [C-5A and the Fast Deployment Logistics Vessels] means the capability of moving quickly troops, supplies and equipment from the United States to any overseas area of crisis."

The C-5A airplane, of which the first was unveiled on March 3, 1968, is an aircraft of unprecedented size. It is a four-engine jet, capable of carrying a maximum load of 141 tons, or somewhat more than three times the maximum load capability of the Boeing-707 intercontinental jet. One C-5A plane can carry 600 or more soldiers with their equipment (844 persons in its civilian passenger version). This plane will also operate from unpaved runway areas that are much shorter than those used by present commercial jets. Fifty-eight aircraft of the C-5A class are being constructed, and when these are completed, the airlift capacity of the U.S. armed forces will be ten times greater than in 1961. When the first of these planes was brought from its hangar, President Johnson observed: "For the first time our fighting men will be able to travel with their equipment to any spot on the globe where we might be forced to stand—rapidly and more efficiently than ever."

With the C-5A for moving the troops, the heavy equipment for Vietnam-type wars is to be transported by FDL vessels. These ships have been in the planning for some time, and, in 1968, the allocation of funds for them was announced. Thirty of these vessels, costing an estimated $1 billion, are to be constructed. These vessels, carrying heavy equipment in containers, would be deployed around the world, able to rendezvous with the troops coming in on the C-5A jets. The combination of these two types of transport would, for example, make it possible for 20 planes to move an entire infantry division to, say, the west coast of Africa from the east coast of the United States in under 10 hours. There, the troops could immediately operate with heavy equipment waiting on the FDL vessels. Senator Stennis of the Senate Armed Services Committee made the nature of these combined forces clear, during a Senate debate on April 19, 1968:

> . . . We have the C-5A coming on to quickly transport the troops and some of the equipment. However, from the beginning, a part of the plan was to have an airlift and a sealift. If the second component is left out we do not have what the Army needs to carry its equipment to where it may be needed.
>
> This is not to pre-position in all parts of the world. This would tend to reduce any need for pre-positioning because with airpower and seapower we would have the ability to respond to attacks with all the equipment and supplies our troops need . . .

Senator Stennis' reference to responding to "attacks" surely does not refer to attacks on the United States. The long-range transportation capabilities of the C-5As and the FDLs clearly mark them as technological arms for wars of military-political intervention in diverse areas of the world, as enumerated by Mr. McNamara. It is also noteworthy that the FDL contract was awarded not to the shipbuilding industry but to the aerospace industry. This is in keeping with the long record of the state-management in building up the capital and the design and production capability of the aerospace industries. At least one major aerospace management, having received the contract, then approached conventional shipbuilders, asking them to do a substantial part of the work required under these contracts. Evidently, FDL contract allocation to the aerospace industries by the state-management continues the pattern of building up sub-firms for central management of major contracts.

The characteristics of the war in Vietnam are important in themselves, but they are also important as clues to the capabilities and limitations of the entire Vietnam wars program. One of the principal allegations of American officials has been that the war in Vietnam essentially involves aggression from the North. A compilation of data from diverse official U.S. sources indicates that even with the most generous estimates of the extent of infiltration of forces from North Vietnam, it is difficult to hold them accountable for more than a minority part of the men fighting in South Vietnam against United States and South Vietnamese forces. An evaluation based upon various U.S. official estimates shows that from 1959–1965, when the Saigon regime was in danger of defeat, the North Vietnamese component of the anti-Saigon forces could not have been more than 20 percent.

"Confirmed" total of military personnel infiltrated from
    North to South from 1959 to February, 1965   19,550
      (State Dept. White Paper)
"Estimated additional" figure   17,550
Total infiltration figure   37,100

Total Number Viet Cong
    (State Department White Paper, p. 3)   95,000–115,000
Viet Cong casualties, 1961–65
    (Gen. Harold Johnson, U.S. Army Chief of Staff)   75,000
Total Number Viet Cong operating in February 1965
    or killed since 1961   170,000–190,000

$$\frac{\text{Total number of infiltrators}}{\text{Total number of Viet Cong}} = \frac{37,100}{170,000\text{–}190,000} = \frac{1}{5} \text{ at most}$$

SOURCE: American Friends Service Committee, *The U.S. in Vietnam,* Philadelphia, Pa., 1966, p. 7.

Thereafter, until 1969, an increasing number of North Vietnamese troops participated in military operations in the South. Still, such forces cannot account for the scale and the character of the military operations against the South Vietnamese and the Americans in the South.

An important aspect of the Vietnam war is the substantial corruption among the conservatively-led Saigon military forces. Thus, as early as November, 1966, a two-months' study, undertaken for a committee of the Congress, noted that corruption was taking up to 40 percent in money value of U.S. assistance to Vietnam, and that the United States probably would never know the full extent of military and other assistance that went into black market and other improper use. By April, 1968, it was discovered that a black-shirted anti-corruption youth organization was operated by leaders who were themselves discovered to be guilty of the very sorts of illegalities which the organization was founded to prevent.

The policy of political-military intervention pursued by the United States, with its range of intensity of military options, has brought a substantial enlargement of branch offices of the Pentagon in many parts of the world. By June, 1966, for example, the number of American personnel in the U.S. Embassy in the Dominican Republic had risen from 47 to 115, while local employees were up from 42 to 286. It was reported that: "Almost every week the Embassy acquires another building for its expanding activities. Since last summer 6 wings have been added to the white tree-shaded chancery." Countries of the world that become clients of U.S. military-political intervention see the enlargement of Pentagon management along with an expansion of military-political operations.

From a small force of 700 noncombatant military "advisors," the U.S. military operation came to encompass 639,000 men (plus many thousands of U.S. civilians in Vietnam) by 1969. This escalation of the U.S. military operation in Vietnam is a tribute to the regularity with which military-based options have been selectively and consistently preferred as solutions to problems in Vietnam. After all, the Vietnam war went through many stages, each confronting the United States government with an array of problems involving a mixture of military, political, economic, and social issues. Characteristically, preference has been shown for military-based solutions to these problems, increasing military operations as other options have been cast aside.

So relentless has been the pursuit of and pressure for a military win that, at many points, efforts to terminate the war by negotiated settlement were clearly frustrated by decisive military acts. The history of frustrated negotiations for peace in Vietnam is given in a volume by David Kraslow and Stuart H. Lury, *The Secret Search for Peace in Vietnam* (Random House, 1968). This history is testimony to the readiness of the state-management to persist relentlessly in efforts to score a military win in Vietnam, thereby validating the Pentagon doctrine promising political success through military options applied with skill.

It is difficult to discover the limits beyond which these men are not prepared to go. For example, disregarding the warning of many American scientists, American armed forces have employed diverse chemical weapons in Vietnam, thereby establishing a deadly precedent which could be turned against an American population at some future time.

The record of Senate hearings in mid-1968 on the Tonkin Gulf incident suggests that there is substantial doubt as to whether there was, in fact, an attack on U.S. warships in Tonkin Gulf at the time it was supposed to have happened on August 4, 1964. The Senate Foreign Affairs Committee hearings, in May and June of 1968, disclosed ambiguity in the basic instrument readings used to determine the presence and the operations of North Vietnamese warships.

The conduct of the U.S. war in Vietnam was vividly depicted by an American officer during the Tet offensive in 1967. He declared: "We must destroy the city in order to save it." This readiness to use military power, even to destroy the country in order to "save" it, has brought a great array of drastic disruptions to South Vietnamese society. For example, the essential food of that country is rice. *Business Week* of December 4, 1965 reported as follows: . . . "In 1963 South Vietnam exported 300,000 tons of rice, and in 1964 this dropped to 40,000 tons. But this year, Vietnam has had to import 200,000 tons, most of it from the U.S. Next year, imports from the U.S. are expected to continue at the same level. In addition, Saigon has contracted to buy 75,000 tons next year from Thailand, to be paid for with U.S. aid dollars." The disruption of agriculture, brought about by the destruction of villages and the wholesale removal of populations, has undermined the basic agricultural activity of the society—rice production.

The war in South Vietnam should be understood as a model for the Vietnam-type war program in another major respect: the readiness of the United States to lavish resources unstintingly on efforts to overcome the three prongs of guerrilla warfare through various forms of technologically-based military power. The Pentagon's Director of Guerrilla Warfare Research, Seymour D. Dietchman, indicated in November, 1966, that the United States would have to have up to 2 million troops operating over a 5-year period to score a military win in Vietnam.

By August, 1968, the United States armed forces had flown 107,000 bombing missions against North Vietnam, and the combined services had dropped 2,581,876 *tons* of bombs and rockets. This covered the period of February, 1965, to August, 1968. These tonnages of high explosives applied in the Vietnam war are about four times the total tonnage unloaded by U.S. planes in all the campaigns in the Pacific in the Second World War, and amount to more than 12 tons of bombs for every square mile of both North and South Vietnam. It is significant that a substantial part of this explosive power was applied in area bombardments. This means that highly-developed aerial bombardment systems were used in an attempt to overcome the third condition making for guerrilla warfare's success—the inability to identify the guerrillas. Large tonnages of high explosives were dropped in so-called "free fire zones" from which the populace was ordered out.

The Pentagon sought technological devices by which to overcome the advantages held by guerrillas and inherent in their mode of warfare. For example, in July, 1966, the journal *Armed Forces Management* disclosed procurement orders for a series of new weapons including the following: "Snake Eye"—a low-drag bomb; "Sad Eye" —an air launched cluster bomb; "Wet Eye"—a chemical bomb being developed; "Wall Eye"—a TV-guided air-launched bomb for accurate guidance on particular targets; "Rock Eye"—a cluster bomb to contain anti-personnel and anti-tank charges; "Fire Eye"—an improved bomb for delivering a new burning agent against ground targets.

During 1967, the Pentagon introduced the use of infrared binoculars and similar devices in order to facilitate night driving at reasonable speeds, as well as to aid in the firing of rifles and other weapons at night. A mobile two-man radar unit, mounted on the back of a jeep, could use a combination of sound and video screen to detect men as far as three miles away. A successor to the infrared sniper-scope was on hand during 1968—a new device called the star scope, based on the principle of amplifying very small quantities of light. These are part of a whole family of sensing devices developed for use in jungle warfare situations. Another portable device, mounted in aircraft, detects the presence of human beings by sensitivity to normal body odor. An infrared fence has been invented, with photoelectric cells and infrared projectors to sound an alarm. Simpler protective devices in the nature of a "break wire" attached to control boxes about the size of cigarette packages exist; if the wire is broken, an alarm sounds. Many sorts of lightweight armor have been developed for both airborne and ground personnel. New types of shoes have been introduced to protect soldiers from being impaled on boobytraps consisting of sharpened stakes in the ground. Lightweight rations were developed to make it possible for foot soldiers to survive over extended periods with food they could readily carry.

In the area of weaponry, extensive operations have been carried out using chemical warfare methods. These were catalogued in June, 1966, in *Viet-Report*. New major weapons have also been developed. Thus, by September, 1968, aircraft manufacturers were encouraged to design new fighter planes in an effort to "close" a recently-discovered "fighter gap."

By December, 1966, it became apparent that U.S. forces, for all the military power that they applied, were unable decisively to undermine their opponents' capability in large-scale operations. That is, the technological and military capability of the United States had not been able to eliminate the three prongs of successful guerrilla warfare or the operation of regular forces, which continued and were extended by virtue of military assistance extended to North Vietnam by the U.S.S.R. and China. All this is especially striking if one takes into account the scale and technical character of the military assistance given to North Vietnam. Although the Soviets are said to have given North Vietnam about $1.7 billion of weaponry aid annually, it still remains that the North Vietnamese have had no air force for either offensive or defensive operations. The North Vietnamese and NLF troops have, characteristically, operated with portable weapons, primarily hand-carried, and there is little evidence from 1963 to 1968 that heavy weapons, such as artillery or tanks, have been used by them. Of course, the enemy has thereby been unable to do the sorts of bombing U.S. forces could do. Therefore, U.S. forces have been virtually untouched by the sorts of weaponry that *they* have used for their primary attacks against the North Vietnamese and the NLF. Under these conditions, it has not been possible to define the military circumstance using conventional weapons under which the United

States could conceivably score a military victory against their opponent. Indeed, as the war proceeded, it became evident that each increase of U.S. forces or military power was being countered by either appropriate numbers of North and South Vietnamese or additions to the opponents' military matériel, or both. The result was highly visible by February 20, 1968, as Tom Wicker summarized the experience of the Tet offensive in *The New York Times:*

> . . . The inescapable facts are that the South Vietnamese government and its American ally were unable to protect the cities and their populations to begin with. When the attacks came, they proved unable to overcome them without the destruction of whole areas and the mass production of dead and homeless civilians. And when all the firepower has done its deadly work, neither Saigon nor Washington will be anywhere near able to take care of the human tide of misery and despair that will be the result . . .
>
> The sad and terrible truth of the decision to blow up South Vietnam's cities in order to defend them is that neither Washington nor Saigon has anything to rely on but firepower. With that, they can destroy South Vietnam, but they can never save it from Communism, or anything else.

The readiness of the United States to apply immense military power in South Vietnam carries another possible implication: that small countries (or parts of a country) might one day attempt to get hold of nuclear weapons to wield an "equalizer" against U.S. military forces. In May, 1967, an advisory panel to the Atomic Energy Commission cautioned: ". . . a black market was likely to develop in fissionable materials, with criminal or terrorist groups attempting to divert the materials to secret production of atomic weapons." This advisory panel, headed by Dr. Ralph F. Lumb, was established to assess the effectiveness of policies and procedures both domestically and internationally for safeguarding nuclear materials. Besides finding substantial weaknesses in the existing procedures, the panel feared potential irregularities that could develop in the future, owing to the enlarged scale of civilian nuclear operations, as well as their proliferation within the United States and abroad.

I refer again to weapons of mass destruction because I wish to underscore that in a small country, the line between conventional and nuclear and similar weapons may be overridden under the pressure of military operations. Where large powers threaten the existence of a small country, or part of the population of a small country, some of those threatened may, in a desperate attempt to overcome inequalities in technology and wealth, resort to inexpensive weapons of mass destruction. Bacteriological as well as nuclear weapons could be resorted to under such circumstances. (As noted in the previous chapter, it will be possible for many small countries, even countries as small as Israel, to make their own nuclear weapons in the foreseeable future.)

The entire range of United States government behavior in Vietnam has defied explanation in terms of many conventional theories. By the end of 1968, it was perfectly clear that the military-political thrust of the United States government was patently unsuccessful in terms of declared objectives. There had been no military victory, nor could anyone describe the conditions or the timetable for a conventional military victory. This war had cost the United States about one hundred billion dollars in direct military outlays, besides the cost of a series of economically, morally, and politically damaging effects. Inescapably, the issue is: Who pressed this Vietnam war program? Who insisted that it be carried out, even though the military-political impasse of 1968 was already visible in 1965 and in 1963? Some interpreters of industrial capitalism have suggested that the Vietnam war is but a continuation of the imperialism that flourished in many places in the world around the turn of the 20th century.

In November, 1966, the United States government's Agency for International Development published a catalog of investment information and opportunities. This volume is an index of available reports pinpointing investment prospects in many countries of the world. The section on Vietnam reflects an impoverished condition of investment prospects in that country.

Baran and Sweezy, in their book *Monopoly Capital* (Monthly Review Press, 1966), understood the Vietnam war as being but a continuation of classic colonialist policy. However, the classic theories of economic imperialism fail to explain the behavior of the United States in Vietnam. There is no evidence of recent or planned trade or investment in Vietnam by major U.S. firms of the sort and the scale that might prompt an effort to bring substantial pressure on United States government policy. One reviewer of the Baran and Sweezy volume noted in the June–July, 1966 issue of *Viet-Report:*

> . . . Unfortunately for this theory, which has a familiar ring, not one of Standard Oil's 54 tentacles (as listed in the book) have a grip on South Vietnam, nor on any other country of Southeast Asia. Neither did any of the other corporate giants possess more than negligible investments in South Vietnam until this year. Diem, after all the bad things that have been said about him, was distrustful of modern industry. He laid a barrage of red tape in the path of any investor foolish enough to try to establish a foothold here. Not until General Khanh's shortlived reign was the first Vietnamese stock exchange opened in Saigon. Total foreign investments in South Vietnam have until quite recently been entirely trivial. Nor does the country contain important deposits of raw materials for the sake of which an ambitious corporation might urge the American government to make war. There are no investments to protect, no oil, tin, or copper to grab: why then should a corporation like Jersey Standard display the least interest in Vietnam?

Failing evidence that, as a group, major industrial firms had a stake in Vietnam that might be served by large-scale U.S. military intervention, one might fall back on the possibility that perhaps the largest Pentagon sub-firms gain from the war and, therefore, perhaps, pressed for the war. But this speculation falls afoul of the evidence given in Chapter 2, which establishes the Pentagon as their top management. The available evidence points to the direction of major formal control coming primarily from the Department of Defense to these firms, not in a reverse direction. This is not to gainsay the undoubted impact of ex-contractor personnel on the functioning of the Pentagon itself. But this effect must be seen in the context of who manages and who controls. Thus, in multi-division firms, the central office typically co-opts personnel from the divisions. That fact does not lead to the inference that the divisional managers are thereby controlling the central office. Similarly, the movement of sub-managers into the state-management itself does not alter the essential location of control—at the Pentagon and not among the subdivisions.

Furthermore, the stake of the sub-firms is not necessarily in the Vietnam war per se, but in their continuing function as suppliers of the Department of Defense. That status is assured by the state-management's announcements that budgets requested of the Congress would be maintained or even enlarged after the Vietnam war to make up for the reduction of military inventory and deferred starts on new major military systems. In sum, the family of theories that would explain the Vietnam war as the result of one or another group of private firms using the government as an instrument for their advantage fails for lack of evidence.

The existence and normal operation of a state-management over military industry, at the peak position of the federal government, offers a more fruitful explanation of Pentagon and federal government behavior. For this state-management has indeed scored a great success, enlarging the scope and intensity of its decision-power through the Vietnam war operation: it gained control over more money, more men, more real estate, more property, and more industry. Similarly, it is the prospect of maintaining and enlarging decision-power that makes the technological preparation for a Vietnam wars program into a meaningful forecast of such wars to be carried out under the direction of this state-management.

At the end of 1967, Major General Alan T. Stanwix-Hay, Deputy Assistant Secretary of Defense (Matériel), addressed the American Ordnance Association on planning for defense mobilization. He said: ". . . We seek a capability for the selective use of force for all kinds of conflict. Our objective is to offer the President a range of military responses appropriate for each threat. We want that he should have the flexibility to choose and apply force sufficient to gain the end result while holding to a minimum the risk of further escalation to a more destructive level of conflict. . . ." This description of the Pentagon's strategy in the design of armed forces points to preparation of substantial escalation capability within the technological arsenal of the armed forces, even within the range of conventional weapons. This is designed to support the military-political interventionist strategy, which can itself operate at a succession of degrees of intervention:

1. Support of friendly governments.
2. Buying allies (and elections).
3. Supporting military coups at a distance.

4. Supporting military coups by intervention.
5. Physical occupation of a territory.
6. Subduing an opponent by military force.

It should be noted that a limiting condition on success of interventionist strategy is the absence of local allies. Thus, the failure of
the United States-sponsored invasion of Cuba in 1961 was due to the
absence of local allies, or, in terms of guerrilla warfare theory, to the
absence of a surrounding population to shield and assist the fighting
force.

The Vietnam war experience is especially crucial for the future of
the United States, for it casts light on the projected behavior of the
U.S. government. From this standpoint it is worth examining a remarkable address given by Robert McNamara in May, 1966, in Montreal, in which he discussed the relation of military and political security to economic development. Here are key sections from his address:

. . . The planet is becoming a more dangerous place to live on—
not merely because of a potential nuclear holocaust—but also because of the large number of *de facto* conflicts and because the
trend of such conflicts is growing rather than diminishing.

At the beginning of 1958, there were 23 prolonged insurgencies
going on about the world. As of February 1, 1966, there were 40.

Further, the total number of outbreaks of violence has increased
each year: in 1958, there were 34; in 1965 there were 58.

But what is most significant of all is that there is a direct and
constant relationship between the incidence of violence and the
economic status of the countries afflicted.

The World Bank divides nations, on the basis of per capita income, into four categories: rich, middle-income, poor, and very
poor.

The rich nations are those with a per capita income of $750 per
year or more. The current U.S. level is more than $2,700. There
are 27 of these rich nations. They possess 75 percent of the world's
wealth, though roughly only 25 percent of the world's population.

Since 1958, only *one* of these 27 nations has suffered a major
internal upheaval on its own territory.

But observe what happens at the other end of the economic scale.
Among the 38 very poor nations—those with a per capita income
of under $100 a year—no less than 32 have suffered significant
conflicts. Indeed, they have suffered an average of two major out-

breaks of violence per country in the eight year period. That is a great deal of conflict.

What is worse, it has been, predominantly, conflict of a prolonged nature.

The trend holds predictably constant in the case of the two other categories: the poor, and the middle-income nations. Since 1958, 87 percent of the very poor nations, 69 percent of the poor nations, and 48 percent of the middle-income nations have suffered serious violence.

There can, then, be no question but that there is an *irrefutable relationship between violence and economic backwardness.* And the trend of such violence is up, not down.

Now, it would perhaps be somewhat reassuring if the gap between the rich nations and the poor nations were closing; and economic backwardness were significantly receding.

But it is not. The economic gap is widening.

By the year 1970, over one half of the world's total population will live in the independent nations sweeping across the southern half of the planet. But this hungering half of the human race will by then command only one-sixth of the world's total of goods and services.

By the year 1975, the dependent children of these nations alone —children under 15 years of age—will equal the *total* population of the developed nations to the north.

Even in our own abundant societies, we have reason enough to worry over the tensions that coil and tighten among underprivileged young people, and finally flail out in delinquency and crime. What are we to expect from a whole hemisphere of youth where mounting frustrations are likely to fester into eruptions of violence and extremism?

Annual per capita income in roughly half of the 80 underdeveloped nations that are members of the World Bank is rising by a paltry one percent a year or less. By the end of the century, these nations—at their present rates of growth—will reach a per capita income of barely $170 a year. The United States, by the same criteria, will attain a per capita income of $4,500.

The conclusion to all of this is blunt and inescapable: given the certain connection between economic stagnation and the incidence of violence, the years that lie ahead for the nations in the southern half of the globe are pregnant with violence . . .

. . . What is often misunderstood is that communists are capable of subverting, manipulating, and finally directing for their own ends the wholly legitimate grievances of a developing society.

But it would be a gross oversimplification to regard communism as the central factor in every conflict throughout the underdeveloped world. Of the 149 serious internal insurgencies in the past eight years, communists have been involved in only 58 of them—38 percent of the total—and this includes seven instances in which a Communist regime itself was the target of the uprising . . .

. . . The United States has no mandate from on high to police the world, and no inclination to do so. There have been classic cases in which our deliberate non-action was the wisest action of all.

Where our help is not sought, it is seldom prudent to volunteer.

Certainly we have no charter to rescue floundering regimes, who have brought violence on themselves by deliberately refusing to meet the legitimate expectations of their citizenry . . .

. . . In a modernizing society, *security means development.*

Security is *not* military hardware—though it may include it. Security is *not* military force—though it may involve it. Security is *not* traditional military activity—though it may encompass it.

Security *is* development.

Without development, there can be no security.

A developing nation that does not in fact develop simply *cannot* remain "secure."

It cannot remain secure for the intractable reason that its own citizenry cannot shed its human nature.

If security implies anything, it implies a minimal measure of order and stability.

Without internal development of at least a minimal degree, order and stability are simply not possible. They are not possible because human nature cannot be frustrated beyond intrinsic limits. It reacts —because it *must.* . . .

Since this analysis was formulated and announced by the Secretary of Defense, how can we account for the continuation of the Vietnam war and the preparation—under his direction—of a Vietnam wars program?

McNamara's speech is about as eloquent a statement for investing in world-wide economic development, as a strategy for American security, as could be made by a senior U.S. government official. What is the connection between this political position (in Montreal) and the operation of the Pentagon's strategic overkill and Vietnam wars program? In the McNamara view, there is no contradiction between the use of military power, as in Vietnam, and the requirements for world economic development. For McNamara has assumed that the United

States is indefinitely wealthy and productive, that the country can afford guns and butter, and that only a defective system of values among the populace prevents the allocation of American money to world economic development—regardless of the tax rates, the size of the Pentagon budgets, and the cost of the Vietnam war.

There is no reason to believe the personal judgment of McNamara is not exactly that stated in Montreal. However, institutional and not personal factors dominate the scene. This means that Robert McNamara, the architect and first chief of the state-management institution, may have understood that there are limitations on the use of military power for political purposes. Nevertheless, he proceeded not only to perform but to justify professionally the preparation of such military power as was demanded by his institutional role, which effectively checkmated possible United States action for world economic development on a serious scale.

The selection of general political policies for the government of the United States obviously involves not only the Department of State but the President as well. What of the state-management? The Secretary of Defense as "Chairman of the Board" of the state-management is directly responsible to the President of the United States, who is thereby "President" of this firm. The State Department, during the last twenty years, has developed an ideology that gives first priority to the use of military methods for political purposes, with the result that it is difficult to differentiate the sorts of judgment and policy preferences that prevail in the Department of State from those of the military establishment.

During the last years, it has often emerged that Department of Defense personnel stood for greater caution in the use of military power than their State Department counterparts. Apart from such variations in judgment, however, the common ground is fundamental, and that is agreement across the top echelon of the federal executive that military power, in diverse forms, is the most appropriate instrument for coping with political problems abroad.

In organizational operation, as well as ideologically, the Department of State and the Department of Defense are linked by powerful bonds and are not easily differentiated as components of the state machine, though possesssing differing histories and distinct current responsibilities. When Robert McNamara spoke in Montreal, he dealt with a subject one would expect to hear discussed by a Secretary of State. It is significant not only that McNamara's functions were deeply political in nature, but that the Department of Defense also included a senior section on International Security Affairs, under an Assistant Secretary of Defense. This political arm of the Department of Defense has given the organization its own capability in this sphere of interest, as well as linking it to the Department of State and other related departments of the federal executive branch. Moreover, the Pentagon and its allied security agencies, including the Central Intelligence Agency, are heavily engaged in politics of all sorts around the world. They make policy by "operating" in the field, often independently of the State Department.

While the Secretary of Defense is equal in rank with other Secretaries of major government Departments, he is nevertheless "more equal" than the others, insofar as he controls the expenditure of more than half the federal government's budget. It is this institution, and its central policies, that dominates the field and gives thrust to the Vietnam wars program as a system of policy and practice.

The Vietnam wars program requires conscription. With uniformed armed forces of 639,000 in Vietnam and adjacent areas by 1969, the Pentagon—with mainland support elements—committed about one million men to that war alone. This does not include civilians employed in industry or by the Pentagon. The continuation of the Vietnam wars policy system, therefore, presses the state-management to implement virtually a total military conscription policy—with all its consequences. One of these consequences is maintaining and extending state-management power over the young men of the nation into an indefinite future.

7

The Ideology of
the Para-State

Since 1945, an intricate network of theory and justification has been constructed in support of giving priority to military organization, military methods, and military budgets. During the 1960's, the relevant ideology was marvelously elaborated, following the introduction of so many intellectuals into the newly established state-management. The ideology is composed of three main elements: first, justification concerning defense; second, socially validated propositions concerning the operation of the American economy; and third, articles of faith concerning the state-management itself, and its methods. The propositions reviewed here are significant not only in their own right, but because they are widely accepted as valid descriptions of reality or as limits of possible public policy.

CONVENTIONAL IDEOLOGY CONCERNING
DEFENSE

Addition to offensive military capability increases military power (or deterrence). Among the major military powers, addition to offen-

163

sive capability now means addition to nuclear and similar capability: the number of nuclear weapons, the size of nuclear warheads, and the number and variety of delivery methods for these explosive devices. Each of the great nuclear powers already possesses large overkill capability. Additions to offensive capability in the overkill range cannot add to military power (or deterrence): overkill of 1,000 is not greater than overkill of 100 or of 1.

Defensive systems can be designed to effectively protect sufficient numbers of people to ensure an ongoing society even after a nuclear war. Under present conditions, all defensive strategies and technologies can be either saturated, overwhelmed, or evaded by a variety of nuclear and other offensive military systems. When overkill power (U.S. and U.S.S.R.) exceeds 100, then a 99 percent effective defense still leaves at least one-kill capacity, and that is sufficient. There are no grounds for anticipating defense at 100 percent efficiency.

With a technological breakthrough, perhaps the United States could still be defended even against nuclear attack. There are no grounds for expecting that a physical shield could be constructed against the concentration of energy release that is made possible with nuclear weapons, nor against the varied devices by which nuclear and other weapons of mass destruction could be delivered. The human body is simply not constructed to be able to withstand the diverse lethal devices that have been fashioned by application of modern science.

If the United States had the will to do it, then it could maintain a lead in all relevant science and technology for attaining military superiority. Let us assume that we know what a "lead" would mean in this case, namely, that in the United States, discoveries would be made in all militarily relevant spheres of science and technology. On such a basis, the United States could have more variety in weapons systems than any other country. That, however, would be no assurance of military "superiority" or the feasibility of "defense." If superiority means having more overkill, then it is a theoretical difference that has no practical meaning. Monopoly possession of a scientific breakthrough cannot be assured, since the laws of nature cannot be classified or copyrighted.

The total strength of U.S. armed forces is maximized by improving the strength of each component of these forces. Total United States military power can no longer be defined as the sum of the parts. A better warhead, a better missile, a better vehicle produces just that, but does not alter the effects of major powers' each possessing multiple overkill capability over the other.

The United States must be competent to cope with all military contingencies. Once overkill capacity is dispersed among many countries, it is no longer clear what military "competence" consists of. The physical security of nuclear-armed societies depends on assurance that these and biological weapons will not be used.

Pre-eminent military power is the decisive requirement for successful conduct of American foreign policy. When potential opponents each possess overkill power, neither can be pre-eminent. In non-nuclear war, political considerations, as in South Vietnam, can dominate the field and frustrate military pre-eminence for the nation that wields by far the greatest firepower.

The Department of Defense makes rational decisions for defending the United States and employs resources to yield high returns to the taxpayer. The total cost of military operations in Vietnam, at this writing, probably exceeds $100 billion. This is almost half the capital funds required for the creation of a major economic development program in the United States for the thirty million Americans who are living economically and socially substandard lives. Further, the major field operations under McNamara and the Joint Chiefs, conducted with unprecedented resources in money and matériel, have been a military and political failure. The taxpayer is getting a "no-win" in Vietnam, "no-win" against poverty at home, and no strategic defense of the U.S.

In the strategic sphere, the Department of Defense has built a nuclear arsenal with an overkill capability of more than 6 tons of TNT per person on the planet. This is militarily irrational on the offensive and is no shield on the defensive.

Military organizations yield stability abroad. The most recent data assembled by the U.S. Arms Control and Disarmament Agency show that the less developed nations of the earth have been spending more for arms than for education and public health. This sort of priority curtails economic development and breeds movements of rebellion against regimes responsible for human neglect. The military assistance given by the United States and other nations produces regional instability rather than national security for smaller states.

Military matters are too complex for ordinary people and must be left to the technologists. The nature of modern weapons and armed forces, and decisions to use them, are, in fact, political issues, not technical problems to be solved by "experts." For example, the decision to make nuclear weapons equivalent to a million tons of TNT rather than equivalent to (only) 20-thousand tons of TNT was a political decision. It was based on the assumption that a nuclear system including many individual warheads, each of which could destroy a major metropolis, would be a more believable threat. Decisions to use or not to use nuclear weapons are entirely political matters. The ability to design a complex control mechanism does not give a man a special capability for deciding whether a society should survive.

Even though nuclear wars cannot be fought to a victory, small wars with conventional weapons can be fought, held within bounds, and won. Since the end of the Second World War, all wars between nation-states fought with conventional weapons have been stopped by the intervention of either the United Nations or separate groups of states. In every instance, the war was not permitted to reach a military conclusion. Military victory was not permitted. This was caused by the universal fear that "small" wars fought with non-nuclear weapons might not be held within those bounds. That is, the fear of escalation into nuclear war has restrained conventional wars. There is another sort of conventional war, a war within states, like the civil war in Vietnam. The Vietnam war demonstrated that even immensely superior firepower, in this case wielded by the United States, is not decisive when the military opponent operates on a guerrilla basis—the military expression of a popular political movement.

If we did not have a large defense establishment, the United States might be overrun or destroyed, or both. Since the end of the Second World War, what we have had is not a defense establishment, but rather a war-making machine of unprecedented destructive power. This has been demonstrated in Hiroshima, in Nagasaki, and later in Vietnam. It is impossible to know exactly what might have happened if the United States had not built up its nuclear overkill capability. It has never been suggested that any other nation could literally overrun the U.S. Who would try this? Why? And how could they get here? This much, however, is clear. If this overkill force is used, it would mean the end of the United States and perhaps of human life on the planet. The new condition of military power is that the security of the United States depends on the assurance that nuclear and similarly destructive military power is not used, and on the elimination of these weapons altogether. So much emphasis has been given during the last decades to a search for military advantage that the problem of international relations without the use of major military power has gone unattended. Yet it is precisely in this direction that the United States and every other major country must look for security in a multi-overkill world.

Improvements in military technology have given American commanders more information upon which to base rational decisions for the defense of the United States. It is true that there is a growing capability for obtaining, storing, and arranging information in the Pentagon. None of this, however, has altered the condition of mutual overkill and the limit that this places on meaningful military capability. None of the new information-gathering and analysis systems makes it possible to alter the condition of no purchasable defense.

By investing in modern technology it is possible for American military chiefs to control worldwide forces on behalf of the political purposes of the United States. When the U.S. Navy's spy ship Pueblo was being boarded and seized off South Korea, it took hours before the Joint Chiefs of Staff and the Secretary of Defense were alerted in Washington. During the subsequent time of emergency, there is no record of any return communication to the Pueblo from senior commanders. Similar snafus took place in the "Bay of Pigs" operation and in the case of the intelligence ship Liberty, which operated in the eastern Mediterranean during the 1967 Israeli-Arab six-day war. In all these cases, and without intervention by any other nation to confuse communications, Pentagon commanders, using the most elaborate communications equipment, could not control the operations of their forces. These and many other similar incidents during the last years have cast doubt on the conventional assumption that the Pentagon is indeed able to exercise reliable control on a push-button basis over forces around the world. However, the idea that this can be done remains a continuing assumption of U.S. military and political chiefs and is a factor in leading them to take risks which would otherwise seem unreasonable.

The Army builds men. Therefore service in the Armed Forces improves the physique and education of the men who serve. In 1967, the armed forces rejected 40.7 percent of the men examined because of physical and educational defects. Therefore, the young men who have been most deprived of health care and education are left untouched by the armed services. Military operations tend to damage soldiers. Furthermore, the greatest number of military specialty occupations are, of course, specific to military requirements and are not necessarily transferable to civilian use.

New military technology and organizations create new options for American policy. This is true, but as the new options tend to be military ones, they actually impose severe limitations on United States policy choices. That is, since the state-management has the largest share of the federal budget, attention is focused on military options at home and abroad, while the preemption of resources further limits the development of non-military policy capability.

Military organizations advance technology. For example, the use of antibiotics was speeded during the Second World War. Military organization advances militarily relevant technology. However, insofar as one-half and more of key American research manpower is invested in military technology, there have been growing deficiencies in the nonmilitary technologies. Of course, great efforts were made to limit U.S. fatalities during wars; thus, antibiotics were introduced as quickly as practicable. But that is surely no justification for overkill war preparation or for having wars. The destruction of life and property in any modern war more than offsets whatever technological advances may have occurred that could be put to use elsewhere. In the nuclear era, the issue of technological spillover from military activity has become a completely secondary matter compared to the danger of a nuclear war that would simply cancel the prospect of further organized life.

Military preparedness is the true measure of American strength. What is strength? Strength for what? Military preparedness after spending $1,000 billion since the Second World War has not given the United States a plausible shield against destruction from the outside. Still, the United States does have massive capability for war-making. If Vietnam is an indication of what that means, then this is a great destructive capacity, but not necessarily capability for winning.

It's a tough world, and military power is the only language "they" understand. It is true that the world has become a cruel place. It takes toughness, in the sense of courage of mind and spirit, to confront the fact that military power can no longer be wielded as a competent instrument of national security and to act on the implication of this transformation. But we do not see much of that toughness around just yet; and there is little toughness abroad, in the sense of strong commitment to achieve great, constructive goals.

The unspoken idea here is that everyone understands that nuclear military power implies a capability and a readiness to destroy other societies. That surely evokes fear and concomitant hatred for the potential destroyer. Great fear evokes great hate. The result is a mutual overkill confrontation that turns readiness to kill into readiness for one's own suicide. Nuclear arms have converted military "toughness" into mutual weakness.

IDEOLOGY ON AMERICAN ECONOMY

The United States is an affluent society and therefore does not have to choose between guns and butter. While the United States is rich, it is not inexhaustibly rich. A massive Gross National Product of $900 billion tends to overshadow the fact that an important part of this money is payment for economically parasitic activity rather than for productive growth. Military and space work is paid for, but yields a product which cannot be used for further production or as part of the current level of living. By this functional test, military work is parasitic. The contrast is with productive growth: producing goods or services that can be used for further production or for the present level of living. Thus a printing press or a loom multiplies its worth.

The use of a common money unit to measure all economic activity masks the functional difference between parasitic and productive growth. The concentration of skilled brains and hands in the United States on parasitic growth explains why there is deterioration in many facets of life while the growth of a money-valued GNP is celebrated.

As long as the Gross National Product rises, income and resources are available for new programs. This is not necessarily true. Insofar as GNP increases occur in sectors of parasitic growth, then the increased quantity of money-valued goods and services is not available for productive uses.

The productive resources of this nation are so great that an indefinite number of public programs, foreign and domestic, can be pursued simultaneously. Actually the United States, despite a GNP per person of over $4,000 per year, is limited in its work-capabilities by a finite stock of manpower, especially skilled manpower. When this manpower has been completely allocated, then further economic growth, of whatever sort, that requires skilled manpower cannot be performed.

Under such conditions, the creation of more money, or the appropriation of money, for additional work will not get work done. Thus, with the lion's share of the nation's research and development talent preempted by the armed forces and the organizations that serve them, it is unfeasible for American railroads to operate other than Toonerville Trolleys on passenger services. The same military priority system does make it possible to have commercial airplanes that are adaptations of military airplanes. Similarly, it is now impossible for the United States to do what is needed to maintain health services: for example, we need about three new medical schools *per state,* while present programs are for the construction, by 1975, of thirteen new medical schools for all fifty states. There will be a further decline in health services for the American people.

Despite such demonstrations, the assumption that the productive resources of the nation are indefinitely great remains a piece of conventional wisdom that is widely trusted by senior officers of the U.S. government and by their ideologists.

At this writing, parasitic military spending by the United States amounts to over $80 billion per year, over one-half of the federal budget. If one adds the capital investment required for an antiballistics missile system, the civil defense program that must accompany it, multiple independent re-entry vehicles, the C-5A aircraft program, and the counterinsurgency forces, one discovers an additional capital outlay for parasitic growth of not less than $650 billion. If the work were to be done over a five-year period, this would require more than doubling the military budget. To the extent that such plans are given first priority, an inevitable consequence will be to make unavailable all manner of crucial resources for other work in this society.

Individual, corporate, and government money-making is a competent test of economic productivity. We may ask: productive in what sense? Is the outcome productive growth or is it parasitic growth? And productive in what moral sense? After all, values do count for something. If the money-making activity is done in the furtherance of illegality, if it is done in complicity with violation of the laws of war (i.e., war crimes), then is that to be regarded as acceptable economic performance? Constraints are indispensable. Money-making *per se* cannot be regarded by society as a sufficient end in itself.

The diminishing level of United States Treasury gold reserves is an economic-technical detail, and the present condition is simply a stepping stone to a new and better monetary order. On the contrary, the decline of the gold reserve is a very real threat to the value of the dollar. The decline is the consequence of a chronic imbalance of payments that has been generated by parasitic military spending abroad. If the trend is not arrested and reversed, the consequences for the world position of the United States will necessarily be similar to, or worse than, those Great Britain has suffered.

The nationally widespread distribution of defense spending improves personal incomes and adds to money in circulation—which is especially meaningful to the low-income areas of the country. The fact is that the regional distribution of federal spending for military and space programs, as contrasted with non-defense federal spending, differs significantly from one area to another. On the average, high-income states have received a larger-than-proportionate share (based upon spending per capita) of money for military and space programs, while low-income states have received a larger proportionate share of spending from civilian programs. This means that a shift in federal activity from defense to non-defense activities would, in itself, contribute towards a relative improvement in the economic activity, hence income position, of the low-per-capita-income states of the nation. (Murray L. Weidenbaum, "Shifting the Composition of Government Spending: Implications for the Regional Distribution of Income," Peace Research Society: *Papers,* 1966.)

IDEOLOGY ON THE STATE-MANAGEMENT

Military industry and research help civilian industry via "spillover" in knowledge and design factors. True, the development of computers for civilian use got something from the investment made in computers for military use. True, the commercial jetliner came, in part, from the Air Force's jet refueling tanker. True, we have nuclear energy capability that may be increasingly useful for civilian purposes. Do these economically meaningful "spillovers" justify the use of over three-fourths of the government's research and development budget for military and allied purposes?

None of these "spillover" effects justifies the gross depletion and deterioration in many of our civilian industries. I recorded the first draft of this book on a tape recorder that was made in Japan, not America. Americans did major theoretical work in solid-state physics and enormous work on its technological application. But those technological applications have been, mainly, military applications. That is why, for the first time, new, mass-produced, durable-goods products are designed, produced, and marketed outside the United States. The inexpensive transistor radio, TV set, and tape recorder are products of the electronics industry of Japan, a country where the young electronics engineers have no place to go except to civilian-industry employers.

Military priority produces domestic stability because of high-level economic activity. On the contrary, sustained military priority and the unavailability of resources for much civilian investment is producing insurrection at home. The "domestic stability" induced by large military forces is incompatible with the values of freedom in society.

Military priority over a long period makes impossible the reconstruction of the cities and the investment in human capital and in new work places that is essential if thirty million Americans are to be economically developed. About 7.5 million American families live in poverty. One estimate of the capital outlay required for their economic development is $50,000 per family. Thus, a capital fund of $375 million is required to raise the impoverished of our own country to productive status. That capital fund, and the manpower it must represent, are both unavailable and inaccessible today and in the foreseeable future, so long as the present military priority is sustained.

Military-industrial firms are new industries with a high level of technical competence and represent a general enrichment of the technical and managerial resources of the nation. Close scrutiny suggests that managements of the subsidiaries of the national military-industrial firm are infused with a trained incapacity for operating civilian enterprises functioning in the civilian market place. Attempts by these managements to enter civilian markets have mainly failed. The failures did not result from personal incompetence. Rather they stemmed from the fact that the management methods, costs, and technological requirements for the military market are inappropriate in the civilian sphere. Thus, the management style, technology, equipment, and practices required for producing certain nuclear submarines at $12 per pound are hopelessly inappropriate for producing commercial oil tankers at less than $1 per pound.

Military-industrial firms can readily convert to civilian work if that is required. The evidence of the 1963–1964 period, when there were minor curtailments in military contracts, instructs us to the contrary. It will be necessary to motivate these organizations strongly to attempt possible conversion planning. Beyond that, it will be necessary to plan for salvaging the individuals involved in the military-industrial sector with appropriate retraining and relocation programs to aid them in transferring them to civilian work.

We might just as well maintain military priorities, for even if we tried to realign priorities, Congress would not allocate the funds needed. In 1939–1940, the Congress of the United States appropriated 42 percent of the federal budget for social welfare, community development, health, education, housing, and allied purposes. The same set of purposes recently received about 12 percent of Congressional appropriations. There is no science from which to forecast that if Congress could do it in 1940, it could not do it again today. There is nothing in the nature of Congress as an institution that precludes changing an order of priorities.

Concentration of decision-power in the federal government is inevitable and, as in the Department of Defense, desirable, in the name of economic-industrial efficiency. Efficiency indeed. Under the guidance of the Secretary of Defense, the F-111 airplane was supposed to cost up to $3.9 million. The latest estimate is $12.7 million. This ratio between expected and actual costs is fairly typical of industrial performance for the Department of Defense. Wherever the customer or competitor constraints of a commercial market are operative, this sort of cost performance would compel either a change of management, or bankruptcy, or both. In the land of military-industry, gross inefficiency has become normal. And so the polite thing is to be learned about the programs for "cost effectiveness" and the miracles generated by "cost-benefit analysis," thereby detracting attention from staggering cost-excesses that would be self-penalizing elsewhere. There is little evidence to be found in these spheres of ordinary workaday economy and efficiency.

If university professors and students would work on research problems of interest to the Department of Defense, then all will be well for the national defense, and for the universities and for the nation as well. This is not necessarily true. There are strong grounds for supposing that long concentration on military priorities, with the proliferation of military research activity, threatens the integrity of the university and undermines the traditional function of the university: teaching people and generating new knowledge.

The operation of the Department of Defense and its connections with industry are in good order as long as this is under civilian control. Holders of the highest offices of the state-management are nominally civilians. They are not professional military officers and they ordinarily wear civilian clothes to work. However, the difference between "military" and "civilian" in the government becomes blurred when the largest part of the federal budget is controlled by the Pentagon, whose control systems ramify into industry, the universities, and other areas of American society.

Whatever else may be said about the state-management, a managerial type of government is a bearable price to pay for a welfare state in a technological society. The fact is, more than two-thirds of spending by the federal government is for current and past military operations. In 1968, only 12 percent of the federal budget was used for health, education, welfare, and community development. By preempting manpower and money in the name of defense, the state-management has led the way in restricting the money and manpower left over for the human care of human beings. Furthermore, there is little evidence to support the proposition that only a centralized, federally controlled managerial organization is able to plan and execute activities designed to improve the condition of life.

Whatever may be said about the power-expanding propensity of the state-management, its activities are finally controlled by the Congress. It is true that the Congress votes the money required by the state-management. But the state-management has found ways of participating in these Congressional decisions. On February 20, 1969, the Associated Press reported that the Pentagon spends about $4 million a year for a lobbying force of 339 men, or about one lobbyist for every two members of Congress. With such continuing representation on Capitol Hill, the Pentagon is in a fine position to get its message across. Also, the state-management can use its unequaled capital-investment capability so that location decisions for new industrial and base operations improve Pentagon popularity among important congressmen.

> Lockheed, the largest defense firm, last year opened a plant in Charleston, S.C., home of Representative L. Mendel Rivers, chairman of the House Armed Services Committee. Last year also, General Dynamics, second largest defense plant (sic), placed an electronics subsidiary in Camden, Ark., after Senator John L. McClellan, chairman of the Government Operations Committee, had visited the Fort Worth plant where General Dynamics makes the F-111 (TFX). Senator McClellan has said that he asked the president of General Dynamics to take a look at what Arkansas had to offer when he was being shown around Fort Worth by that gentleman. (*The Nation,* October 21, 1968.)

Apart from its large size, the Department of Defense is just another government bureaucracy. The size of its budget and its control over people give this bureaucracy very special capabilities. Most important is its production decision-power. This latter set of powers identify this bureaucracy as a self-expanding industrial management.

The very diversity of the state-management's operation gives the President more choices in policy-making. Constitutionally, the President of the United States is a key decision-maker with respect to use of American military power. However, the President's alternatives are, in turn, defined by the great importance of the Pentagon. The result is that military options dominate the array of options considered.

A state-management is inevitable on account of the complex technologies that are used in military systems. Actually, the state-management orders the characteristics of military technology. Military technology has no life of its own. It is instrumental to the state-management, which was created to serve particular political requirements as perceived by President Kennedy and his aides upon entering office (see the discussion in Chapter 5).

Managers from military contracting firms go to work in the Pentagon. With their corporate associations they can exert important policy pressure on the operation of the state-management. The critical consideration is not where individuals come from but which institution has crucial decision-power. The state-management decides on which submanagements in the Pentagon industrial empire get work orders. The state-management also decides which firms shall undergo the greatest expansion. These are the controlling production decisions and they are made at the state-management level.

Consider the parallel condition in the ordinary multi-division industrial firm. In that environment, the central office characteristically draws upon management men from the various divisions of the firm. Thereby, the divisions of the firm do not control the central office. That is so because it is the central office that is the location of critical decisions on capital investment and other key production decisions. The state-management in the Pentagon is similarly related to the managements of the sub-firms in its industrial empire. Many people have assumed that movement of former "defense contractor" managers to the Pentagon is evidence of their control over the Pentagon; the unstated underlying assumption is that the various military contracting firms are, in fact, private and autonomous. That is precisely not the case. These firms' operations for the Pentagon are controlled by the state-management.

Since there is no profit calculation by the state-management on its own functioning, it is not capitalism. All the main attributes of industrial capitalism (other than the profit calculation) are present in the state-management. There is a hierarchical organization, separation of decision-making from production, and sustained pressure to enlarge decision-power of the management group. In the modern corporation, recorded profit has often ceased to be an autonomous indicator of the success of a management. Instead, profit has become a factor that is determined, within a wide range, by management decisions on allocation and size of key costs. The state-management gets the effect of profit-accumulation and investment (i.e., enlarging its decision-power) without an intervening process of selling products and accumulating an actual money profit. This management draws on the continuous flow of fresh capital granted to it by the Congress of the United States.

The state-management has made extensive use of systems-analysis and other techniques for assuring economic and technical effectiveness. This common understanding, elaborately cultivated by the state-management since 1961, does not account for important parts of the state-management's performance. Here is a list of 65 major defense projects which were canceled during the period 1953 to 1968 because they were found to be unneeded or unworkable. These 65 projects cost more than $10.5 billion before they were canceled. This "Sorry, but we changed our mind" list, furnished by the Pentagon, shows the name of the project, the year it was started, and the year canceled, and the amount of money that had been invested by the time of cancellation. This list of canceled contracts does not include the F-111 airplane fiasco which involved an enormous investment, under direct control of McNamara's office, in airplanes that finally did not function according to plan and may cost American citizens several billion dollars when all the outlays have been finally calculated.

PROJECT	YEAR STARTED	YEAR CANCELED	FUNDS INVESTED ($ MILLIONS)
Aircraft			
Army:			
XV3 Convertiplane	1952	1960	10.1
Navy:			
Seamaster	1951	1959	330.4
F-8U-3	1956	1958	100.0
HSL-1	1950	1955	94.0
F-5D-1	1954	1957	49.0
A-2D-1	1950	1954	47.0
T-40	1954	1958	33.0
A-2J-1	1948	1963	20.0

PROJECT	YEAR STARTED	YEAR CANCELED	FUNDS INVESTED ($ MILLIONS)
J-40-engine	1944	1953	18.0
F-10F-1	1950	1953	15.0
F-2Y-1	1949	1955	15.0
Air Force:			
ANP [Nuclear Air Craft]	1951	1961	511.6
F-108	1958	1959	141.9
XF-103	1950	1957	104.0
F-107	1954	1957	100.0
J-83 engines	1956	1959	55.0
C-132	1952	1957	54.0
T-61 engine	1957	1959	37.4
YH-16	1951	1954	23.4
X-21	1960	1966	36.0
X-19	1962	1966	16.0
XB-70	1958	1967	1468.1
Missiles			
Army:			
Hermes	1944	1954	96.4
Dart	1952	1958	44.0
Loki	1948	1956	21.9
Terrier, Land Based	1951	1956	18.6
Plato	1951	1958	18.5
Mauler	1960	1965	200.0
Navy:			
Sparrow I	1945	1958	195.6
Regulus II	1955	1958	144.4
Petrel	1945	1957	87.2
Corvus	1954	1960	80.0
Eagle	1959	1961	53.0
Meteor	1945	1954	52.6
Sparrow II	1945	1957	52.0
Rigel	1943	1953	38.0
Dove	1949	1955	33.7
Triton	1948	1957	19.4
Oriole	1947	1953	12.5
Typhon	1958	1964	225.0
Air Force:			
Navaho	1954	1957	679.8
Snark	1947	1962	677.4
GAM-63 Rascal	1946	1958	448.0

PROJECT	YEAR STARTED	YEAR CANCELED	FUNDS INVESTED ($ MILLIONS)
GAM-87 Skybolt	1960	1963	440.0
Talos (Land Based)	1954	1957	118.1
Mobile Minuteman	1959	1962	108.4
Q-4 Drone	1954	1959	84.4
SM-72 Goose	1955	1958	78.5
GAM-67 Crossbow	1957	1958	74.6
MMRBM	1962	1964	65.4

Ships

Navy:

Type II towed Torpedo Countermeasures	1945	1955	13.0

Ordnance, Combat Vehicles and Related Equipment

Army:

Vigilante	1952	1961	26.6
Tank medium and heavy T-95	1955	1960	18.0
Truck, cargo, 2½ Ton	1946	1965	5.9
Truck, cargo, 16 Ton	1959	1965	4.8[1]
Truck, tank, 5000 gal.	1959	1966	[1]
Truck, wrecker, 20 ton	1959	1966	[1]
Area Scanning Alarm (E 49)	1957	1966	3.9
Infantry Mortar, 107mm, XM95	1960	1967	10.7
AN/USD 5 Drone	1957	1962	103.3
AN/USD 4 Drone	1957	1960	40.0
Aerial Tramway	1947	1957	13.5
Auto Integrated Switch	1958	1965	39.9

Navy:

NRRS Sugar Grove	1957	1962	70.0
Hi Energy Boron (ZIP)	1952	1959	123.0

Air Force:

AN/ALQ-27	1957	1959	142.0
Hi Energy Boron (ZIP)	1956	1959	135.8
Dyna-Soar	1960	1963	405.0

[1] The three trucks listed comprise the 16-ton series of the GOER program which was terminated in June 1965. Work was officially terminated on the tanker and wrecker in February 1966. The cost of the program was $4.8 million.

The idea that economy has in fact been attained because of an announcement to do so simply cannot be taken seriously. During the 1960's, the very period of the formal establishment of the state-management, the reliability of major new military systems costing tens of billions of dollars was lower than the reliability of systems constructed during the 1950's. During this period, a great deal of work had been done toward improving the reliability of, for example, the individual electronic components. How can the reliability of single components go up while the reliability of systems goes down? This can happen as a result of great increase in the complexity of these systems. The error of a system is not the sum of the errors of the linked components. Rather, the system error is the product of the errors of components. Thereby, sufficient increase in the number of linked components can, through the multiplicative effect of linked error, offset improvements in reliability of single components. Something of this sort must have happened to help produce the remarkable decline in reliability of weapons systems that was reported by Richard A. Stubbing in January, 1969. Mr. Stubbing has been an analyst on military systems for the Bureau of the Budget. His paper on reliability of electronics systems during the 1950's and the 1960's presented a vivid set of data from which he concluded: "Less than 40 percent of the effort [during the 1960's] produced systems with acceptable electronic performance—an uninspiring record that loses further luster when cost overruns and schedule delays are also evaluated."

By means of their influence on the operation of the Pentagon, military-industry firms seem to get away with large profits. It is true that many military-industry firms have earned unusually large profits on their investments—larger than has been the case in private industry. The Stubbing report on military-system reliability showed that military-industry firms that have produced systems of lowest technical reliability had also earned highest rates of profit. To explain this, it is necessary to see the military-industry empire as one big firm dominated by the state-management. In that case "profits" are, in effect, grants of capital from the top management to the sub-managements —reflecting decisions to differentially enlarge or support subdivisions of the empire. This understanding of the matter explains the otherwise inexplicable decisions by the state-management (publicly recorded in May, 1969) to make considerable grants of capital to the General Dynamics and the Lockheed companies, after both of them had gone well beyond original cost estimates on particular military work. In both instances these grants of funds from the state-management represented decisions to maintain or enlarge the two enterprises as parts of the military-industrial system. (See the reports in *The New York Times* and *The Washington Post* of May 3, 1969.)

Waste is deplorable anywhere, but in military matters it is to be expected because of the essential nature of the undertaking. Therefore, one has to accept the abandonment of many projects along the way as simply part of the price one pays for trying to build a modern military defense. On September 3, 1968, *The Washington Post* headlined an article on Pentagon industrial procurement with "Much of Pentagon's $45 billion spending buys nothing." I do not agree with the judgment contained in that headline. Decision-power is being purchased by the state-management's industrial expenditures, even where these are related to goods that are finally scrapped.

Even though the Pentagon may itself be unduly ambitious in its new weapons proposals, there are nevertheless outside checks on its operations—for example, from the Bureau of the Budget, which works directly for the President. The Bureau of the Budget has had about three hundred staff members, of whom thirty, or 10 percent, have been assigned to the Department of Defense. That means that half of the spending activity by the federal government gets 10 percent of the surveillance. Evidently the Pentagon's budgets have been treated as sacrosanct and have been given almost automatic approval. Neither has there been any sustained check from the committees of the Congress, since these committees on Armed Services and Appropriations have not only included strongly pro-Pentagon members, but have operated with virtually no staff of their own to give them independent investigative and policy-formulating ability.

War is inherently wasteful. However, the program planning and budgeting systems introduced by the state-management and the widespread training of the Pentagon staff in cost effectiveness techniques are bound to restrain inappropriate, unplanned use of public funds. On December 8, 1966, it was disclosed that, during the previous year, the Pentagon had spent $20 billion on the war in Vietnam, that being exactly twice the budgeted expenditure. Furthermore, this doubled expenditure had not been previously announced (apparently, not even inside the government) and, as a result, had the effect of seriously upsetting important parts of the fiscal policy operations of the federal government. One Washington report had it that the $10 billion of additional spending was concealed to make the war seem cheaper than it was, particularly before the election in November, 1966. Finally, under law, the Department of Defense and every other government department can only spend the money allocated by the Congress for designated purposes. Where did the Pentagon get the $10 billion to spend for military operations in Vietnam that had not been voted for this purpose by the Congress? What laws were violated by the use of $10 billion of funds assigned to other purposes? Who was responsible for this violation of law, and what has been done, if anything, by the Department of Justice to bring the culprits to the bar of justice?

The Pentagon, even though it is a large organization, is nevertheless a part of the American system of government and is responsible to the President, the Congress, and, ultimately, to the American people. In November, 1967, the Senate Foreign Relations Committee commented on the near-absolute power acquired by the President to commit the United States to war. The Committee held:

> The concentration in the hands of the President of virtually unlimited authority over matters of war and peace has all but removed the limits to Executive power in the most important single area of our national life. Unless they are restored, the American people will be threatened with tyranny or disaster.

The concentration of authority, while formally in the hands of the President, is exercised through the Department of Defense. In the Pentagon the new state-management has a centrally important role as a concentration of decision-power at home and abroad.

I have reviewed many of the key propositions which are used to justify the operation of the Pentagon and its state-management. Under critical scrutiny these ideas turn out to be little more than a web of half-truths (and sometimes less than half-truths), precariously balanced on each other to give the aura of a solid ideology. When dealt with singly, the whole net of interlocked mythology crumbles, and we must simply face the facts: first, "defense" is no longer possible—that is, there is no reliable way of preventing destruction of the United States by a determined attacker; second, the American economy and society are depleted and not benefited by military priorities; and, third, these priorities are very serviceable for enlarging the decision-power of the state-management. Despite their invalidity, these ideologies are persistently advanced, owing to their contribution to the ideologues and to the state-management with which these men have identified themselves.

8

The Cost of the Para-State to American Society

Since the end of the Second World War, the United States government has spent an astronomical $1,000 billion for military purposes. This is equal to the value of all residential and business structures in the United States. Of this amount, over one-half has been spent since the beginning of the Kennedy-Johnson administration in 1961. The true cost to the nation is more realistically measured by what has been foregone; that is, the goods and services that could have been available to the people of the United States if priority had not been given to the Pentagon's objectives.

The full cost of the Vietnam war, one of the priority projects of the state-management, according to private congressional sources, was as much as $40 billion during 1968. That sum could have been used for very different purposes.

1. Each month of Vietnam war cost could have financed the complete training of over 100,000 scientists.
2. Each month of Vietnam war cost would finance the annual food bill for ending hunger among 10 million Americans.

3. Each month of Vietnam war cost could more than double the resources of the Agency for International Development for its annual economic programs throughout the world.
4. Each month of Vietnam war cost could create four new Rockefeller Foundations.
5. Each month of Vietnam war cost could pay the full year's cost of state and local police in all the states of the union.
6. The annual cost of the Vietnam war could enable more than doubling the social security benefits paid to 20 million Americans.

If Americans wished to embark on a systematic effort to end poverty (economic underdevelopment) in the United States, this would require investment in "human capital" and in job-creating capital. The money and manpower used up in a Vietnam war would finance the annual cost of a national effort which would obviously enhance the quality of life for all. Such a national effort could be completed within ten years. The cost of the Vietnam war alone to American society cannot be readily comprehended even in those terms. From 1965 to 1969, this war cost the federal government about $108 billion. Taking into account the veterans' benefits and interest on the national debt incurred because of this war, the cost is finally about three times the initial spending.

By 1965, the following opening paragraphs from my book *Our Depleted Society* appropriately diagnosed the American condition, even before the accelerated depletion that was induced by the Vietnam war.

The United States now is the scene of a drama different from that implicit in her confident ideology. A process of technical, industrial, and human deterioration has been set in motion within American society. The competence of the industrial system is being eroded at its base. Entire industries are falling into technical disrepair, and there is massive loss of productive employment because of inability to hold even domestic markets against foreign competition. Such depletion in economic life produces wide-ranging human deterioration at home. The wealthiest nation on earth has been unable to rally the resources necessary to raise one fifth of its own people from poverty. The same basic depletion operates as an unseen hand restricting America's relations with the rest of the world, limiting foreign-policy moves primarily to military-based initiatives . . .

The price of building colossal military power and endlessly adding to it, has been the depletion of American society, a process now well advanced in industry, civilian technology, management, education, medical care, and the quality of life. The prospect of "no future" has become a permanent part of government security policies that depend mainly on the threat of using nuclear weapons. Never before were men made to feel so powerless, so incapable of having a voice over their own fate . . .

Americans have believed that our nation is so wealthy and so productive that there is no possible contradiction between massive military buildups and growing affluence for all. The United States can afford guns and butter; besides, doesn't defense spending put money into circulation? This was learned from three years of U.S. involvement in World War II—an experience different from twenty years of Cold War. The contradiction between guns and butter is now real and measurable. Our able young men cannot, at once, be trainees for the Atomic Energy Commission and physicians in training; they cannot be teaching the young and also designing missile components. The salary money spent by the missile builder goes into circulation, but that does not in the least add to the stock of talent available for civilian work that needs to be done. "Guns" take away from "butter" even in the United States.

In an industrial ecenomy, two classes of technical activity limit the current and future quality of the industrial system. The first is the *scale and quality of research and development;* the second is the *quality of the physical plant* used for production. The physical plant fairly well determines the productivity of both capital and labor, and research and development affect the development of productivity and product innovation.

In November, 1968, the McGraw-Hill Company completed its regular five-year inventory of metalworking machinery in U.S. industry; it disclosed that 64 percent of the metalworking machine tools used in U.S. industry were ten years old or older. The age of this industrial equipment (drills, lathes, etc.) marks the United States' machine tool stock as the oldest among all major industrial nations, and it marks the continuation of a deterioration process that began with the end of the Second World War. This deterioration at the base of the industrial system certifies to the continuous debilitating and depleting effect that the military use of capital and research and development talent has had on American industry. The machine tool industry is merely one of the American civilian industries with modest research and development programs (excepting a literal handful of the very largest firms) and with unstable, hence inefficient, production systems.

The aging stock of machine tools constrains productive growth within the entire industrial system, because all metalworking industries utilize machine tools to a greater or lesser degree. While the United States carries out research and development (R&D) programs on a scale unmatched by any other country, it is important to evaluate this activity in terms of the concentration points of the R&D effort, as well as the size of the U.S. population and the scale of its economy. Thus, in November, 1967, the international Organization for Economic Cooperation and Development (based in Paris) found that the United States had 700,000 scientists, engineers, and technicians working in research and development. However, 63 percent of this activity was on behalf of the military. Thus, approximately 259,000 R&D personnel were estimated to be engaged in civilian work. This compares most unfavorably with the western European research and development staff which totals 466,000, an overwhelming part of which is engaged in civilian research and development.

If military and allied expenditures are removed from the U.S. research and development outlay, then U.S. civilian research costs amount to about 1.5 percent of the Gross National Product, or the same percentage as Belgium's, and not much more than the 1.4 percent spent by the United Kingdom, the 1.2 percent spent by France, and the 1.1 percent spent by West Germany.

There is another type of constraint imposed by military priorities in research and development that is difficult to express in measurable units, and that is the consequence of the "classification" of information that restricts access to many sorts of knowledge. This means that insofar as particular fields of knowledge are elaborately developed for military purposes, there is a better than fair chance that important parts of these fields will be subjected to secrecy controls. This is mirrored in the formation of classified bibliographies and classified libraries, to which only persons with appropriate security clearances can have access. When research activity is split up in this fashion, it is bound to have a braking effect on the sector which is relatively free, if only because much duplication of work will be done by those not having access to restricted information.

The industrial impact of military priorities is further indicated by the fact that in 1967, for the first time in American history, the import of machine tools exceeded their export. Thus, there has been a far more rapid growth in the machine tool industry in countries such as Japan and West Germany than in the United States.

Industrial deterioration is also visible in the iron and steel industry. An article by Professors Adams and Dirlam on "Big Steel Invention and Innovation" (*Quarterly Journal of Economics,* May, 1966) indicated that the United States iron and steel industry has not only lagged significantly in research and development, but, further, has been notable for "backwardness" in adopting new technology. Steel industry management has called attention to the high U.S. prices of new equipment—compared with prices paid by German and Japanese steelmakers. Management has also emphasized the impact upon them of the "wage-price spiral," which is strongly impelled by high military spending.

During the last 20 years, these trends have reinforced the lead that Japanese manufacturing industry has taken in several areas, ranging from shipbuilding—including shipbuilding technology—to civilian electronics. Thus, the head start the Japanese gained in manufacturing the small transistor radio continues to hold in the mass production and international sale of more complex recording devices, television sets and small desk-top electronic computers. The same focus on civilian use of electronics is demonstrated by the major innovations made by Japanese engineers in the development of artificial limbs, especially their control mechanisms.

In an industry as traditional as watchmaking, which enjoys a mass market in the United States, American industry has somehow been unable to match the Swiss competition over the years, and the American market has been feeling the effects of the major import of quality watches not only from Japan but from the Soviet Union as well. The Soviet watch industry ranks second in the world in production quantity. (While visiting the Soviet Union in 1959, I recall taking special note of the array of Soviet designed machine tools on exhibition for turning out parts for the watchmaking industry. Thus, the present level of Russian watch production is a consequence of homework done some years ago to lay the basis for the current, competent watchmaking industry.)

There are other American services, requiring a modern technological base, that also show evidence of substantial depletion: American rail services have hardly begun to move up to the standard of technological capability demonstrated by the rail industry of the Japanese, French, and others, while postal service in the United States has deteriorated to the point where transit time has been lengthened rather than shortened.

In 1965, the Congress enacted the High Speed Transportation Act. The Secretary of Commerce, charged with implementing the Act, sought to initiate a research program in the field and to engage the services of various laboratories and individuals. Here is what the Secretary of Commerce reported after one year:

> Vietnam has affected the program in other ways as well. The aerospace industry which has exhibited great interest in advanced technology in high speed ground transportation has found itself much more preoccupied with defense needs. This has affected the availability of research contractors and of qualified personnel for employment within the Department of Commerce. As a result the research and development program has taken a slower pace.

The slackened pace mentioned by the Secretary was appreciable, for only $24 million of the $35 million authorized by the Transportation Act was requested for fiscal year 1967, and the Secretary of Commerce indicated that requested ". . . appropriations through fiscal year 1968 will be substantially less than the $90 million authorized by the Act." Such industries and services are only parts of a total industrial system. But they are important in their own right, and the technological and economic depletion manifest in these fields is explicable only by the fact that fresh research and development talent and fresh productive capital have been relatively unavailable in these spheres over a period of more than twenty years. Major industries must be technologically and economically renewed if the United States is to have a competent, viable industrial system.

As late as January, 1967, it still seemed possible to the federal government, and to various economic commentators, to consider Vietnam a relatively inexpensive war, the proof being that ". . . there have been no shortages as in past wars." That comment is correct with respect to the supply of automobiles and household appliances, but certainly not correct with respect to the supply of modern, attractively priced production equipment for U.S. industry. Nor is it correct with respect to many basic services, such as shelter, medical care, or education, which we will discuss below. Thus, the notion that the United States can have both "guns and butter" is, in fact, an assumption not borne out by the record of the last decade. In an important paper on "The Economics of the Vietnam War" (*New University Thought,* Summer, 1968) my colleague Terence McCarthy summed up the cost of the Vietnam war as follows:

> $54 billion in direct military costs plus billions of dollars of sales of government assets and rundown of military inventories [up to February 1968—S.M.];
>
> raised the annual rate of Vietnam war expenditures to $29 billion in calendar 1968 [private Congressional sources suggest the actual cost of the war to the United States in calendar 1968 as $40 billion —S.M.];
>
> reduced the purchasing power of the consumer's dollar by almost 9 per cent;
>
> distorted the economy by adding only 1.6 million production workers to manufacturing payrolls compared with 2.3 million to government payrolls;
>
> caused a loss in housing construction of at least 750,000 dwelling units;
>
> raised interest rates to the highest levels in a century;
>
> deepened the poverty of the poor by increasing food prices 10 per cent [up to February 1968—S.M.];
>
> raised the interest bearing federal debt by $23 billion;
>
> produced a $20 billion federal deficit in fiscal 1968 even assuming a tax increase;
>
> rendered impossible required expenditures on renovation of America's decaying cities;
>
> increased the adverse balance of payments insupportably;
>
> cost the nation the gold cover of its dollar;

forced the establishing of a two-tier price for gold throughout the world;

generated the greatest threat of inflation since the Civil War . . .

Undeniably, this set of economic consequences generated by the Vietnam war is unique in 20th-century American economic experience. This has much to do with the fact that by 1965, before Lyndon Johnson heated up the Vietnam war, the United States was already well advanced in many forms of industrial and other depletion. The society-wide depletion process was accelerated when the Vietnam war was undertaken in a period of relatively full employment after twenty years of cold war. (By contrast, the U.S. involvement in the Second World War endured for somewhat more than three years and called into the labor force 8 million men who were unemployed up to that time, as well as additional millions of women who had not previously been considered part of the labor force.)

The infant mortality rate (deaths per 1,000 live births during the first year of life) is accepted as a basic indicator of the quality of *health services* throughout the world. In the United States, by 1967, the Assistant Secretary of the Department of Health, Education and Welfare, Dr. Philip R. Lee, announced that "Only 15 years ago this nation ranked 5th in the world in infant mortality. The latest figures from the Harvard School of Preventive Medicine show America now ranks 25th. Even worse, we have virtually stood still while other nations have steadily improved their survival rates." He further indicated that the death rate in the 15-to-64 age-bracket is higher in America than in other industrialized nations, and that death from heart disease is twice the rate in comparable nations. These mortality levels do not reflect unavailability of medical knowledge or a low level of medical technology in general. Rather, these rates indicate the lack of requisite manpower and physical resources for applying known medical technology within American society. A striking example of this failure to apply medical technology was obtained from the slums of New York City, with respect to infant mortality rate. In September, 1967, it was reported that ". . . for the first six months of this year the rate in Central Harlem was 44.4 and in East Harlem 42.6, or 5 times the 8.2 rate in a Bronx health district, the lowest in the city."

This means that if the rate that obtains in that part of New York City with the best infant mortality performance applied elsewhere, then the United States would have the lowest infant mortality rate in the world, and 40,000 infants would be saved each year.

Tuberculosis has long been recognized as a poverty-linked disease. In the United States as a whole, from 1965 to 1967, the incidence of new TB cases averaged 24.2 per 100,000 people, while in New York City as a whole the rate was 47.7—exceeded only by the Chicago rate of 56. The New York level was determined in large part by the TB rates—six to ten times the national average—found in slum areas. There is no ambiguity; the termination of slum living is what is needed to bring down the TB rate.

Another indication of restriction on resources for health care was recorded in the President's Special Message to the Congress on Children and Youth (February 9, 1967), when President Johnson stated: "Nearly 2 out of 3 disadvantaged children between the ages of 5 and 14 have never visited a dentist. They have 5 times more decayed teeth than their more fortunate classmates." This means that about 3 million children are so disadvantaged. The President followed this analysis with a recommendation to ". . . authorize a pilot program of dental care for 100,000 children in areas of acute poverty." Accordingly, the provision made would cover only 3 percent of the children in the group needing dental care.

Hospitals and allied facilities in the United States are frequently operated under conditions judged deficient, when measured by standards formulated by the American medical profession. This is closely connected with a shortage of physicians and nurses. In 1966, at Kings County Hospital in New York City, a resident physician commented: "I look around for somebody who looks sick, people with heart attacks usually make themselves known, but we've had heart attacks wait 8 or 9 hours on wooden benches before being seen." Such scandalous conditions in the emergency wards of major city hospitals are unavoidable with a shortage of doctors and nurses. Patients at Kings County Hospital are accustomed to waiting; patients with fractures have waited up to eight hours, according to Dr. Jerold Haftan, Director of Emergency Services.

According to the Secretary of Health, Education and Welfare, the nation should graduate 11,700 physicians each year, 3,500 more than in 1966, in order to avoid a drastic drop in the number of available doctors. (This figure does not take into account termination of the importation of physicians, which has mounted from 1,600 to as much as 2,700 a year.) In 1965, I calculated that in order to improve health care services in the United States as a whole, to raise them to the level prevailing in the state of California, it would be necessary to construct about 150 new medical schools, or, on the average, three new medical schools per state. The actual program for new medical school construction is for 13 new medical schools to be built by 1975. Predictably, the United States is confronted with the diminishing availability of medical services. In March, 1966, American hospitals offered posts for 13,463 interns. The medical schools of the United States could supply 7,588, leaving the hospitals to seek interns abroad or to make do with fewer M.D.'s than needed.

The importation of physicians hardly begins to make up for the difference between supply and requirement. However, it is significant to note other effects of the importation process. If 2,700 physicians are imported to the United States in a given year, this means that the output of approximately 27 medical schools is being imported—that is, the United States is being saved a capital outlay of $540 million by having not built 27 medical schools, which, in addition, would cost $135 million to operate annually. The importation of physicians imposes these costs on other countries, helps deter the construction of the medical schools necessary to the United States, and renders the United States vulnerable to any termination of the importation process which might very well occur, as a number of countries in Asia and Latin America block the departure of their physicians for service in the United States.

The supply of nurses, of immense importance for operating modern medical facilities, is very poor in the United States, with an average of one out of four nursing posts vacant. However, in certain large cities—New York City being an important case in point—the condition is disastrous. Thus, with 7,800 authorized and budgeted nursing posts, the city's own hospital system has recently been able to fill only about 2,000 of them.

In New York City, the condition of deterioration in the supply of physicians and nurses within major hospitals reached the point where, in mid-1966, the city government was forced to consider closing a major general hospital because of failure to maintain medical services at a level acceptable to the profession. Thus, with only seventeen registered nurses among the personnel caring for 1,800 patients at Bellevue and Metropolitan hospitals, the administrators of municipal hospitals in New York City found themselves with virtually unmanageable problems.

Further consequences of this shortage of physicians and nurses include the inability of the United States to make use of innovations in medical technology. The prospect of the development of an effective artificial heart means that by 1975 about 10,700 physicians and about 4,600 surgeons would be required to do the work of planting hearts in the approximately 100,000 Americans a year who would presumably be eligible for such treatment. How the heart surgery teams are to be generated in the few years that remain before an artificial heart is designed is a problem that will remain unsolved as long as the relative supply of physicians is as short as it is. A similar problem is already visible in the case of kidney failure, where 6,000 lives a year are being lost in the United States because of the lack of money for producing the dialysis machines as well as the lack of trained personnel needed to operate them. The cost of machine and the annual cost of the man-hours needed to operate it amount to an outlay of about $28,000. As a result, of the estimated 7,000 terminal patients who could benefit from dialysis, only about 1,000 can be treated with existing facilities. This imposes a remarkable moral problem: who shall live and who shall die? How is the selection to be made among the 7,000 medically eligible for treatment?

Deterioration and depletion are also epidemic in the nursing homes operated around big cities. As is to be expected, this is especially so in nursing homes for low-income people. Thus, the elderly men and women who must depend on social security checks and little more often find themselves in nursing homes hardly worthy of the name, subjected to gross indignities, overcrowding and rat infestation.

With large numbers of Americans, notably in military service, living abroad for extended periods, the American population is being exposed to exotic diseases which hitherto have only rarely appeared within the United States. Thus, American health officials note that plague has reached epidemic proportions among civilians in South Vietnam and fear the importation of the disease into heavily populated areas of the United States. Perhaps this is a collateral penalty for allowing rat infestation in American slum areas to continue, for these animals are the principal carriers of plague.

Another view of health in the United States comes from the report *Hunger U.S.A.,* formulated by a Citizens' Board of Inquiry into Hunger and Malnutrition in the United States (Beacon Press, Boston, 1968). The report indicates that about 10 million Americans are subject, in varying degrees, to significant malnutrition. This extends, for example, to the discovery that the protein deficiency disease, kwashiorkor, which is widespread in Africa, is found on Indian reservations in the United States, within various southern states, and has even shown up in New York City, where a physician who had emigrated from Africa recognized such a case in one of the city hospitals. Senator McGovern wrote in 1968:

> At the time of this writing, the country is being shocked by pictures of golden-haired Biafran children who are on the verge of death from the extreme protein-calorie deficiency condition called kwashiorkor. But here on our own Indian reservations we have children suffering from kwashiorkor! In our ghettos and our depressed rural areas, we have children who grow up on low-protein diets that are almost exclusively such foods as beans, potatoes, and gravy—a diet that frequently results in irreparable brain damage.

In South Carolina, testimony before the Citizens' Board of Inquiry on Hunger and Malnutrition disclosed:

> There were cases of rickets in most countries in South Carolina and a fairly large number of pre-school children had some degree of kwashiorkor, a protein deficiency disease mostly associated with West Africa. . . . Mrs. Victoria DeLee, a Negro civil rights worker in Dorchester County, South Carolina, has said there have been cases there where children have starved to death. Asked by incredulous panelists if that is what the doctor said was the cause of death, Mrs. DeLee replied, "That's what the doctors called it."

Recent studies indicate that severe protein malnutrition in infants has the effect of inhibiting brain development and hence limits the child's future capacity to learn. No course on contemporary American problems is complete without a reading of Homer Bigart's remarkable series of articles on hunger in America in *The New York Times* (February 16, 17, 18, 19, and 20, 1969).

In education: In New York City, the wealthiest city in the world, out of 927 school buildings surveyed by the city's Department of Buildings, 425 have been found to be in violation of the city's building code. Investigations, in late 1968, disclosed that there was gross overcrowding and that 85,000 youngsters had been attending classes in 109 New York City school buildings constructed before 1900. The principal of one school testified that he began the year with a pupil enrollment of 1,100, and that a few months later it had grown to 1,494, forcing him to double sessions in the school while reducing the instruction time allowed each child. Public school teachers are in short supply as well, and the National Education Association has recommended a comprehensive program to increase the supply of teachers. However, the U.S. Office of Education has simultaneously denied the existence of a teacher shortage and reported that approximately one million trained teachers had sought better-paying jobs outside the school systems. This supports the understanding that there is no absolute shortage in these spheres, but only a relative shortage, since those activities society has given priority to (as measured by money paid for work performed) seem to be well supplied with staff. Clearly, educational systems have not been given priority.

In 1968, an investigation by a group of eminent citizens who comprised the Detroit High School Study Commission reported: "Our high schools are appallingly inadequate—a disgrace to the community and a tragedy to the thousands of young men and women who we compel and cajole to sit in them." This group reported that ". . . school buildings are outmoded and overcrowded and teachers overburdened." The group recommended an annual increase of $21 million a year to the $210 million school budget, to expand high school facilities and teaching staffs.

While the United States has failed to improve the quality of its own "human capital," it has been resorting to a variety of devices to secure the labor force necessary for priority industries. Thus, New England firms in military work have engaged labor recruiters in European countries to hire machine operators for them from abroad.

The deterioration found in the relative supply of physicians, nurses, and teachers has begun to appear in certain classes of researchers. For example, by the end of 1967, the American Institute of Physics warned than an increasing shortage of newly trained physicists was threatening the further development of physics in the United States. The Institute report noted:

> [although] physics attracts only those who are good in mathematics, or who select physics as a career, there is also the possibility that many children who are fighting to get into the best colleges fear they will not get as high a mark in physics as in some other subject.

This, in turn, is linked to the position of the art of teaching mathematics in the United States. An international study reported that, in 1967–1968, the United States ranked approximately twelfth among nations in the quality of instruction in mathematical subjects.

For many years, the American Medical Association dominated the scene in the decision-making on the number and character of medical schools and hence on the availability of physicians in the nation. Major investments in medical schools, however, are no longer subject to decisions by the AMA, for they do not control the capital funds or the annual operating funds for these purposes. Such funds come primarily from the federal government and the states. The priority given to parasitic economic growth by government has been the root cause of the inadequacy of capital investment for medical and educational purposes.

During the ten years ending in 1968, 561,000 subsidized, low-rent *dwellings* were built in the United States. This does not even amount to 10 percent of the number required to replace dwelling units now rated as grossly substandard on grounds of health and other basic considerations. While Congress has passed various bills authorizing the construction of low-rent housing, the funds necessary for carrying this work forward have not been made available, again because of the priorities given to the requirements of the Pentagon. Since housing deterioration proceeds at a rate of about 600,000 units a year, the rate of deterioration will still exceed the rate of construction even under the program adopted by Congress in 1968. Therefore, by the end of the proposed three-year period of activity, there would still be about six million substandard housing units in the nation.

Available technology could supply reasonably good, modern *transport facilities* for U.S. metropolitan areas, requiring a capital outlay of about $10 billion. The funds are simply not available in the face of the priority given to the demands of the state-management.

In June, 1967, the Urban League prepared a statistical presentation on *the relation of Negroes to whites with respect to income, unemployment, education, health, and housing.* This study compared the condition of the Negro population of the United States to the average condition of the white population during 1955–1965. The study found that there had been some improvement with respect to relative position in education, that is, more educational opportunities were available for Negroes, and thus the gap between them and whites could be lessened. However, in every other sphere—income, employment, health and housing—the difference between the two populations had widened.

The state-management's priorities definitely do not include the termination of economic underdevelopment in the United States. The long-term poor in American cities include 200,000 children in New York City who, on the testimony of the Welfare Commissioner, cannot afford a candy bar. In 1966, pediatricians in the Montefiore Hospital in the Bronx diagnosed a case of kwashiorkor in a 10-month-old child. The Indians of the United States, long left outside the economic growth of the affluent society, live under conditions of extreme squalor. Homer Bigart, of *The New York Times,* has described hundreds of Chippewa Indians in North Dakota as living through the winter "in hovels unfit for pigs."

A further consequence of state-management affluence in American society is vividly illustrated by the results of the Selective Service examinations. By October, 1966, the journal *American Education* noted that two-thirds of the 18-year-old Negroes who had taken the Armed Forces qualification tests in the previous eighteen-month period had failed them on educational grounds. The national combined failure rate is 25.3 percent, with considerable variation from state to state and with major differences between whites and Negroes. Thus, even in the states with the best performance, the disparity of results for Negroes was considerable. In the state of Washington, the combined failure rate on this test of elementary literacy and basic knowledge was 5.8 percent; in the District of Columbia the failure rate was 55 percent. In the state of Washington, 25 percent of the Negroes failed, but only 5.5 percent of the non-Negroes failed.

In 1965, when I called attention to the massive disqualification of young men for selective service on educational and medical grounds, the data and analyses were received with substantial skepticism by a considerable number of readers. Subsequent developments have only reinforced that analysis. By 1967, 40.7 percent of all young men examined for induction into military service were disqualified for educational or physical deficiencies, or both. In this remarkable fashion, a type of retribution has been visited upon the operators of the Pentagon.

The American *physical environment* has been allowed to decay further, little capital being appropriated to efforts to diminish soil erosion or air pollution, because of the military priorities of the state-management. In December, 1966, John Gardner, Secretary of Health, Education and Welfare, reported: "There is not a major metropolitan area in the United States without an air pollution problem today."

Testing operations on behalf of the supersonic airliner, which is a major state-management project, have not only produced considerable disruption of ordinary life for those citizens in the testing area, but also have caused extensive geologic damage to United States national parks. Prehistoric cliff dwellings have been damaged by the sonic boom ordinarily produced by the testing operations. If supersonic aircraft are normally operated with present technology, a trail of sonic booms generated across the United States would guarantee far-reaching and continual damage.

In 1962, I calculated the cost of *world economic development* in my book *The Peace Race*. I found that the cost of a serious economic development effort, worldwide, would be $22 billion a year. The Vietnam war during 1968 cost almost two times that amount. Perhaps even more striking than that is the relation between the worldwide cost of economic development and the spending for military budgets by developing countries in a recent year. By 1966–1967, the "less developed countries" were spending $17.4 million for their armed forces out of their own budgets. This exceeded their combined spending on education and health—$16 million. For the people of Asia, Africa, and Latin America, the priority to arms in their own budgets effectively frustrates their own economic development. For the arms budgets use up just the quantity of capital (men, machinery, and so forth) needed to substantially accelerate the development process, so that the gap between the rich and the poor nations could start narrowing. In all this, the Pentagon with its "military assistance" and arms sales programs has played a crucial part, thereby depleting economic development for the poorest of the poor.

Some apologists for the military priorities policy point out that defense budgets in developing countries constitute a smaller percentage of their GNP than the defense budgets of the United States or the Soviet Union. However, it should be noted that $15 out of a per capita income of $150 has a much greater impact on the life of an individual than a 10 percent tax of, say, $185 taken from a per capita income of $1,850. Comparison between the military budgets of developing countries and those of industrialized states in absolute amounts, or in percentage of the GNP, tends to be misleading. A more meaningful relationship would be to show the amount of the military budget of an unindustrialized country as a percent of the value product of the industrialized sectors of its economy, for it is from the industrialized or economically developed sector that new capital is obtained. Viewed in this way, the percent outlay for military purposes would be at least doubled for developing countries, thus revealing the percentage of their GNP used for parasitic economic growth as the same or greater than the percentage prevailing in the United States.

Military organization in underdeveloped countries has a destructive effect on the economic relations between the industrialized and developing countries. Ordinarily, capital investment has a multiplying effect on output per person and per unit of physical capital used in production. That is the basis for ability to repay loans by developing countries when the fresh capital has been used for productive growth. However, when a developing country turns a technically significant part of its national plant to the service of economically parasitic military growth, then the net depleting effect of this growth impairs the ability of developing countries to pay off loans from abroad from a steadily increasing margin of new salable output. Neither do the skilled manpower and machinery invested in military activity yield any marketable product.

Developing countries are also burdened by the tendency of world machinery prices to rise more rapidly than raw-materials prices. Price inflation (including increased costs for machinery) in industrialized countries (in which their military priorities play a key part) thus visits a penalty on the poor countries, requiring them to repay loans with products of diminished exchange value. As a result, fresh loans are often arranged to enable payment of interest and principal on older capital loans by developing countries.

When the economic development of these societies is restricted, this, in turn, diminishes meaningful professional opportunities for their newly educated young people. During the 12-year period of 1956 through 1967, immigration into the United States of scientists, engineers, and physicians tripled, rising from 5,373 at the beginning of the period to 15,272 in 1967. "But the immigration from the developing countries more than quadrupled, from 1,769 in 1956 to 7,913 in 1967." This conclusion, from the report on scientific "brain drain" from developing countries by the Congressional Committee on Government Operations, reflects a tragedy for the developing countries, as their most precious capital, highly trained skilled manpower, does not return to the societies that produced them. In this way, the developing countries, in fact, make a major capital export to the United States, since in an industrial society the really important capital is human capital. It is also the most expensive to produce, since it involves the rearing and educating of children until they become capable of being employed. The Congressional Committee reported: "The very high contribution of the developing countries to U.S. medical manpower is equivalent in number to the entire output of 15 U.S. medical schools graduating the largest number of M.D.'s in 1967." Thus, as mentioned above, the developing countries alone export to the United States more medical doctors each year than will be produced by the enlargement of the United States medical school population that is planned through 1975. The result of all this is apparent.

The World Health Organization has declared a worldwide goal for 1970 of one doctor per 10,000 people. To maintain the same ratio within the next ten years, 8,500 new African doctors will be needed. But World Health Organization experts concede that such an achievement is presently impossible. In the Congo, for example, the drastic shortage of doctors has been identified as a major limiting factor on the area's progress. The prognosis, therefore, is for continued deterioration in health services in developing countries. There is a recognized connection between health, population growth, and economic development. Recently, Drs. Taylor and Hall of Johns Hopkins University concluded: "Sound demographic, economic and scientific evidence indicates that health programs promote economic development and directly stimulate the demand for, and practice of, family planning." The judgment is that the problem of population growth can become manageable in a context of economic development which includes an increasingly competent level of health care. Thus, the United States, with its shortage of manpower for health services, contributes substantially to worldwide problems by attracting medical personnel in tragically short supply from the developing countries of the world. The effect is a form of national piracy, regardless of the cloaking justification of the rights of free international movement by individuals. Altogether, the prognosis for the developing countries is grave. Thus, there are few men who forecast anything other than the imminence of major world famines for the next decades. For example: a panel of the President's Science Advisory Committee reported in 1967: "A compound annual growth rate of 4 percent in food production and 5.5 percent in income must be achieved by the developing nations if they are to meet their food requirements during the period 1965 to 1985." Actually, these countries have been increasing their food production by only 2.7 percent annually and their incomes by 4.5 percent.

In the developing countries, gross shortages appear in virtually every form of basic commodity and service. Thus, housing is in far more limited supply in developing nations as compared with the United States or western Europe. But the United States, for its part, has been incapable of supplying the requisite technology that might be helpful toward remedying the housing conditions of Latin Americans, Africans, and Asians. For with its Pentagon-first priority system, the

United States has been incapable of even attending to the slum conditions that exist in its own cities.

Analysts of economic development have repeatedly cited the foreign military-aid activities of the big powers as one of the single most important factors in deterring democratic political development. Thus, the estimate of two students of Pakistani affairs is that:

> In the long run, the worst aspect of military aid is the complete change it produces in the balance of social and political forces in favor of conservatism and established vested interests. The dragon seed sown by military aid has produced a crop of military officers whose social roots are in the most conservative strata of our society. There is no countervailing force to hold them in check. Once in power they do not allow for easy and peaceful democratic political evolution. In Western societies the trade union movement is an effective countervailing force; the longer tradition of democracy, perhaps, also plays its part. In a country like India, where these two factors are to some extent operative, a military coup d'état would not be all fair sailing. But in countries like Pakistan, where the trade union movement is relatively weak, the peasant movement non-existent and political evolution rudimentary, the picture is rather more grim. Perhaps there is no factor so inimical to the growth of democracy in underdeveloped countries as the militarization of our societies.

Another type of competence foregone by the United States because of its state-management priorities has been *planning for the economic health of the country* under conditions of peace, rather than under conditions of war and war preparation. In 1964, the Pentagon and the White House shot down Senator McGovern's bill for establishing a National Economic Conversion Commission. In October, 1968, it was indicated that about 6,000 civilians, mostly research and development employees, would be discharged from various government installations in an attempt to cut back civilian spending to meet Congressional "economy" requirements, and that there had been virtually no planning for relocating these men. This is a remarkable fact, since it is certainly the case that engineers, scientists, technicians, and other professionals are in short supply, and that a planned program for using these people elsewhere would yield considerable benefits. Until now there has been no action ordered by the federal government to plan for the re-employment of these men. However, the Pentagon does have a fairly elaborate set-up for relocating even its civilian staff within the military establishment when a base, for example, is declared surplus.

In sum, there is no clear way of giving a cumulative, quantitative reckoning of what has been foregone in American society because of the sustained priority given to the requirements of the state-management. The economic reckoning can be given in terms of past behavior, but it is the capability and incapability for the future that is probably the most important. Of all these matters, I judge the present inability of the United States to produce economic development at home and abroad as the most important economic capacity that has been foregone because of priorities given to the state-management's military concerns. The inability to develop economically is a source of major divisiveness, especially along racial lines, within American society and among nations. This incapacity will continue as long as the state-management is accorded first priority. The United States thus runs the risk of an internal race war, while some analysts expect great international wars of the future to be based on a war of the races; an international war rooted in a condition of economic underdevelopment will be highly correlated with racial hatreds.

The critical reader at this point might very well ask: "But is all this necessary? Would it not be possible for American economy and society to repair the conditions of the cities, of education, of health care, to stop the deterioration in various civilian industries, while still carrying on the same scale of military and allied activity? After all, the wealth of the United States is very great."

Altogether, the prognosis is not favorable for a guns-plus-butter performance in the United States. So long as Americans accept the priorities of the state-management, the repair of the areas of deterioration within American society reviewed in this chapter cannot be accomplished. For example: while it is true that more money-income for the poor could provide them with more food and more consumer goods of many kinds, this would not produce the big changes that constitute economic development. These require capital outlays that consist, not of aggregated small consumption decisions, but of investment decisions by the Congress, the body that wields the important block of social-responsibility money in this society. So long as the priority there continues to be for the Pentagon, serious economic development for thirty million Americans and the renewal of depleted industries and services are foreclosed.

The most durable constraint on the ability of the United States to repair deterioration is the present use of the finite stock of manpower available to the society. The U.S. has no unemployed doctors, nurses, teachers, engineers, or city planners. Everybody trained in these occupations is working. Thus, it is difficult to conceive of relieving present shortages in health services, education or housing, or restoring fresh water, or improving waste disposal, while the United States, by salary and similar rationing, assigns skilled heads and hands to meet the requirements of an expanding state-management. I recall that an ABM system, only one of the new military systems planned for by the state-management, would require a capital outlay of about $650 billion. This, together with other state-management projects, would consume annually a quantity of resources so great as to require doubling federal taxes, or exacting payment in the guise of price inflation.

9

1984 by 1974? Or, Can the State-Management Be Stopped?

The state-management was formed and enlarged under the direction of President John F. Kennedy. He and his advisors centralized and consolidated control over military industry. Thereby, they gathered into very few hands the top economic, political, and military power in the United States. These men were evidently captured by the prospect of wielding political decision-power by applying America's technical brains and industrial capacity toward forging a super military machine, capable of "flexible response" in diverse situations. This was their first priority. So they escalated the nuclear overkill forces, created the "Green Berets" to fight guerrillas, enlarged the Army to eighteen divisions, and lavished money, manpower, and industrial might on the military without stint.

The armed forces were redesigned and enlarged in accordance with war plans that included required capability for fighting three wars at once: a NATO war; a war in Southeast Asia; and a smaller Western-Hemisphere operation. It was beyond the imagination of the designers and managers of such a military machine that their will might be frustrated by a small, impoverished people, lacking in sophisticated munitions, without armor or an air force or a navy—as in Vietnam. The Kennedy administration, helped into office by a proclaimed "missile gap" (later conceded to be unsubstantiated), never admitted the human irrationality of piling up nuclear overkill. If that were conceded, then it would be hard to prevent the emergence of the idea that the overkill buildup was a rational procedure to a different end— enlarging the state-management's control over research and the nation's industry. It is not likely that such a stated purpose would be well received by many Americans.

The Kennedy establishment, suffused with boundless confidence in its own competence and wisdom, created in the state-management their new instrument of power in American society. How different from the old General-President Eisenhower—who tried to warn his successor and the nation against excesses of power by the "military-industrial complex" of his time. The Kennedy administration swiftly made this warning obsolete by creating a new institution—the state-management in the Pentagon. How all this was carried off to the accompaniment of claims of "cost effectiveness" will surely engage the historians of this period. Apart from the political behavior of the Kennedy administration, however, the meaning of its handiwork is most significant in terms of the underlying relation of the new institution to the structure of American economy and society.

Is the growth of the Pentagon and its state-management a necessary condition of industrial capitalism or can industrial capitalism evolve without priority to such a war-oriented institution? There are two main elements in this issue. The first concerns the use of government: does industrial capitalism have to use government as a necessary instrument for its operation? The second element concerns war-making and war priority. With or without the use of government as an instrument of economic control, can industrial capitalism prosper without recourse to military production on a large scale?

Throughout the world, government has been used as an instrument of production decision-making in industrial capitalist societies. In the older capitalist nations, government was made an important center of economic decision-making since the Great Depression, when the theories of John Maynard Keynes showed how government could be used as a regulator of economies. Government initiative was thereafter used with increasing confidence to restrict fluctuations of industrial capitalist economies and to produce significant expansion and contraction of economic activity. In the newer lands of industrial capitalism, including state-centered capitalism (socialism), government has often been used from the very first as a center of economic initiative and management. Clearly, the use of government as an instrument of production decision-making is characteristic of both private and state capitalism, of both older private capitalist and the newer "socialist" economies.

Is war production essential for the viability of the capitalist state? This part of the theoretical problem proposed here has to be examined in light of the particular experience of the United States and of other countries, especially since the Second World War. During the 1950's and 1960's, the outstanding industrial growth performer in the world was Japan, with almost no military establishment (1 percent of the Gross National Product for military purposes in 1966), followed closely by West Germany, with its limited military capability (4.1 percent of GNP in 1966). Also, the data of western European countries allied to the United States indicate that they have done very well economically from 1945 to 1969, while using substantially smaller parts of their GNP's for military purposes than the United States. The case of the Scandinavian countries is outstanding in this respect. Sweden, in particular, is a land of economic well-being and economic growth, a land where poverty has been virtually eradicated; it also spends 4.3 percent of its GNP for military purposes.

All this suggests that countries with military budgets ranging from almost 0 to 4 percent of Gross National Product as compared with 8 to 10 percent in the United States, have been prospering in an outstanding fashion, while operating burgeoning industrial capitalist economies. The following data portray intensity of spending on arms and rate of growth in output per employee. If there were a necessary and positive relation between large arms budgets and economic growth in capitalist economies, then the countries of most intense military spending would show greatest economic growth rate. That is not confirmed by the following data:

	MILITARY SPENDING, PERCENT OF GNP 1966	PERCENT GROWTH RATE IN OUTPUT PER EMPLOYEE 1950–1965
United States	8.5	2.4
West German Federal Republic	4.1	5.3
Japan	1.0	7.7

SOURCE: U.S. Arms Control and Disarmament Agency, *World Military Expenditures 1966–67*, Research Report 68-52, Washington, D.C., 1968, pp. 9 ff.; U.S. Department of Commerce, *Statistical Abstract of the U.S.: 1968*, Washington, D.C., 1968, p. 842.

While government has been widely used as an instrument of economic decision-making, economic growth in viable capitalist economies has been possible without large-scale military activity.

The Second World War peace settlements contributed importantly to the subsequent low level of German and Japanese armed forces. In conventional wisdom that should have been associated with capitalist economic lethargy in those countries—which was not the case at all. Nor can it be said that these countries have prospered as they have because they are economic satellites of the United States, operating under control of either private American industry and finance or U.S. government control. Japan is an example of a nation that has made investment by foreigners in its economic system a very difficult affair. From 1960 to 1964, Japan's annual rate of growth in output per employee reached 9.8 percent.

Some people may respond intuitively with the comment that Japan's high growth rate reflects the low level of economic activity from which Japan started after the Second World War. True, United States bombers wrecked major parts of Japan's cities and industry. Still, that economy produced a great navy and air fleet, including thousands of the formidable Zero fighter planes, before the military debacle. This was no industrially underdeveloped country. The 1950–1965 Japanese growth rate had something to do with the concentration on productive economic growth. If Japan had gone the U.S. (and U.S.S.R.) route after the Second World War, then priority to parasitic growth would have restrained economic development there as well.

On the other hand, if the United States were to change priorities in favor of productive growth, then the repair of depletion in many spheres of life would require spending about $76 billion per year for these purposes. Serious U.S. participation in world economic development would cost about $22 billion per year (see my book *The Peace Race*). Almost $100 billion of new, productive activity would give the United States annual growth rates in the range of 8 to 10 percent—comparable to Japan.

Do capitalist nations require military production as a priority economic activity—because they are capitalist? The available evidence says "no."

How, then, can we account for the priority attention that has been given to military expenditure and military organization in the United States during the last decades? If that is not assignable to a generally necessary, inherent feature of capitalism, what special conditions of American economy or society account for this development? I think an explanation must begin with the Great Depression. At that time, the civilian government in Washington was unable to extricate the nation from the economic depression by civilian economic policy as then practiced. With hindsight, many people have held that a more aggressive policy of government economic investment would have turned the trick, but at the time there was not enough confidence and general agreement in the pursuit of Keynesian-type economic intervention. The result was that the American Great Depression was terminated as the United States became involved in war production, and finally, in the Second World War itself. Since the war involved full mobilization of U.S. resources, this terminated unemployment for millions of Americans and brought many others into the greatly enlarged labor force. The result was an unprecedented outpouring of goods of every kind, with a parallel increase in the level of living. All this occurred with massive output of military matériel—enough for wars in Europe and the Pacific. This experience led many Americans to believe that military production and organization was the occasion of economic prosperity and that this nation could have both guns and butter.

Nevertheless, from a 1945 military budget of $80.5 billion, there was a reduction to $13.3 billion by 1950. With the beginning of the

Korean war in mid-1950, the American government and population became convinced that a military containment policy directed toward Stalin's Russia was required for American security. From that time on, military budgets underwent substantial general expansion, particularly for constructing and operating a considerable nuclear delivery system that would be competent for "massive retaliation."

The Kennedy administration introduced a major innovation. It formulated the requirement that United States armed forces must be suited for fighting three wars at once: a NATO war, a Southeast Asia war; and a smaller military engagement in Latin America. These war plans produced the forces described in Chapters 3, 5, and 6. All this was paralleled by the organization of the state-management institution in the Department of Defense. The combined effects of these decisions included military priorities, the Vietnam wars program, and general depletion of American society.

Whenever the Congress wishes to check the grandiosity of the state-management, more prudent military security forces could be designed for the United States. This is exemplified in the memorandum on "Proposed Reductions in Military Overkill and Waste," which I submitted to Congress in May, 1969. (See Appendix C.)

Evidently, the state-management in the United States is the result of a nationally and politically specific set of developments. This does not detract from the importance of the institution, but it does tell us that the operation and formation of this institution is not necessarily intrinsic to industrial capitalism itself. Knowing this is significant for an assessment of possible options within American society concerning the state-management and its operation. Since the future of the state-management is not determined by a built-in economic necessity of industrial capitalism, this leaves the future of the institution as a political issue. The issue is clearly political because the Congress has the key regulatory power by its control over the state-management's capital. Just as the Congress can enlarge the state-management by appropriating more money, the same mechanism could enable the Congress to check or diminish the state-management's power.

Who needs the state-management, and who opposes it? Here is an enumeration of principal groups within American society that have supported the state-management (by backing its policies), despite the contradictions and depletions that have arisen from its operations:

The administrative staff of the state-management,

Career men, military and civilian, in the armed forces,

People employed in military industry,

People working in the military research-and-development establishment,

Communities and parts of communities dependent on military industry and bases,

Many members of Congress representing areas of high military activity,

Believers in a world Communist conspiracy against the United States,

People of strongly authoritarian personality, who identify with martial leadership.

The directorate of the state-management is committed to its professional role not only because it is there, but also because military organization is the purest hierarchical organizational form and therefore its enlargement produces a maximum extension of decision-power over the people directly involved.

The men and women accounted for by these categories are appreciable in number, even discounting the last two categories of political belief. But the 8 million persons directly employed in military work, and those indirectly connected to military work, who may be three to five times as many, are still not a majority of the American population. The importance of these groups, however, is not accounted for simply by numbers. The various "think tanks"—research establishments supported by the military—include about 12,000 employees. Research activity carried on within universities for the Pentagon accounts for the full-time professional work of about 20,000 people. Taken together, this is a relatively small group of people in a society of 200 million. But their influence is considerable, since they are a part of those institutions upon which the whole society depends for the creation of new knowledge and teaching of the young.

The Congress has been a crucial supporter of the state-management, since the Congress must vote the capital funds without which the Pentagon could not function. Beyond that, however, many members of Congress are actively involved in securing industrial contracts for firms located in their districts or states. In some areas, groups of Congressmen have formed regular committees, with designated persons to look after these matters of liaison with the Department of Defense. These relationships are, in part, facilitated by the large staff of liaison officers which the Department of Defense deploys in the halls of Congress. Further, many Congressmen get involved in efforts to locate and continue the operation of military bases in their districts or states. In part, this is viewed as a continuation of a classic sort of "pork-barreling"—efforts by energetic Congressmen to secure government-financed public works for their districts. Finally, many Congressmen belong to the military reserve.

On the other hand, there are definable groups in America that constitute the state-management's potential opposition, whether from interested or disinterested motives:

The more educated part of the population,

Education and health professionals,

A major part of the clergy,

Part of the management and labor force of civilian business and finance,

Parts of the racial underclasses,

People with strong commitment to values of humanism and personal freedom,

Opponents of the Vietnam war and its conduct.

During the 1960's, public opinion polls repeatedly disclosed that the degree of criticism of government policies concerning Vietnam and similar matters was correlated with educational level. The most intense criticism of militarist policies was found in the college-educated part of the population. In 1968, about 30 percent of the American population was attending schools, and over 6 million were students in American colleges and universities. University enrollments have increased by about 70 percent from 1960 to 1968, promising to almost double by 1985.

Neither of the defined groups of fairly committed Americans comprise a clear majority of American society. Other factors, notably the impact of Pentagon operations on American society, as well as ideology and belief, are significant in determining the balance of political forces in the United States. The Pentagon's military failure in Vietnam shattered the major myth of its military invincibility. The political and moral criticism of the war, including the outcry against U.S. casualties, exposed the Pentagon to opposition that cut through occupational-class lines. The failure of the "guns and butter" promise, plus rapid price inflation produced disillusion with the morality of government, even among those hitherto committed to patriotic acquiescence to government policy. These considerations, cutting across occupational, class, and political lines, could lead to a national majority rejecting the Pentagon, and its parasitism at home and abroad, as the dominant institution of government.

If the state-management institution and its priorities are continued, then the following may be expected: increased international competition in nuclear weapons and delivery systems, with emphasis on shorter response time and, hence, more reliance on mechanisms and greater probability of nuclear war by accident; continuation of the Vietnam wars program elsewhere; acceleration of domestic depletion as a consequence of greatly enlarged Department of Defense budgets; decline in the international value of the dollar as a consequence of unacceptable accumulation of dollars abroad owing to world-wide United States military spending. Even in the absence of society-destroying nuclear war, these effects would, in turn, greatly aggravate the race problems in the United States, for domestic economic development would be foreclosed. The same depletion process would produce increasing rebellion against the authority of government and its allies. Altogether, these would be profoundly destabilizing effects in society, possibly including mass violence and civil war mainly along racial lines.

These consequences from the continued operation of the state-management and its priorities would be forestalled only in the measure that declining support for the state-management is translated into political action that is competent to substantially reduce its decision-power. The critical test of this is either a drastic reduction in money allotted to the Pentagon by the Congress or significant withdrawal of popular readiness to implement Pentagon decisions, or both.

Despite the fact that the state-management operates with durable bases of support in nation-wide management and production systems, even that base is substantially weakened by the growing contradiction between ideology and performance. Thus, the contrast between Pentagon-supporting theory and visible reality, as summarized in Chapter 7, weakens the self-assurance even of the state-management staff and supporters—an essential ingredient to continued operation of the system.

Until now, the most durable source of support for sustaining and enlarging the operation of the state-management has been the pattern of antagonistic cooperation between the U.S. state-management and its Soviet counterpart. On each side, there is an appeal to the respective society to grant resources necessary for attaining superiority in particular weapons systems—qualitatively and numerically. On both sides, the appeal is similar—that the competitor is proceeding along lines that must be matched or exceeded under penalty of being disadvantaged. These appeals continue, successfully thus far, despite the fact that neither state-management is able to break through the limits on "defense" and military "superiority" that were imposed by the application of nuclear weapons to offensive military purposes. Despite this, the mutual appeal to fear—pointing to the hostile behavior of the antagonist—has become the single most powerful ingredient making for sustained build-up of the state-managements and their military organizations on each side.

On the American side this pattern is likely to continue until two things are perceived: first, that military priority imposes an unbearably high cost in the form of a depletion process, while the military cannot deliver on their promises of military advantage or a defensive shield; and second, that a politically vigorous part of the population has to marshal a cross-population coalition to compel the Congress to suppress the Pentagon and its society-destroying programs.

Certain constraints may operate on the state-management, consisting of pragmatic actions to prevent breakdowns within society that have been caused by the state-management's normal operations. Some ability to act in this way exists in various establishment institutions. For example, the federal government acted through the State Department and the Treasury to protect the international value of the dollar when that was imperiled in 1968 as a result of a decline in the U.S. gold reserve. The limited effects of such patchwork is that the various depletions, contradictions, and deteriorations within society, caused by the operation of the state machine, will continue and grow so long as the state-management is given high priority in money, manpower, and policy prestige.

By October, 1968, the Pentagon had initiated an elaborate study of military policy options for the new President. The study called attention to the problem of overseas bases which cost about $5 billion a year to operate. Half of this sum was counted as a drain on the U.S. balance of payments. However, a recommendation to curtail the operations of such military bases on a large scale is not to be expected from the state-management or the Joint Chiefs of Staff, nor from a State Department that has been so strongly Cold War-oriented. However, the loss of $2.5 billion in the national balance of payment account remains a very serious matter, and it is difficult for the Treasury or the Federal Reserve to attempt to safeguard the value of the dollar through the measures open to them, as long as military policies, which cost so much to implement, continue. But the bases policy is bound up with what I have called the Vietnam wars program, and with the general political posture of the United States vis-à-vis the Soviet Union and China as well. These policies could only be altered by a reassessment of the basic assumptions that underlie them. Therefore, the following discussion is addressed to the nature of the state-management and to the consequences of its operation, in order to assess its prospects.

It should be underscored at the outset that the civilian officers controlling the military establishment, including the state-management, do not constitute what is termed elsewhere "civilian control over the military." This is because the crucial factor is the institution's nature, not the style of clothing worn by its top directors. The overwhelmingly military character of the state-management dominates the institution, not the personal-professional identity of its chiefs. Furthermore, since the military budget in the United States has come to equal one-half, and more, of the budget of the federal government, military activity has come to permeate many aspects of American society (as discussed in Chapters 3 and 4), with the result that the whole society begins to take on something of the character of a "garrison society." The term garrison society, or garrison state, describes a nation in which the line of demarcation between military and civilian activity is difficult to define, a condition that is a consequence of the size and pervasive character of the state-management's activity. Therefore, an analysis of the nature of the institution is imperative.

The power of the state-management derives from the readiness of millions of people to accept and execute the orders issued by the Department of Defense, as well as from the formal political authority and financial power inherent in it. Thus, the power of the state-management in the area of research performed in the universities is not only derived from the funds offered and orders issued, but from the acceptance of these funds and the compliance with these orders by professors and students within the universities. That is, the strength of the institution rests in large measure on at least the tacit support of a large part of the population.

The economic characteristics of the state-management are usually glossed over by the ordinary folk wisdom that a dollar spent is a dollar spent and that military spending puts money into circulation and thereby adds to national income. But spending of dollars by the state-management has characteristics without counterpart in a private firm's operation. Thus, a private management usually attempts to enlarge the scope and intensity of its decision-making by investing capital, recovering the money that has been invested through the sale of products, thereby having profits in hand for further investment. Extension of control or the enlargement of decision-making by management is made possible by the profit that this cycle of investment, recovery, and re-investment brings.

In the case of the state-management, the process is altogether different. There, capital is invested, but in the form of funds appropriated by Congress—a proportion of the national income of the society. These funds, and the material resources they represent, once "invested," give direct returns in extension of control, taking the form of military power. There is a return, an enlargement of economic as well as military decision-power, but no return of money from applied capital. No profit-yielding market transaction is involved in the direct use of capital funds by the state-management to acquire military matériel and organizations, the direct manifestation of enlarged decision-power. In the absence of a profit accumulation process, and with one-half the federal taxes as a source of funds, there is little incentive in the state-management to conserve cost in its operations. Characteristically, the theory of the cost-minimizing firm is inapplicable to understanding the operations of the state-management or its subdivisions. While the state-management itself earns no profit, selected submanagements are granted capital funds—in excess of costs—by the central office. These capital grants are termed "profit" in the conventional accounts of the subfirms, although this "profit" is surely not the entrepreneur's reward for risk-taking.

The capital of the state-management is obtained by alleging the existence of external "threats." This word implies both imminent dangers and the promise of future danger. Pentagon spokesmen typically evoke fear by alluding to some "threat" from the outside. Thus, the justification for Pentagon budgets is imperiled by the possibility, not to mention the actuality, of a workable détente between the great powers.

The state-management has to obtain resources from a society that can sustain full employment through generally accepted civilian public policies. The attempt to preempt resources from a high employment economy for economically parasitic growth places great pressure on the relation between currency in circulation and the supply of goods, thereby generating unacceptable price inflation at home. Sustained high military expenditures threaten the value of the dollar at home and abroad. However, the state-management is not itself endangered by a diminution in the value of the dollar, whether from domestic or external causes. For whatever the relative value of the dollar may be, the state-management receives the goods and the services these dollars purchase, and for its purpose that is sufficient.

Civilian economy and civilian management, financial and industrial, all have a clear interest in a currency of stable (predictable) value and in having an economy that functions within predictable and acceptable limits of variation. The state-management needs neither condition in order to function or in order to expand its decision-power.

The military-industrial complex of President Eisenhower's generation was superseded by the state-management. That complex was still essentially a market operation, a network of relations between buyers and sellers. One could not easily abolish the market that was the military-industrial complex. But the operations of the state-management might, for example, be legislated against, since its operation is contingent on a budget passed by the Congress each year. Control of that budget would bring control over the state-management.

The state-management has a propensity for virtually unlimited extension of its decision-power. This is reflected in its budgets, hardware, and political planning. In December, 1968, the Pentagon leaked to the press the fact that it was going to ask for a budget of $100 to $110 billion for the next year. Included in this budget, besides funds for items and organizations already existing, were requests for funds for a new series of enterprises and weapons systems. Among the new items were an enlarged antiballistic missile system, a new strategic bomber, a larger successor to the Minuteman missile, a larger successor to the Polaris missile carried by the submarines, a new continental air defense system, an altogether new intercontinental ballistic missile system—far larger than any of those now in hand, a new type of "quiet" submarine—to cost $150 to $200 million each, and on and on. In response to alleged external "threats," Congressional committees are asked to vote astronomical funds. Rarely do they get an answer to the crucial question: "Does the system as it exists, or as proposed, actually constitute a true defense for the United States?" It is reasonable to suppose that most citizens approve of large allocations for the Department of Defense on the understanding that they are buying an effective shield against external attack.

The state-management's mode of operation has had the effect of enmeshing an ever-widening part of society. For example: consider the political significance of Texas having been transformed between 1965–1968 into a state with the second-largest military industry in the country. Following this change, is this state likely to dispatch Representatives and Senators to Washington who would be critical of the state-management? In a similar vein, would an anti-DuPont candidate be elected in Wilmington, Delaware? Evidently, the state-management's industrial operations produce effects that are in the manner of a closed-loop growth system—automatically reinforcing and enlarging its operation.

The top managers of the new Washington organization have developed a degree of self-confidence that appears to an external observer as arrogance. For example, the readiness of these men to use immense resources for strategic missile systems, ABM systems, and for the continuance of the war in Vietnam demonstrates that these decisions were made in spite of the considerable body of research and analysis that concluded that these expenditures and activities could neither shield the United States nor bring a military victory in Vietnam. The top echelons of state-management have listened to themselves and proceeded on the confident assumption that their mode of operation, including their planning system, their functional budgeting system, and their cost-effectiveness studies, would produce a military machine that would perform precisely as planned. From that standpoint, the meaning of the Vietnam war experience cannot be overestimated, for this was a true field experiment on a grand scale that tested the efficacy of the main decision-processes of the Department of Defense. It is difficult to understand how these decision-processes and the criteria that justified them, which produced the military failure in Vietnam, could still be counted on to produce military success elsewhere.

It is necessary to appreciate the "cost effectiveness" procedures of the state-management afresh, seeing them not as a device for cost reduction in the sense of civilian enterprise, but rather as an instrument for redeploying the resources and facilities of the military establishment in order to better facilitate the extension of decision-making by the state-management.

The global control ambitions of the state-management are revealed by the subjects for which the Department of Defense invited research bids during the last years. The following is the text of a 1965 bid request in the *Department of Commerce Daily Bulletin:*

> Service and materials to perform a research study entitled "Pax Americana" consisting of a phased study of the following: (a) elements of National Power; (b) ability of selected nations to

apply the elements of National Power; (c) a variety of world power configurations to be used as a basis for the U.S. to maintain world hegemony in the future. Quotations and applicable specifications will be available upon request, at the Army Research Office, 3845 Columbia Pike, Arlington, Va., until 1 May 1965.

Another study request invited attention to an ". . . investigation of the feasibility and desirability in the 1970 time frame, of providing selected U.S. allies a significant nuclear defense capability without necessity for maintaining U.S. control or custody over weapons systems or their employment." The first research invitation invites possible plans for worldwide decision-power to be exercised by the state-management; the second invites the plans for proliferating nuclear weapons, not only in sheer numbers, but in terms of passing on their control to other nations. Concerning the latter, it is interesting to consider that support for the treaty to limit proliferation of nuclear weapons may be, in effect, directed primarily against the state-management, since the Pentagon has demonstrated a definite interest in advancing the proliferation of nuclear weapons, making other national armies dependent upon them.

In the operation of the state-management, very great status has been given to the activities of individuals, notably former Secretary of Defense McNamara and certain of his aides. Nevertheless, the main characteristics of the state-management inhere to the institution itself, independently of the particular personalities in charge. Within this institution, particular individual technical failures do not necessarily produce professional disgrace. For example, Secretary of Defense McNamara, during the period 1964–1968, repeatedly predicted "improvements" in the American military and political position in Vietnam. His forecasts were largely misleading, but that did not result in his removal from office. Instead, additions were made to U.S. forces in Vietnam. Tom J. Farer, Professor of Law at Columbia University and one-time McNamara aide, has described the tone of the state-management center.

When I worked there [in the Pentagon] during the Kennedy era, the office of the Secretary of Defense seemed to be . . . an island. We were zestful, moved by controlled excitement, occasionally even euphoric, not with any crass sense of power, but with vistas of elimination of nuclear terror by means of the systematic application of human reason. We were true believers, and McNamara was our prophet.

The consequences of seven years of McNamara's stewardship were quite independent of his intention to eliminate nuclear terror. The main effects were determined by the creation of the new state-management institution and by the build-up of armed forces to fight a nuclear war and two conventional wars at the same time.

The crucial role of the institution as against the individual is also seen in the way that the state-management institution has persistently rejected policy alternatives whose implementation would have halted or reversed the extension of the decision-power of that state-management. If the advice of men like Jerome Wiesner had been taken in 1961, an attempt would have been made to operate a strategic deterrent system based on a small number (say 200) of intercontinental missiles, without building the gigantic overkill force that now gives the United States a delivery capability of 4,200 intercontinental nuclear warheads. But that alternative would have limited the size of the strategic Air Force and also the aerospace industry, which had to be expanded to carry out the new missile program.

State-management control over the dissemination of information and the interpretation of information is far more important and subtle than simple "news management." As the Great Society legislative program began to unfold in 1965, the administration promised that all would proceed in good order, even while the Vietnam war continued and the military budget was enlarged. By the end of 1967, this estimate was revealed to be sharply contrary to economic feasibility and reality. Soon the Great Society became a not-so-great society. All the while, however, the state-management executives never relented in their public avowals of American ability to deliver both guns and butter to American society. An official myth was never publicly denied, even in the face of a sharp contrast between promise and performance. This could not be done because to erase the myth publicly would have required a reassessment of priorities, including the budget of the Department of Defense. It was left to a conservative

Southern Democrat, Senator Ellender, in January, 1967, to tell the truth about the federal budget:

> The truth of the matter is that in many important respects, the Congress and the nation are in the hands of the military. Add to this group the Department of State and you have a combination that calls the shots. The Admirals and the Generals, strongly backed by the Department of State, seem to have the ways and means of getting just about what they want, regardless of the monetary difficulties afflicting the nation. In contrast to the immensity of a $75.5 billion budget for the military, we need only take a glance at the budget estimates for the conservation and development of our natural resources. We find here a national commitment of only $2.5 billion. It is to the conservation of its land and water that the nation must look if we hope to remain strong and prosperous in the decades ahead, but our investment in this field will represent only a tiny portion of the huge sums to be expended by the military during fiscal 1968."

The other side of the state-management's concern with its decision-power is to prevent the conversion of its industrial empire to civilian use. By April, 1968, Professor Walter Heller, former Chairman of the Council of Economic Advisors, wrote: ". . . If we put our economic knowledge to work in sensible post-war planning, an end to the Vietnam war will be, not just a political and moral, but also an economic blessing" (*Harpers,* April, 1968). This blessing requires not only the termination of the entire Vietnam wars program, but a well-developed capability for dealing with conversion problems as well. It was the Department of Defense that took the lead and set the tone for the opposition to legislation for the establishment of a National Economic Conversion Commission, proposed by Senator George McGovern and thirty other Senators in 1963 and again in 1964. They argued that a National Economic Conversion Commission was unnecessary, because the defense industries would be quite capable of carrying out economic conversion when required—although industrial cutbacks in 1963 revealed major defense contractors throughout the country to be woefully incapable of converting their labor forces and facilities to commercial use. Sensible planning for economic conversion was additionally forestalled by a Committee on the Economic Impact of Defense and Disarmament which reported to President Johnson early in 1966 that a formal effort to prepare the country for economic conversion to peace was unnecessary. While this seems unreasonable when viewing depletion in the economy, inhibition of conversion capability makes solid sense in terms of the maintenance of the state-management's power.

The power extension of the state-management even impairs the classic operation of imperialism. Thus, wrecking a country and its economy, as was done in Vietnam, is obviously counter to business investment interests. Classically, industrialists and bankers have preferred to make investments in areas that are both built-up and stable or have the prospect of becoming built-up and stable. This may be concluded from the massive investment that American management concentrated in Western Europe and in Canada after the Second World War. Nevertheless, the state-management scored a substantial success in terms of enlarging the scope and intensity of its decision-power through the Vietnam war, and this success pattern has been pressed by the implementation of the Vietnam wars program. This new imperialism involves direct use of military force to enlarge decision-power. The state-management, pressing for power with its methods, has overridden the interests of the older form of private-enterprise imperialism, based upon capital investment and trade.

For all its immense resources and access to high-grade personnel for its planning and operations management, the state-management has come to be a fundamentally fantasy-oriented organization. Its strategic military plans are oriented to nuclear supremacy, but the mutual attainment of overkill frustrates all ambitions of that sort. Its "conventional war" plans are oriented to winning guerrilla wars with immense firepower superiority, when the Vietnam war has shown this expectation to be only a Pentagon illusion. The Pentagon calculated that with superior military power, world political development could be substantially controlled, but American hegemony in critical places —as in much of Western Europe—has been leaking at the seams, just as Soviet hegemony has frayed in many parts of the world. Above all, the state-management has promised that, through its operations, the United States could be defended, and that is precisely what they have not been able to do. It took the Cuban missile crisis to produce the moment of truth: there is no shield when nation-states confront each other with great nuclear forces.

Structurally, the military economy is cross-class, that is, it represents a vertical slice of society, not simply a modern version of the celebrated "merchants of death" of the First World War vintage. While the top echelon of the state-management does the crucial planning and decision-making, its power depends upon the support and energetic participation of sub-managers, scientists, engineers, and trade union members in the great array of bases, research and development establishments, and weapons-manufacturing industries. One effect of this has been to produce a cross-class lobby for the Pentagon and its budgets. This cross-class bloc depletes the rest of the society.

There has been a similar pattern of cross political-ideological support for the operation of the state-management. Obviously, most conservatives have supported military budgets without limit in the name of defense against Communism. But an important bloc of support for the state-management is composed of moderates, political liberals, and leftists, whose ideology favors more authority for central government. Characteristically, this is justified by the proposition that central government alone has the capacity for regulating economic behavior and for planning and executing the economic amelioration which many liberals and leftists profess to desire. In the name of these ends, ever-increasing budgets for the federal government are supported, even though these growing budgets are for predominately military purposes. Thus, pro-big-government liberals and leftists, often critical of certain Pentagon policies, function as the loyal left opposition for the state-management.

The highly structured Pentagon, with its state-management, immense funds, collateral organizations in government and in industrial and other spheres of life, and its decisive influence on national and international affairs has become a true "state within a state," a para-state.

The normal operation and expansion of the para-state and its state-management has been based upon the wholesale selling of fear—fear of nuclear war, fear of Communism (even after the post-Stalin thaw) —as a lever for prying more and more support from the public and

Congress for ever-larger military budgets. Here is the list of defense inadequacies that the operators of the most powerful military machine in the world claim have existed since 1960:

> Missile gap
> Bomber gap
> Anti-ballistic missile gap
> Fighter plane gap
> Megatonnage gap
> Submarine gap
> Survival gap
> Strategy gap
> Security gap

Each of these claims evoked the genuine feelings of helplessness that ordinary people might have at the prospect of war in the nuclear age. However, the implied promise of the militarists is that they can erase the particular threat that is signaled by each "gap" and really provide security, if only they are granted more money for still another device or program. Whether explicit or merely implied, such claims are a cruel hoax. Military security in the nuclear era is obtainable only by workable agreements among states that weapons will not be used and that their actual numbers will be reduced. The very existence of quickly triggered, nuclear-powered antagonists, each prepared to use society-destroying weapons, is the final menace to the existence of the human species. This threat, which encourages antagonistic cooperation among nuclear opponents, is the one military threat that the para-state systematically omits from its budget-supporting list of "threats."

The para-state, directed by its new class of managers and technologists, both breeds and needs foreign and domestic crises. The direction of massive public funds towards parasitic growth and warmaking helps to create and sustain depletion in the value of the dollar; to create inflation; to inflame race relations; to destroy morals; to cause serious deficiencies in civilian technology, education, and health care; to sustain the draft; and to aid in the deterioration of domestic and international observance of lawful behavior.

The Pentagon-sponsored arms race—without defined limit—has become a prime cause of war crises. Obviously, a procession of nuclear confrontations and Vietnam wars is no viable strategy for American security. But that is the built-in disposition of the Pentagon and its priorities. Americans of every class and interest group—except for those who prefer to take their chances with nuclear and Vietnam wars—will respond with increasing criticism and opposition to the Pentagon's wars, to Pentagon-caused depletion, and to the state-management's control ambitions. Every class and interest group in America whose well-being depends on the operation of a civilian economy and society—with all its problems, stresses, and strains— requires the curtailment of the Pentagon and its power. The longer such an organization persists, with Congress granting it virtual blank-check-drawing rights on the U.S. national income, the more difficult will be the task of checking its power.

Rarely does a single social force have a controlling influence in changing, swiftly, the character of life in a large and complex society. The expansion of the Pentagon and its state-management is such a force. Failing decisive action to reverse the economic and other growth of these institutions, then the parent state, if it is saved from nuclear war, will surely become the guardian of a garrison-like society dominated by the Pentagon and its state-management.

What greater threat—present and potential—is there to the security of Americans, to their life and liberty?

APPENDIXES

Appendix A

GENERAL EISENHOWER AS FOUNDER OF THE
"MILITARY-INDUSTRIAL COMPLEX" IN 1946

[The following is the full text of a memorandum by General Eisenhower, acting in his 1946 capacity of Chief of Staff of the United States Army. The policy statement formulates the idea of a close, continuing relationship between the Army and civilian scientists, industry, technologists and the universities. This document evidently served as a policy guide thereafter. By January 1961, then President Eisenhower, observing some of the consequences of the collaboration he had set in motion in 1946, tried to caution his successor and the nation to be watchful of the military-industrial complex. This document is from the Henry L. Stimson Papers in the Sterling Library of Yale University.

S.M.]

Memorandum for Directors and Chiefs of War Department General and Special Staff Divisions and Bureaus and the Commanding Generals of the Major Commands:

Subject: *Scientific and Technological Resources as Military Assets.*

The recent conflict has demonstrated more convincingly than ever before the strength our nation can best derive from the integration of all of our national resources in time of war. It is of the utmost importance that the lessons of this experience be not forgotten in the peacetime planning and training of the Army. The future security of the nation demands that all those civilian resources which by conversion or redirection constitute our main support in time of emergency be associated closely with the activities of the Army in time of peace.

The lessons of the last war are clear. The military effort required for victory threw upon the Army an unprecedented range of responsibilities, many of which were effectively discharged only through the invaluable

231

assistance supplied by our cumulative resources in the natural and social sciences and the talents and experience furnished by management and labor. The armed forces could not have won the war alone. Scientists and business men contributed techniques and weapons which enabled us to outwit and overwhelm the enemy. Their understanding of the Army's needs made possible the highest degree of cooperation. This pattern of integration must be translated into a peacetime counterpart which will not merely familiarize the Army with the progress made in science and industry, but draw into our planning for national security all the civilian resources which can contribute to the defense of the country.

Success in this enterprise depends to a large degree on the cooperation which the nation as a whole is willing to contribute. However, the Army as one of the main agencies responsible for the defense of the nation has the duty to take the initiative in promoting closer relation between civilian and military interests. It must establish definite policies and administrative leadership which will make possible even greater contributions from science, technology, and management than during the last war.

In order to ensure the full use of our national resources in case of emergency, the following general policies will be put into effect:

(1) *The Army must have civilian assistance in military planning as well as for the production of weapons.* Effective long-range military planning can be done only in the light of predicted developments in science and technology. As further scientific achievements accelerate the tempo and expand the area of our operations, this interrelationship will become of even greater importance. In the past we have often deprived ourselves of vital help by limiting our use of scientific and technological resources to contracts for equipment. More often than not we can find much of the talent we need for comprehensive planning in industry or universities. Proper employment of this talent requires that the civilian agency shall have the benefit of our estimates of future military problems and shall work closely with Plans and the Research and Development authorities. A most effective procedure is the letting of contracts for aid in planning. The use of such a procedure will greatly enhance the validity of our planning as well as ensure sounder strategic equipment programs.

(2) *Scientists and industrialists must be given the greatest possible freedom to carry out their research.* The fullest utilization by the Army of the civilian resources of the nation cannot be procured merely by prescribing the military characteristics and requirements of certain types of equipment. Scientists and industrialists are more likely to make new and unsuspected contributions to the development of the Army if detailed directions are held to a minimum. The solicitation of assistance under these conditions would not only make available to the army talents and experience otherwise beyond our reach, but also establish mutual confidence between ourselves and civilians. It would familiarize them with our fundamental prob-

lems and strengthen greatly the foundation upon which our national security depends.

(3) *The possibility of utilizing some of our industrial and technological resources as organic parts of our military structure in time of emergency should be carefully examined.* The degree of cooperation with science and industry achieved during the recent war should by no means be considered the ultimate. There appears little reason for duplicating within the Army an outside organization which by its experience is better qualified than we are to carry out some of our tasks. The advantages to our nation in economy and to the Army in efficiency are compelling reasons for this procedure.

(4) *Within the Army we must separate responsibility for research and development from the functions of procurement, purchase, storage and distribution.* Our experience during the war and the experience of industry in time of peace indicate the need for such a policy. The inevitable gap between the scientist or technologist and the user can be bridged, as during the last war, by field experimentation with equipment still in the developmental stage. For example, restricted-visibility operations with the aid of radar, such as blind bombing and control of tactical air, were made possible largely by bringing together technologists who knew the potentialities of the equipment and field commanders familiar with combat conditions and needs. Future cooperation of this type requires that research and development groups have authority to procure experimental items for similar tests.

(5) *Officers of all arms and services must become fully aware of the advantages which the Army can derive from the close integration of civilian talent with military plans and developments.* This end cannot be achieved merely by sending officers to universities for professional training. It is true that the Army's need for officers well trained in the natural and social sciences requires a thorough program of advanced study for selected military personnel, but in addition we must supply inducements which will encourage these men in the continued practical application of scientific and technological thought to military problems. A premium must be placed on professional attainments in the natural and social sciences as well as other branches of military science. Officers in each arm and service must familiarize themselves as much as possible with progress and plans made in other branches. Only then can the Army obtain the administrative and operative talents essential to its task and mutual understanding by the arms and services of their respective problems.

In general, the more we can achieve the objectives indicated above with respect to the cultivation, support and direct use of outside resources, the more energy will we have left to devote to strictly military problems for which there are no outside facilities or which for special security reasons can only be handled by the military. In fact, it is our responsibility deliberately to examine all outside resources as to adequacy, diversity, and geographical distribution and to ensure their full utilization as factors of security. It is our job to take the initiative to promote the development of new resources, if our national security indicates the need. It is our duty to support broad research programs in educational institutions, in industry, and in whatever field might be of importance to the Army. Close integration of military and civilian resources will not only directly benefit the Army, but indirectly contribute to the nation's security, as civilians are prepared for their role in an emergency by the experience gained in time of peace. The association of military and civilians in educational institutions and industry will level barriers, engender mutual understanding, and lead to the cultivation of friendships invaluable for future cooperation. The realization of our objectives places upon us, the military, the challenge to make our professional officers the equals in knowledge and training of civilians in similar fields and make our professional environment as inviting as those outside.

In the interest of cultivating to the utmost the integration of civilian and military resources and of securing the most effective unified direction of our research and development activities, this responsibility is being consolidated in a separate section on the highest War Department level. The Director of this section will be directly supported by one or more civilians, thus ensuring full confidence of both the military and the civilian in this undertaking. By the rotation of civilian specialists in this capacity we should have the benefit of broad guidance and should be able to furnish science and industry with a firsthand understanding of our problems and objectives. By developing the general policies outlined above under the leadership of the Director of Research and Development the Army will demonstrate the value it places upon science and technology and further the integration of civilian and military resources.

Signed by General Eisenhower
on April 27, 1946.

Appendix B

PRESIDENT EISENHOWER'S FAREWELL TO THE NATION

Address by President Eisenhower [1]

My fellow Americans: Three days from now, after half a century in the service of our country, I shall lay down the responsibilities of office as, in traditional and solemn ceremony, the authority of the Presidency is vested in my successor.

This evening I come to you with a message of leavetaking and farewell and to share a few final thoughts with you, my countrymen.

Like every other citizen, I wish the new President and all who will labor with him Godspeed. I pray that the coming years will be blessed with peace and prosperity for all.

Our people expect their President and the Congress to find essential agreement on issues of great moment, the wise resolution of which will better shape the future of the Nation.

My own relations with the Congress, which began on a remote and tenuous basis, when long ago a member of the Senate appointed me to West Point, have since ranged to the intimate during the war and immediate postwar period and, finally, to the mutually interdependent during these past 8 years.

In this final relationship the Congress and the administration have, on most vital issues, cooperated well to serve the national good rather than mere partisanship and so have assured that the business of the Nation should go forward. So my official relationship with the Congress ends in a feeling on my part of gratitude that we have been able to do so much together.

II

We now stand 10 years past the midpoint of a century that has witnessed four major wars among great nations. Three of these involved our own

---

[1] Delivered to the Nation by television and radio on Jan. 17 (White House press release).

SOURCE: U.S. Department of State, *Bulletin,* Vol. 44, Feb. 6, 1961.

country. Despite these holocausts, America is today the strongest, the most influential, and most productive nation in the world. Understandably proud of this preeminence, we yet realize that America's leadership and prestige depend not merely upon our unmatched material progress, riches, and military strength but on how we use our power in the interests of world peace and human betterment.

III

Throughout America's adventure in free government our basic purposes have been to keep the peace, to foster progress in human achievement, and to enhance liberty, dignity, and integrity among people and among nations. To strive for less would be unworthy of a free and religious people. Any failure traceable to arrogance or our lack of comprehension or readiness to sacrifice would inflict upon us grievous hurt both at home and abroad.

Progress toward these noble goals is persistently threatened by the conflict now engulfing the world. It commands our whole attention, absorbs our very beings. We face a hostile ideology—global in scope, atheistic in character, ruthless in purpose, and insidious in method. Unhappily the danger it poses promises to be of indefinite duration. To meet it successfully there is called for not so much the emotional and transitory sacrifices of crisis but rather those which enable us to carry forward steadily, surely, and without complaint the burdens of a prolonged and complex struggle—with liberty the stake. Only thus shall we remain, despite every provocation, on our charted course toward permanent peace and human betterment.

Crises there will continue to be. In meeting them, whether foreign or domestic, great or small, there is a recurring temptation to feel that some spectacular and costly action could become the miraculous solution to all current difficulties. A huge increase in newer elements of our defense, development of unrealistic programs to cure every ill in agriculture, a dramatic expansion in basic and applied research—these and many other possibilities, each possibly promising in itself, may be suggested as the only way to the road we wish to travel.

But each proposal must be weighed in the light of a broader consideration: the need to maintain balance in and among national programs—balance between the private and the public economy, balance between cost and hoped-for advantage, balance between the clearly necessary and the comfortably desirable, balance between our essential requirements as a nation and the duties imposed by the Nation upon the individual, balance between actions of the moment and the national welfare of the future. Good judgment seeks balance and progress; lack of it eventually finds imbalance and frustration.

The record of many decades stands as proof that our people and their Government have, in the main, understood these truths and have responded to them well in the face of stress and threat. But threats, new in kind or degree, constantly arise. I mention two only.

IV

A vital element in keeping the peace is our Military Establishment. Our arms must be mighty, ready for instant action, so that no potential aggressor may be tempted to risk his own destruction.

Our military organization today bears little relation to that known by any of my predecessors in peacetime, or indeed by the fighting men of World War II and Korea.

Until the latest of our world conflicts, the United States had no armaments industry. American makers of plowshares could, with time and as required, make swords as well. But now we can no longer risk emergency improvisation of national defense; we have been compelled to create a permanent armaments industry of vast proportions. Added to this, 3½ million men and women are directly engaged in the Defense Establishment. We annually spend on military security more than the net income of all United States corporations.

This conjunction of an immense Military Establishment and a large arms industry is new in the American experience. The total influence— economic, political, even spiritual—is felt in every city, every statehouse, every office of the Federal Government. We recognize the imperative need for this development. Yet we must not fail to comprehend its grave implications. Our toil, resources, and livelihood are all involved; so is the very structure of our society.

In the councils of government we must guard against the acquisition of unwarranted influence whether sought or unsought, by the military-industrial complex. The potential for the disastrous rise of misplaced power exists and will persist.

We must never let the weight of this combination endanger our liberties or democratic processes. We should take nothing for granted. Only an alert and knowledgeable citizenry can compel the proper meshing of the huge industrial and military machinery of defense with our peaceful methods and goals so that security and liberty may prosper together.

Akin to and largely responsible for the sweeping changes in our industrial-military posture has been the technological revolution during recent decades. In this revolution research has become central; it also becomes more formalized, complex, and costly. A steadily increasing share is conducted for, by, or at the direction of the Federal Government.

Today the solitary inventor, tinkering in his shop, has been overshadowed by task forces of scientists in laboratories and testing fields. In the same fashion the free university, historically the fountainhead of free ideas and scientific discovery, has experienced a revolution in the conduct of research. Partly because of the huge costs involved, a Government contract becomes virtually a substitute for intellectual curiosity. For every old blackboard there are now hundreds of new electronic computers.

The prospect of domination of the Nation's scholars by Federal employment, project allocations, and the power of money is ever present and is gravely to be regarded.

Yet, in holding scientific research and discovery in respect, as we should, we must also be alert to the equal and opposite danger that public policy could itself become the captive of a scientific technological elite.

It is the task of statesmanship to mold, to balance, and to integrate these and other forces, new and old, within the principles of our democratic system—ever aiming toward the supreme goals of our free society.

V

Another factor in maintaining balance involves the element of time. As we peer into society's future, we—you and I, and our Government— must avoid the impulse to live only for today, plundering for our own ease and convenience the precious resources of tomorrow. We cannot mortgage the material assets of our grandchildren without risking the loss also of their political and spiritual heritage. We want democracy to survive for all generations to come, not to become the insolvent phantom of tomorrow.

VI

Down the long lane of the history yet to be written, America knows that this world of ours, ever growing smaller, must avoid becoming a community of dreadful fear and hate and be, instead, a proud confederation of mutual trust and respect.

Such a confederation must be one of equals. The weakest must come to the conference table with the same confidence as do we, protected as we are by our moral, economic, and military strength. That table, though scarred by many past frustrations, cannot be abandoned for the certain agony of the battlefield.

Disarmament, with mutual honor and confidence, is a continuing imperative. Together we must learn how to compose differences, not with arms but with intellect and decent purpose. Because this need is so sharp and apparent I confess that I lay down my official responsibilities in this field with a definite sense of disappointment. As one who has witnessed the horror and the lingering sadness of war, as one who knows that another war could utterly destroy this civilization which has been so slowly and painfully built over thousands of years, I wish I could say tonight that a lasting peace is in sight.

Happily I can say that war has been avoided. Steady progress toward our ultimate goal has been made. But so much remains to be done. As a private citizen I shall never cease to do what little I can to help the world advance along that road.

VII

So, in this my last good night to you as your President, I thank you for the many opportunities you have given me for public service in war and peace. I trust that in that service you find some things worthy; as for the rest of it, I know you will find ways to improve performance in the future.

You and I, my fellow citizens, need to be strong in our faith that all nations, under God, will reach the goal of peace with justice. May we be ever unswerving in devotion to principle, confident but humble with power, diligent in pursuit of the Nation's great goals.

To all the peoples of the world, I once more give expression to America's prayerful and continuing aspiration:

We pray that peoples of all faith, all races, all nations, may have their great human needs satisfied; that those now denied opportunity shall come to enjoy it to the full; that all who yearn for freedom may experience its spiritual blessings; that those who have freedom will understand, also, its heavy responsibilities; that all who are insensitive to the needs of others will learn charity; that the scourges of poverty, disease, and ignorance will be made to disappear from the earth; and that, in the goodness of time, all peoples will come to live together in a peace guaranteed by the binding force of mutual respect and love.

Appendix C

PROPOSED REDUCTIONS IN MILITARY OVERKILL AND WASTE

Memorandum to the U.S. Senate Armed Services Committee, May 2, 1969

From: Seymour Melman

1. The proposed budgets for national defense for fiscal year 1970 amount to $80,815 million (allowing for proposed modifications in the Johnson administration budget by Secretary of Defense Laird, March 16, 1969). This is the largest item in the federal budget and exceeds annual spending for military purposes except those at the peak of the Second World War.

2. In his first official press conference in January, 1969, President Nixon announced that, in his view, what the United States required is sufficiency in the realm of defense. Sufficiency means adequacy. Definite, explicit criteria are required in order to define what is enough.

3. Since 1961 the design of the armed forces of the United States has been oriented towards a three-fold requirement:

   (1) a war in the NATO area;
   (2) a war in the China area;
   (3) a lesser military action in Latin America.

Further: the requirement has been that U.S. armed forces should be capable of fighting wars in each of these areas at the same time. This means the conduct of one nuclear war and two conventional wars at once.

4. This combination of military operations does not refer to the defense of the United States. A nuclear war is an end-of-society war. The war in Vietnam, as a model of conventional far-Eastern war is clearly a military, political, economic and moral disaster—a major drain on American society and highly destructive of this nation both materially and morally. Such wars, in combination, are the military requirements in terms of which the Congress has voted funds from 1961 to 1969: to prepare 18 Army

241

Divisions as against 11 in 1961; 11,000 deliverable nuclear warheads for intercontinental effect, as against 1,100 in 1961; 34,000 aircraft, as against 30,000 aircraft in 1961.

5. An evaluation of "sufficiency" for the armed forces of the United States requires a basic definition of the nature of security commitment that is to be served by U.S. military power. The following are alternative criteria of sufficiency for U.S. armed forces:

(1) Operation of a strategic deterrence force.

(2) Guarding the shores of the United States.

(3) Capability for participation in International peacekeeping operations.

6. This memorandum proposes a set of modifications in the Fiscal Year 1970 budget for U.S. military forces on the ground that the above criteria are a sound basis for judging sufficiency of U.S. military security forces. It should be underscored that these criteria do *not* include war plan elements of the following sort: there is no intention here of preparing a nuclear force in such numbers and of such powers as to be calculably competent for a first strike operation against another nuclear power; these criteria for military sufficiency exclude the intention of preparing armed forces for wars of intervention as in Vietnam.

7. It is emphasized that *after* the substantial reductions recommended here are made for reasons of merit, the armed forces of the U.S. would consist of 2,300,000 men, and would operate missile, aircraft and naval forces of staggering power. *These reductions are directed toward deescalating additions to already massive overkill forces.*

Proposed Reductions of Department of Defense and Related Spending by Deescalation of Present Overkill Forces and Other Wasteful Practices.

A. *Incremental costs of the Vietnam war.* The additional military spending owing to the operation of the Vietnam war refers to the using up of ammunition, matériel, and people directly or indirectly connected with the Vietnam war. This amounts to $20 billion per year. The Congress should reduce the budget of the Department of Defense by this amount as an instruction to the Department and to the President to terminate this war.

$20.0 bill.

B. *Reducing additions to strategic overkill.* It is generally appreciated that no present or foreseeable research effort will make it possible for the armed forces of the United States, or any other nation, to destroy a person or a community more than once. Nevertheless, the nuclear forces and delivery systems of the United States have been built up with multiples of overkill. The exact number is, of course, unknown since we have not observed a full-scale nuclear war. Such observation is not required, however, to understand that with present capability for delivering 11,000 nuclear warheads to the territory of the Soviet Union refers mainly to 156 Soviet cities of 100,000 or over. The systems include various long and short-range missile systems; aircraft and submarines. To continue a buildup of these forces is grossly wasteful, not to mention irrational. Accordingly the following reductions in proposed budgeted expenditures are recommended:

(1) *New nuclear weapons production.* The proposed budget for the Atomic Energy Commission includes funds for further production of nuclear materials and for further production of nuclear weapons. This activity should simply be stopped as being militarily and humanly irrational (*Federal Budget*, p. 80).

$1,518 mill.

(2) *Research, development, test and evaluation.* The descriptive material in the Budget (pp. 265, 266) indicates that the major part of new military research activity is oriented to new strategic weapons delivery systems. This is part of the proliferation of overkill forces which has no rational justification whatsoever (except to keep managerial-industrial empires intact). Accordingly a substantial reduction is recommended in this budget line.

$5,000 mill.

(3) *Poseidon and Minuteman III.* These "new generation" intercontinental missiles would make possible a multiplication of nuclear warheads beyond the present 11,000, and perhaps allow for an increased calculated accuracy. A few hundred yards closer to calculated target in such weapons should be appreciated against the fact that their destructive power extends over miles. Accordingly, a reduction is recommended to cut off this enlargement of overkill forces.

$1,000 mill.

(4) *ABM.* The proposed antiballistic missile system has been the subject of exhaustive debate. The technical workability of the system is under grave doubt on the grounds of complexity and in terms of the experience with an unsuccessful attempt to build an anti-aircraft defense system. The anti-aircraft system involves much simpler requirements, and we know from a principal designer of this system (Dr. Jerome Weisner of MIT) that this system has failed. There is the further prospect that the construction of an ABM system will serve to severely escalate fear among nations and hence drive forward an already irrational arms race. Accordingly, the budgeted items for their purpose (*Budget,* pages 264, 265, 266) are recommended for elimination.

$904 mill.

(5) *Chemical and Biological warfare.* Since 1961 the United States has been producing and stockpiling increasing quantities of these lethal materials. Outside Denver, 100 million doses of nerve gas have been

placed in open storage in steel containers. The mass production of these and biological warfare materials mean more overkill weapons systems. In addition, the very existence of these materials in quantities exposes the people of the United States itself to grave hazards because of possible accidents in the handling of lethal, self-propagating organisms. It is therefore recommended that this production be stopped.

$350 mill.

(6) *Advanced Manned Strategic Aircraft.* In the face of already existing massive overkill capability the proposal to build additional and new high-speed bombers is organizational and industrial empire building and little else. This should be terminated.

$102 mill.

(7) *Bomber defense system (SAGE).* It has long been understood that the Soviets do not have meaningful long-range bomber capability. When this is coupled with the known defects in the operation of the SAGE-type system there is no reason for incurring the large cost that building this would involve since it would apparently add nothing meaningful to the defense of the United States (see discussion in the *Congressional Quarterly,* June 28, 1968).

$1,000 mill.

(8) *Surface-to-air missiles.* Former Pentagon staff have indicated that substantial savings could be made by holding back on major spending for ineffective anti-aircraft missiles, and deferring production on apparently inadequate designs (see the discussion on surface-to-air missiles in the *Congressional Quarterly,* op. cit.).

$850 mill.

(9) *The Manned Orbiting Laboratory.* This is an Air Force venture that is NASA's task on the scientific side, and an addition to overkill if used to add to nuclear delivery. Hence, reduction is recommended (see R. Benson, "How the Pentagon Can Save $9,000,000,000," *The Washington Monthly,* March, 1969).

$576 mill.

C. *Reduction in additions to conventional war overkill.*

(1) *Vietnam war manpower.* The Vietnam war now uses 639,000 soldiers, sailors, airmen. As the Congress instructs the Department of Defense and the President to refrain from operating wars of intervention, these 639,000 men would not be required. Their termination (annual cost of about $10,000 per man) would leave the United States with armed forces of 2,900,000 and an opportunity to effect a major reduction in an unnecessary military outlay.

$6,390 mill.

(2) *Surplus military manpower.* Analysts in the Department of Defense have reported (see *Congressional Quarterly*), that substantial savings could be made in manpower in all the services by a 10 percent

cut in "support" forces which use a lion's share of military manpower, and have been unjustifiably large compared with other armies of the world. In addition manpower savings could be effected by imposing a requirement to reduce the large category of "transient" personnel. These combined reductions in the Army, Navy and Airforce would make possible a reduction of $4.2 billion, allowing for a cost of $10,000 per man year.

$4,200 mill.

(3) *Tactical aircraft programs.* Specialists in the aviation field have indicated that elimination of overly-elaborate and impractical electronic systems, and concentration on simpler (hence more reliable) aircraft would make possible savings on a large scale.

$1,800 mill.

(4) *Attack carriers.* The United States now operates 15 attack carrier forces. Their justification is based on the assumption of fighting three wars at once. Even a beginning of reasonable economy in the use of these forces (see details in *Congressional Quarterly*) make possible substantial budget reductions.

$360 mill.

(5) *Anti-submarine carrier forces.* These forces are known to have severely limited capability in their military function, casting grave doubt on the worth of continuing them, according to Pentagon specialists.

$400 mill.

(6) *Amphibious forces and Fast Deployment Logistics Ships* (FDL). The amphibious forces are massively overbuilt (see *Budget,* p. 75) and are presumably oriented to a Western hemisphere war mission. These could be substantially reduced without reducing a massive military capability. The FDL's are part of an expanded Vietnam Wars program that should be stopped by the Congress (see *Congressional Quarterly*).

$500 mill.

(7) *C5-A jet transport.* This plane has been specifically designed to transport large numbers of troops for the Pentagon's world-wide policing and Vietnam Wars program. This capability should be curtailed.

$500 mill.

(8) *Military assistance.* For some time it has been apparent that the U.S. military assistance program has been a major factor in encouraging and sustaining dictatorial and backward regimes in many countries. This outlay has no demonstrable relation to the defense of the United States and should therefore be eliminated.

$610 mill.

(9) *New naval ship construction.* We are informed in the *Budget* for FY 1970 (p. 77) that "The largest single 1970 increase proposed for General Purpose Forces is for a new ship construction program for our naval forces of $2.4 billion total obligational authority." Such massive

expenditures for naval forces is justifiable only in terms of the 3-wars-at-once military perspective. Even first steps towards building a military sufficiency force, as against a military overkill force for 3-wars-at-once requires elimination of this item.

$2,400 mill.

(10) *Economies in Training.* A former Pentagon staffer (Office of Comptroller) recommends changes in training methods that would save an appreciable sum as against present methods and costs (see Benson, op. cit.).

$50 mill.

(11) *Improved buying procedures.* A series of straightforward steps can apparently produce major savings in Pentagon buying by curtailing the pattern of costly cost-overruns. (See Benson paper for details.) Therefore the following Procurement reduction is indicated.

$2,700 mill.

(12) *U.S. NATO forces.* Pentagon staff indicate feasibility of reducing forces in Europe by 125,000 and their backup by 50,000. (See Benson paper.) At $10,000 cost per man, this justifies budget reduction of

$1,750 mill.

D. *Miscellaneous economies.*

(1) *Military construction.* The *Budget* for FY 1970 (p. 266) enumerates diverse purposes for which new military construction has been scheduled. Secretary of Defense Laird proposed a reduction of the $1,948 million military construction item by $634 million, leaving $1,314 million. This should be further reduced in order to limit the further over-expansion of unnecessary military forces within the United States and abroad—in terms of the requirements of defense sufficiency.

$1,000 mill.

(2) *F-14 aircraft.* The Navy has announced a program for constructing a new class of fighter planes to be carried by its major aircraft carriers. These fighter planes are of doubtful worth since there is no present or potential opposing force with fleets of carriers against which U.S. carrier forces and fighter planes will conceivably be operated. Furthermore, the enlargement of the carrier aircraft force involves a major addition to preparations for further Vietnam-type wars. This alone is the issue with respect to this aircraft (not whether the design is right, or whether the contractor is competent). The *Budget* for FY 1970 (p. 264) suggests the amount intended for this purpose. This should be eliminated.

$834 mill.

The sum of these proposed savings in the military spending of the United States for FY 1970 is: **$54,794 mill.**

A Sufficiency Security Force for the United States

A second approach that can be used by the Congress for considering defense expenditures is a yardstick of adequacy for designing a United States security force. A security force should be designed for the United States to service three requirements:

(1) operate and maintain a strategic deterrence force;
(2) give reasonable security for the shores of the United States;
(3) have capability for participating in international peacekeeping operations.

Such a force is designed, with its nuclear capabilities, to give pause to any potential attacker of the United States. Its coastal patrol and allied defense forces give solid assurance against attack on the shores of this country. Finally, the mobile, combat units proposed in this security force give highly competent capability both for the defense of the United States and for participation in international peacekeeping.

I have estimated the direct, combat manpower requirements for an American security force along these lines as follows:

	MEN
Strategic Deterrence Forces	
International Warning Net	25,000
Strategic Weapons System Operations and Maintenance	10,000
Coastal Defense	
Warships for Patrol	7,500
Coastal Air Patrol-Tactical	2,400
Airborne Combat Units for International Peacekeeping	
100 Autonomous Airborne Combat Units	40,000
Tactical Air-Ground Support	16,000
Air Transport	10,000
	110,900

With direct combat personnel of 111,000 there is requirement for support staffs for the ordinary military headquarters and backup functions including: combined headquarters, intelligence, communication, engineering, logistics, procurement, training and recruitment, research and medical. Such support forces can be estimated on the ratio of 5 to 1, or more elaborately estimated on the basis of 7 to 1. On the former basis the total security force with supporting personnel would amount to 666,000; with the larger allowance for support the total force would require 888,000 men. This security force for the U.S. would require high-caliber voluntary enlistees on a career basis. Conscription would be irrelevant and inappropriate. The annual operating cost of such a security force would be about $20,000 million.

Altogether, such a security force for the United States would have formidable military capabilities for deterring any potential nuclear attack, for securing the United States against physical penetration from the outside, and for deploying highly competent airborne battalions for local defense and for international peacekeeping.

The Armed Services Committees of the Congress could consider the design of a security force along these lines, using it as a yardstick against which to gauge present and subsequent budget proposals. It is underscored that this security force is designed to operate *before* international disarmament agreements of any sort are completed.

The recommendations given above for savings in Fiscal Year 1970 military programs of the United States are justified on the following grounds:

1. Present forces are more than sufficient to serve as a competent security force for the United States.
2. The Congress should stop the armed forces from adding to overkill.
3. The Congress should stop preparation for more Vietnam wars.
4. No conceivable armed forces can do more than help to secure the U.S. in a military sense. Defense as a literal shield is no longer purchasable. The Joint Chiefs do not promise to defend the U.S.— they cannot do it. Neither can they promise a nuclear war "victory," for a "successful first-strike" without one's own destruction is not achievable.
5. The Congress, through these budget reductions, can make available a large fund that is needed for productive, life-serving purposes within the United States.
6. Only by these means can the American people cope constructively with the nation's massive problems of economic development and forestall the dread prospect of racial confrontation in this land.

The application of recommended savings to these purposes could probably be accomplished, swiftly, by translating these savings into major tax reductions. This would permit the cities and the states to use their existing taxing mechanisms for tapping this new source of tax power and applying these funds to the urgent needs of our own people.

Appendix D

Excerpts from

AN INTRODUCTION TO THE DEFENSE SUPPLY AGENCY

Prepared by Public Affairs Office Defense Supply Agency
January 1968

For sale by the Superintendent of Documents, Government Printing Office,
Washington, D.C.

DEFENSE CONTRACT ADMINISTRATION SERVICES

Defense Contract Administration Services (DCAS) completed in 1965 its nationwide organization within DSA for the purpose of administering procurement contracts for the three military departments, DSA, NASA, for other Federal and State agencies, and, when authorized, for foreign governments. Previously the military departments and other agencies managed their own contracts.

A few categories of contracts continue to be administered by the military departments. These include contracts for certain major weapon systems, large civil works construction, and shipbuilding.

Nearly 20,000 military and civilian employees who previously performed field contract administration in the military departments were transferred to DSA and absorbed in 11 DCAS Regions across the United States. The Regions are subdivided into district, plant, and area offices, as necessary, in relation to the volume of defense contracts in areas throughout the nation.

Some of the functions of Defense Contract Administration Services are:

1. Contract administration activities, such as financial analysis, review of contractor systems, price and cost analysis, negotiation of contract changes pursuant to the changes clause, final determination of allowability of costs, convenience termination settlements, plant clearance and disposal of contract inventories, and administration of government property.

2. Production activities, such as pre-award surveys, gauging the prog-

ress of contractors' production effort, use of government-owned industrial resources, planning for industrial mobilization, providing industrial manpower relations services, arranging for packaging, providing support for transportation, and providing technical management and assistance for selected contracts for major systems of high priority.

3. Quality assurance activities, such as product inspection and testing, evaluation and continuous verification of contractors' inspection system of quality program, detection of unfavorable quality conditions or trends, and initiation of corrective action.

4. Industrial security program of the Department of Defense to insure effective protection of classified information, including foreign classified information in the hands of contractors. Security clearance of contractor personnel has been centralized in the Defense Industrial Security Clearance Office in Columbus, Ohio.

5. Data and financial management activities, such as payments to contractors and providing financial status and contract delivery status to procuring activities, inventory managers, and internal management.

6. Support to Small Business and Labor Surplus Areas, such as determining contractors' compliance with the small business and labor surplus are a mandatory subcontracting program, prime contractors' source development, and counseling businessman [sic] on how to do business with the Government.

On July 1, 1967, the Defense Contracts Compliance Office, responsible for assuring equal employment opportunity on all Defense contracts as required by Executive Order 11246, became Part of the Defense Supply Agency's Defense Contract Administration Services. This transfer tied together, for the first time, the office responsible for elimination of discrimination by defense contractors and the contracting officials responsible for administering contracts under DCAS.

The new location of the headquarters of the Defense Contracts Compliance Office is at DSA headquarters, Cameron Station, Alexandria, Va. Field offices are located in the headquarters office of the 11 DCAS regions.

	FY 1967	FY 1966
Number of prime and secondary contracts for full administration (as of June 30)	271.8 (thous)	194.7
Value of contracts (as of June 30)	48,912.5 (mil)	40,451.9
Invoices Completed	1,944.5 (thous)	1,108.2
Value of Materiel Inspected and released for shipment	19,352.3 (mil)	11,730.2
Personnel (as of June 30)		
Military	433	399
Civilian	24,323	20,799

(Personnel figures and statistics on contracts which follow are as of June 30, 1967).

DEFENSE CONTRACT ADMINISTRATION SERVICES REGION, ATLANTA
3100 MAPLE DRIVE, N.E.
ATLANTA, GEORGIA 30305
COLONEL LOREN P. MURRAY, USAF, DIRECTOR

Date established: October 1, 1965.

Geographical area covered: Florida, Georgia, Alabama, Mississippi, Tennessee, South Carolina, North Carolina. The Region also handles, as required, administration of contracts in the Caribbean, and Central and South American areas.

Number of employees (civilian): 1797

Military personnel assigned: 51

Number of contracts requiring contract administration action: 10,234

Dollar value of prime contracts administered: $2.1 billion

Examples of materials for which contracts are administered: Missiles, major spacecraft and rocket components, textiles, clothing, munitions and weapons systems, electronics, metal parts, pumps, trailers, telephone equipment.

Location of District Offices: Orlando Air Force Base, Orlando, Florida 32813; 908 South 20th St., Birmingham, Alabama 35205

Other comments: The Atlanta DCAS Region's industry and contractors are fairly well diversified with electronics heavily concentrated in Florida and many munitions, textile and clothing Contractors in Georgia, Alabama, North Carolina, and South Carolina. An important part of the Regional workload involves NASA contracts concentrated at Huntsville, Alabama, and the Kennedy Space Center in Florida.

DEFENSE CONTRACT ADMINISTRATION SERVICES REGION, BOSTON
666 SUMMER STREET
BOSTON, MASSACHUSETTS 02210
COLONEL FRANK A. BOGART, USA, DIRECTOR

Date established: August 1, 1965

Geographical area covered: Connecticut, Maine, New Hampshire, Rhode Island, Massachusetts, Vermont and New York State, excluding New York City and adjoining Westchester, Orange, Rockland and Putnam Counties.

Number of employees (civilian): 3055

Military personnel assigned: 44

Number of contracts requiring contract administration action: 45,603.

Dollar value of prime contracts administered: $6.6 billion.

Examples of materials for which contracts are administered: Rifles, machine guns, rocket launchers, gun mounts, airplane engines, woolen and felt products, ammunition, steel cables, computers and a variety of electronic components including missile systems components, radar and sonar equipment, helicopters and components.

Location of District Offices: 557 Asylum Avenues, Hartford, Connecticut, 06105 and 317 Child Street, Rochester, New York 14611.

DEFENSE CONTRACT ADMINISTRATION SERVICES REGION, CHICAGO
O'HARE INTERNATIONAL AIRPORT, P.O. BOX 66475
CHICAGO, ILLINOIS 60666
COLONEL JOHN P. GIBBONS, USAF, DIRECTOR

Date established: October 1, 1965
Geographical area covered: Wisconsin, Indiana, and northern half of Illinois.
Number of employees (civilian): 2318
Military personnel assigned: 34
Number of contracts requiring contract administration action: 32,218
Dollar value of prime contracts administered: $3.2 billion
Examples of materials for which contracts are administered: Radios, telephone switchboards, chemicals, construction equipment, ammunition, trucks, small engines, generators, clothing, helmets, medical supplies and equipment, petroleum products, food, missile parts.
Location of District Offices: Indianapolis District, Building 1, Finance Center, Fort Benjamin Harrison, Indianapolis, Indiana 46249; Milwaukee District, Commerce Building, 744 North Fourth Street, Milwaukee, Wisconsin 53202.

DEFENSE CONTRACT ADMINISTRATION SERVICES REGION, CLEVELAND
FEDERAL OFFICE BLDG.
1240 EAST NINTH STREET,
CLEVELAND, OHIO 44199
COLONEL NORMAN T. DENNIS, USA, DIRECTOR

Date established: August 1, 1965.
Geographical area covered: Ohio, Kentucky, and northwestern Pennsylvania (Erie, Crawford, and Mercer Counties).
Number of civilian employees: 1842
Military personnel assigned: 30
Number of contracts requiring contract administration action: 20,718
Dollar value of prime contracts administered: $1.9 billion
Examples of materials for which contracts are administered: Trucks, tanks, general purpose vehicles, tires, batteries, rifles, machine guns, jet engines and components, missiles, and electronic components.
Location of District Offices: c/o Defense Electronics Supply Center, 1507 Wilmington Pike, Dayton, Ohio 45401; Federal Office Building, 550 Main Street, Cincinnati, Ohio, 45202

DEFENSE CONTRACT ADMINISTRATION SERVICES REGION, DALLAS
500 SOUTH ERVAY STREET
DALLAS, TEXAS 75201
CAPTAIN W. GLENN NORMILE, SC, USN, DIRECTOR

Date established: June 1, 1965

Geographical area covered: Texas, Louisiana, Arkansas, Oklahoma, and New Mexico

Number of employees (civilian): 1099

Military personnel assigned: 47

Number of contracts requiring contract administration action: 8787

Dollar value of prime contracts administered: $2.2 billion

Examples of materials for which contracts are administered: Petroleum products, clothing and other textiles, trailer mounted engine driven generators, bombs, ammunition including artillery shells, shell casings, special munitions, fire fighting equipment, special purpose trailers, radio, radar, electronic systems and sub-systems, parachutes, optics, components for military missiles, the modification and overhaul of military aircraft.

Location of support offices: Houston Area Office, 2320 LaBranch St., Box 61167, Houston, Texas 77061; Oklahoma City Area Office, 621 N. Robinson St., Oklahoma City, Oklahoma 73102; San Antonio Area Office, 7071B San Pedro, San Antonio, Texas 78216

DEFENSE CONTRACT ADMINISTRATION SERVICES REGION, DETROIT
1580 EAST GRAND BOULEVARD
DETROIT, MICHIGAN 48211
COLONEL KENNETH R. JOHNSON, USA, DIRECTOR

Date established: April 1, 1965

Geographical area covered: State of Michigan and all of Canada

Number of employees (civilian): 1364

Military personnel assigned: 20

Number of contracts requiring contract administration action: 17,486

Dollar value of prime contract administered: $2.3 billion

Examples of materials for which contracts are administered: General purpose and commercial vehicles, armored cars, cranes, guidance systems, radar and communications equipment, pharmaceuticals, tires, batteries, maintenance tents, helmets and helmet liners, rocket components, warheads.

Location of District offices: 21 Ottawa Avenue, N.W., Grand Rapids, Michigan 49502

Other comments: With DCAS Office in Otawa, Canada, DCASR, Detroit is responsible for the administration of almost all United States defense contracts with Canadian industry.

DEFENSE CONTRACT ADMINISTRATION SERVICES REGION, LOS ANGELES
11099 SOUTH LA CIENEGA BLVD.
LOS ANGELES, CALIFORNIA 90045
BRIGADIER GENERAL ARTHUR E. EXON, USAF, DIRECTOR

Date established: December 1, 1965
Geographical area covered: State of California south of Monterey, Kings, Tulare and Inyo Counties; Arizona and Clark County in Nevada
Number of employees (civilian): 3310
Military personnel assigned: 48
Number of contracts requiring contract administration action: 28,619
Dollar value of prime contracts administered: $8.5 billion
Examples of materials for which contracts are administered: Basic and applied research, air frames and aircraft subsystems, missile components, avionics systems, ammunition and weapons, computing equipment, rubber and plastic products.
Location of District Offices: 125 South Grand Avenue, Pasadena, California 91105; 8155 Van Nuys Boulevard, Van Nuys, California 91402; 1548 State College Boulevard, Anaheim, California 92805; Building 4, Air Force Plant 19, 4297 Pacific Coast Highway, San Diego, California 92110; 3800 North Central Avenue, Phoenix, Arizona 85012

DEFENSE CONTRACT ADMINISTRATION SERVICES REGION, NEW YORK
770 BROADWAY
NEW YORK, NEW YORK 10003
BRIGADIER GENERAL WALTER M. VANN, USA, DIRECTOR

Date established: November 1, 1965
Geographical area covered: New York City; Westchester, Rockland, Orange and Putnam Counties, Long Island, and all counties in New Jersey north of Ocean, Burlington and Mercer Counties.
Number of employees (civilian): 3546
Military personnel assigned: 58
Number of contracts requiring contract administration action: 44,598
Dollar value of prime contracts administered: $10.2 billion
Examples of materials for which contracts are administered: Guided missiles, clothing, subsistence, drugs, petroleum, shipboard pumps, electronic receivers, and transmitters.
Location of District Offices: 605 Stewart Avenue, Garden City, L.I., New

York 11530; 240 U.S. Route 22, Springfield, New Jersey 07081.
Other comments: Region handles some overseas contracts.

DEFENSE CONTRACT ADMINISTRATION SERVICES REGION, PHILADELPHIA
2800 SOUTH 20TH STREET
PHILADELPHIA, PENNSYLVANIA 19101
COLONEL GERALD JOHNSON, JR., USA, DIRECTOR

Date established: April 20, 1964 (Pilot Region)
Geographical area covered: States of Pennsylvania (except Crawford, Erie, and Mercer Counties), Virginia, West Virginia, Delaware, Maryland, and the counties of Mercer, Burlington, Ocean, and all counties south thereof in the State of New Jersey, and the District of Columbia.
Number of employees (civilian): 2725
Military personnel assigned: 42
Number of contracts requiring contract administration action: 36,250
Dollar value of prime contracts administered: $7.3 billion
Examples of materials for which contracts are administered: Vehicles, missile systems, weapons, ammunition, aircraft components, turbines, electronics, clothing, medical, and subsistence items.
Location of District Offices: Building 22, Fort Holabird, Baltimore, Maryland 21219; 808 Market Street, Camden, New Jersey 08102; 1610-S Federal Building, 1000 Liberty Avenue, Pittsburgh, Pennsylvania 15222; and 750 Penn Street, Reading, Pennsylvania 19602
Other comments: The Defense Contract Administration Services Region (Pilot Test) was established at Philadelphia on April 20, 1964. It served as the test for all DCASRs until September 1, 1964, at which time the pilot test designation was dropped and the Region was redesignated the Defense Contract Administration Services Region, Philadelphia.

DEFENSE CONTRACT ADMINISTRATION SERVICES REGION, ST. LOUIS
1136 WASHINGTON STREET
ST. LOUIS, MISSOURI 63101
CAPTAIN RAYMOND S. SULLIVAN, SC, USN, DIRECTOR

Date established: October 1, 1965
Geographical area covered: Missouri, in Illinois the counties of Adams, Brown, Cass, Menard, Sangamon, Macon, Moultrie, Douglas, Edgar, and all counties south of these; Iowa, Colorado, Kansas, Minnesota, Nebraska, North Dakota, South Dakota, and Wyoming.
Number of employees (civilian): 1670
Military personnel assigned: 32
Number of contracts requiring contract administration action: 14,953
Dollar value of prime contracts administered: $2.6 billion

Examples of materials for which contracts are administered: Rocket engines and components, aircraft and related components, missiles and launchers, ammunition and related items, helicopter armament systems, clothing and textiles, pharmaceuticals, truck trailers, and building hardware supplies.

Location of District Office: 2305 Ford Parkway, St. Paul, Minnesota 55116

Other comments: The Region performs all contract administration functions for the Defense Plant Equipment Facility at Atchison, Kansas. This is a man-made limestone cave of about 15 acres, considered to be the world's largest single storage unit contained on one level.

DEFENSE CONTRACT ADMINISTRATION SERVICES REGION, SAN FRANCISCO
866 MALCOLM ROAD
BURLINGAME, CALIFORNIA 94010
COLONEL WILLIAM KENNETH ASHBY, USAF, DIRECTOR

Date established: December 1, 1965

Geographical area covered: Northern California, Nevada (except for Clark County), Utah, Montana, Idaho, Oregon, Washington, Alaska and Hawaii.

Number of employees (civilian): 1290

Military personnel assigned: 25

Number of contracts requiring contract administration action: 12,308

Dollar value of prime contracts administered: $1.8 billion

Examples of materials for which contracts are administered: military vehicles, naval guns, communications satellites, components for Polaris and Poseidon missile system and high altitude bombers, military clothing and subsistence, electronic systems and components, and ammunition.

Location of District Offices: Building 178, Treasure Island, San Francisco, California 94130; Building 5D, U.S. Naval Air Station, Sand Point, Seattle, Washington 98115; 1750 South Redwood Road, Salt Lake City, Utah 84104

Other comments: Provides acceptance inspection and arranges for the overseas shipment of the bulk of DoD lumber procurements.

DEFENSE INDUSTRIAL CLEARANCE OFFICE
DEFENSE CONSTRUCTION SUPPLY CENTER
COLUMBUS, OHIO 43215
LIEUTENANT COLONEL WILLIAM W. ROBERTS, USAF, CHIEF

Date established: March 22, 1965

Geographical area covered: World-wide

Number of employees (civilian): 307

Military personnel assigned: 2

Mission: DISCO is a field extension of the Office of Industrial Security, Headquarters DSA CAS. On a nationally centralized basis, the Office determines eligibility for access to classified information, foreign and domestic, by contractor personnel; maintains records of these determinations and the legal documents related to determination of eligibility of industrial facilities for access to classified information; processes visit requests involving NATO and foreign classified information.

Clear actions completed: FY 1967 FY 1966
464,454   391,711

Appendix E

INDEX OF 100 PARENT COMPANIES WHICH WITH
THEIR SUBSIDIARIES RECEIVED THE LARGEST
DOLLAR VOLUME OF MILITARY PRIME CONTRACT
AWARDS IN FISCAL YEAR 1968

RANK	PARENT COMPANY	RANK	PARENT COMPANY
89	Aerodex Inc	40	Day & Zimmerman Inc
74	Aerospace Corp (N)	38	Dupont E I de Nemours & Co
61	American Machine & Foundry Co	59	Eastman Kodak Co
71	American Mfg Co of Texas	76	Emerson Electric Co
6	American Telephone & Telegraph Co	33	F M C Corp
49	Asiatic Petroleum Corp	56	Fairchild Hiller Corp
94	Atlas Chemical Industries Inc	82	Federal Cartridge Corp
99	Automatic Sprinkler Corp America	19	Ford Motor Co
12	Avco Corp	1	General Dynamics Corp
31	Bendix Corp	3	General Electric Co
7	Boeing Co	10	General Motors Corp
75	Cessna Aircraft Co	63	General Precision Equipment Corp
62	Chamberlain Corp	41	General Telephone & Electn Corp
43	Chrysler Corp	28	General Tire & Rubber Co
68	City Investing Co	48	Goodyear Tire & Rubber Co
47	Collins Radio Co	11	Grumman Aircraft Engineering Corp
69	Colt Industries, Inc	78	Gulf Oil Corp
79	Condec Corp	96	Harris-Intertype Corp
81	Continental Air Lines Inc	65	Harvey Aluminum Inc
86	Control Data Corp	93	Hazeltine Corporation
72	Curtiss Wright Corp	37	Hercules Inc

259

RANK	PARENT COMPANY	RANK	PARENT COMPANY
20	Honeywell Inc	57	Pacific Architects & Engineers Inc.
24	Hughes Aircraft Co	32	Pan American World Airways Inc
83	Hughes Tool Co		
30	International Business Machine Co	26	Radio Corp of America
98	International Harvester Co	35	Raymond Morrison Knudsen (JV) *
29	International Telephone & Tel Corp	15	Raytheon Co
85	Johns Hopkins University (N)	23	Ryan Aeronautical Co
18	Kaiser Industries Corp	50	Sanders Associates Inc.
64	Lear Siegler Inc	77	Seatrain Lines Inc
8	Ling Temco Vought Inc	36	Signal Companies Inc (The)
14	Litton Industries, Inc	100	Smith Investment Co
2	Lockheed Aircraft Corp	16	Sperry Rand Corp
87	Lykes Corp	44	Standard Oil Co of Calif
55	Magnavox Co	25	Standard Oil of New Jersey
17	Martin Marietta Corp	92	States Marine Lines Inc
53	Mason & Hanger Silas Mason Co	90	Susquehanna Corp
54	Massachusets Institutechnology (N)	91	Sverdrup & Parcel & Assocs
		52	T R W Inc
5	McDonnell Douglas Corp	67	Teledyne Inc
88	McLean Industries, Inc	46	Texaco Inc
51	Mobil Oil Corp	39	Texas Instruments Inc
80	Motorola Inc.	13	Textron Inc
66	National Presto Industries Inc	58	Thiokol Chemical Corp
34	Newport News Shipbld & Dry Dock Co	42	Uniroyal Inc
		4	United Aircraft Corp
45	Norris Industries	60	United States Steel Corp
9	North American Rockwell Corp	95	Vinnell Corp
		84	Vitro Corp of America
22	Northrop Corp	70	Western Union Telegraph Co
21	Olin Mathieson Chemical Corp	27	Westinghouse Electric Corp
		73	White Motor Co
		97	World Airways Inc

* Raymond International, Inc; Morrison-Knudsen Co., Inc; Brown & Root, Inc; & J. A. Jones Construction Co.
(N) Non-Profit
(JV) Joint Venture
SOURCE: Office of Secretary of Defense, Pentagon, Washington, D.C.

Appendix F

FEDERALLY FUNDED RESEARCH AND
DEVELOPMENT CENTERS *

Federally Funded Research and Development Centers (FFRDC's) administered by universities and colleges received from Federal agencies $908 million in fiscal year 1967 (table 18). These centers, formerly called Federal Contract Research Centers (FCRC), receive all or a substantial part of their support from the Federal Government to perform activities or manage programs that are primarily concerned with research and development and are considered beyond the capabilities of any single established organization. Although these FFRDC's function as relatively autonomous components of the university establishment, some centers make important contributions to the educational and research activities of the parent institution.

The establishment of FFRDC's was an outgrowth of World War II demands of the Federal Government for highly qualified talent to conduct scientific investigations on projects related to military objectives. At that time, neither Federal agencies nor universities were prepared, in terms of personnel and facilities, to undertake the special assignments that were largely concerned with the development of the atomic bomb. Most of the centers were, and continue to be, established at or near universities where they could draw upon the available scientific and technical manpower.

The range of interests of these centers is quite large and their activities involve essentially all the major fields of science. Not only does their work materially affect many of the critical national programs, but it also exerts an important influence on the progress of academic science. A list of such

* SOURCE: U.S. National Science Foundation, *Federal Support to Universities and Colleges,* Fiscal Year 1967, NSF 69-7, Washington, D.C., 1969, pp. 36–40.

Table 18.—*Federal obligations to Federally Funded Research and Development Centers administered by universities and colleges, 1963–67*

LOCATION AND NAME	FEDERAL OBLIGATIONS (THOUSANDS OF DOLLARS)					SPONSORING AGENCY	ADMINISTERED BY
	1963	1964	1965	1966	1967		
Total	$814,082	$862,353	$895,287	$917,631	$907,549		
Arizona:							
Kitt Peak National Observatory[a]	3,750	4,400	6,915	5,791	5,485	NSF	Association of Universities for Research in Astronomy, Inc.
Cerro Tololo Inter-American Observatory (Chile)[a]	1,100	1,100	1,465	1,471	1,713	NSF	Association of Universities for Research in Astronomy, Inc.
California:							
Jet Propulsion Laboratory[b] ..	230,168	226,194	245,094	230,091	222,169	NASA	California Institute of Technology
Stanford Linear Accelerator Center	16,193	24,122	43,943	50,969	30,891	AEC	Stanford University
Lawrence Radiation Laboratory	162,854	169,424	156,254	169,870	174,661	AEC	University of California
Center for Research and Development in Higher Education	....	....	....	....	849	HEW(OE)	University of California
Center for the Study of the Evaluation of Instructional Programs	....	....	....	....	534	HEW(OE)	University of California
Stanford Center for Research and Development in Teaching	....	....	....	....	797	HEW(OE)	Stanford University

Colorado: National Center for Atmospheric Research [a]	6,019	10,036	8,941	11,791	16,576	NSF	University Corporation for Atmospheric Research
District of Columbia: Center for Research in Social Systems	947	934	1,843	1,808	1,936	DOD (Army)	American University
Georgia: Research and Development Center in Educational Stimulation	....	....	....	....	732	HEW(OE)	University of Georgia
Illinois: Argonne National Laboratory [c]	74,947	84,507	86,329	87,255	97,262	AEC	University of Chicago and Argonne Universities Association
Iowa: Ames Laboratory	6,549	7,360	8,464	9,089	9,371	AEC	Iowa State University of Science and Technology
Maryland: Applied Physics Laboratory	42,096	49,124	54,097	52,491	47,172	DOD (Navy)	Johns Hopkins University
Massachusetts: Cambridge Electron Accelerator	5,946 2,632	5,717 3,424	5,851 3,792	6,130 3,517	6,786 3,596	AEC	Harvard University Massachusetts Institute of Technology
Lincoln Laboratory	70,606	78,764	68,683	64,060	66,989	DOD(Air Force)	Massachusetts Institute of Technology
Center for Research and Development in Educational Differences [d]	....	....	....	1,112	1,165	HEW(OE)	Harvard University

Table 18.—*Federal obligations to Federally Funded Research and Development Centers administered by universities and colleges, 1963–67—Continued*

LOCATION AND NAME	FEDERAL OBLIGATIONS (THOUSANDS OF DOLLARS)					SPONSORING AGENCY	ADMINISTERED BY
	1963	1964	1965	1966	1967		
New Jersey:							
Plasma Physics Laboratory	7,542	8,268	6,997	6,556	6,572	AEC	Princeton University
Princeton-Pennsylvania Accelerator	6,224	5,500	7,521	8,825	7,971	AEC	Princeton University
	881	1,790	1,982	1,801	1,775		University of Pennsylvania
New Mexico:							
Los Alamos Scientific Laboratory	93,020	97,680	94,636	103,311	102,213	AEC	University of California
New York:							
Brookhaven National Laboratory[a]	59,180	58,619	63,564	64,407	64,160	AEC	Associated Universities, Inc.
Hudson Laboratory	3,780	3,939	4,195	4,673	4,708	DOD (Navy)	Columbia University
Oregon:							
Center for the Advanced Study of Educational Administration	....	509	534	663	676	HEW(OE)	University of Oregon
Pennsylvania:							
Ordnance Research Laboratory	3,763	4,827	7,025	9,597	8,120	DOD (Navy)	Pennsylvania State University
Learning Research and Development Center	....	....	754	642	1,309	HEW(OE)	University of Pittsburgh
Tennessee:							
Oak Ridge Associated Universities[a]	4,291	5,059	5,695	6,168	5,620	AEC	Oak Ridge Associated Universities

Texas: Research and Development Center in Teacher Education	....				763	HEW(OE)	University of Texas
Virginia: Human Resources Research Office	2,794	3,081	3,382	2,752	2,853	DOD (Army)	George Washington University
Space Radiation Effects Laboratory	....			729	1,815	NASA	College of William and Mary
Washington: Applied Physics Laboratory	3,200	2,275	2,178	5,145	2,836	DOD (Navy)	University of Washington
West Virginia: National Radio Astronomy Observatory[a]	4,550	4,600	3,380	4,719	5,062	NSF	Associated Universities, Inc.
Wisconsin: Army Mathematics Research Center	1,050	1,100	1,273	1,390	1,378	DOD (Army)	University of Wisconsin
Center for Research and Development for Learning and Re-Education	....		500	808	1,034	HEW(OE)	University of Wisconsin

[a] One of six administered by university consortia.
[b] Includes amounts subcontracted principally to industrial firms for performance, as follows: 1963, $107 million; 1964, $145 million; 1965, $163 million; 1966, $144 million; 1967, $119 million.
[c] Administered by both university and consortium.
[d] Discontinued July 1, 1967.

activities undertaken by FFRDC's would include projects such as the following:

Jet Propulsion Laboratory—in California, work involving the development of unmanned lunar and space exploration, including early exploration of planets with automated spacecraft.

Lawrence Radiation Laboratory—in California, studies of controlled thermonuclear reactors to generate energy through fusion of light nuclei and important contributions toward improving the efficiency of nuclear weapons.

Los Alamos Scientific Laboratory—in New Mexico, largely concerned with weapons development, also research in rocket propulsion, reactor technology, and physical research in the medium-energy region.

Argonne National Laboratory—in Illinois, research in high-energy physics using the zero gradient synchrotron, somatic effects of radiation, and engineering of liquid metal fast breeder reactors.

Lincoln Laboratory—in Massachusetts, defense and other military problems involving ballistic missile defense and offense, radar discrimination, satellite communication, and identification of underground nuclear tests.

Applied Physics Laboratory—in Maryland, includes research in such areas as naval surface-launched missiles and missile systems and Navy satellite navigation technology.

National Center for Atmospheric Research—in Colorado, problems of social concern involving long-range weather prediction, weather control, and air pollution.

Learning Research and Development Center—in Pennsylvania, the scientific study of learning and the development of instructional materials and procedures.

As the needs of the Federal Government have changed, so has the universe of FFRDC's. The most recent additions, for example, include centers created under the sponsorship of the Office of Education to conduct research on modern educational problems and to develop methods to improve the educational process. Changes also occur for reasons that essentially have to do with administrative control, funding level, or primary mission.

Because the identification of FFRDC's is the responsibility of the sponsoring agency, certain problems of uniform identification have developed in the past. As a result, an interagency task force was established on January 10, 1967, by the Committee on Academic Science and Engineering (CASE) of the Federal Council of Science and Technology (FCST) to develop criteria for Government-wide classification of FFRDC's and procedures for maintaining a master listing of these centers. After adopting the new criteria, a master list of FFRDC's was prepared and the name was changed from Federal Contract Research Centers to Federally Funded Research and Development Centers to convey the fact that the activities of the centers involved more than research. The criteria adopted concern all FFRDC's managed by universities and colleges, nonprofit institutions, and industrial firms. The task force defined the types of activity and general organizational structure of the FFRDC and established additional criteria in such areas as management and control, level of Federal support, ownership of facilities, and agency-center relationships.

It was recognized by the interagency task force that FFRDC's administered by institutions of higher education generally fall into two categories. One is the "mission-oriented" center, an organizational subunit that is performing research and development or R. & D. management upon the request of the Government. The other is the "large research facility," an installation that may be a national facility and is staffed so that few, if any, scientific and professional personnel are involved in any teaching or graduate training function.

It was also recognized that, although all the centers have sufficient similar characteristics to identify them all under the single general term FFRDC, they do have in many instances significant differences in terms of management, functions, types of activity, levels of funding, areas of primary emphasis, and of course the sponsoring agencies.

Centers differ also with regard to their emphasis on basic research, applied research, and development. Although data concerning types of R. & D. activities for each center are not available in this study, a recent NSF survey shows that most of the AEC's budget for FFRDC's was used in almost equal amounts for basic research and development; of DOD and HEW, largely for applied research; of NASA, mostly for basic research; and of NSF, virtually all for basic research.[1] These data include not only the support of centers sponsored by each agency but also funds for centers sponsored by other agencies. An agency's support for individual centers did not always reflect the same degree of emphasis on type of activity. For example, AEC's Stanford Linear Accelerator Center and the Princeton-Pennsylvania Accelerator are not involved in development activities but are mostly if not exclusively doing basic research, whereas the Los Alamos Scientific Laboratory is doing mostly development.

Another difference among FFRDC's is the practice of some centers, such as the Jet Propulsion Laboratory, to subcontract to industrial firms and other research organizations outside the university sector.

Some FFRDC's continue to carry out mission-oriented work, much of which is classified for security reasons. Others such as the Oak Ridge

[1] National Science Foundation, *Federal Funds for Research, Development, and Other Scientific Activities, Fiscal Years 1967, 1968, and 1969,* vol. XVII, NSF 68–27. Washington, D.C. 20402: Supt. of Documents, U.S. Government Printing Office, 1968.

Associated Universities, which receives most of its Federal support for "other" scientific activities, are assuming many of the characteristics of educational institutions.

Although all of the centers have developed a special relationship with academic institutions, it varies both in degree and kind. It ranges from one which is essentially an administrative-managerial relationship to those involving joint faculty appointments for staff members, programs providing research opportunities, training, facilities, and employment for the faculty and students of cooperating universities and colleges. Some centers outside the university sector, such as Oak Ridge National Laboratory (managed by an industrial firm), also provide special programs for research and research training for faculty and graduate students from institutions throughout the country.

The implementation of the new criteria led to the deletion of some centers and the inclusion of others. The Apollo Guidance Center at the Massachusetts Institute of Technology, the Naval Arctic Research Laboratory at the University of Alaska, and the Navy Biological Laboratory at the University of California are no longer classified as FFRDC's but are included in this report as part of the parent institutions. The new additions include nine university centers funded by the Office of Education (Department of Health, Education, and Welfare), the Cerro Tololo Inter-American Observatory in Chile sponsored by the National Science Foundation, and the Space Radiation Effects Laboratory funded by the National Aeronautics and Space Administration.

FEDERAL SCIENCE OBLIGATIONS TO FFRDC's, 1967

The 33 FFRDC's managed by universities and colleges received $908 million in 1967 (table 19). Of this amount, 88 percent was allocated for R. & D. projects related to agency missions; 11 percent, for R. & D. plant and facilities in support of these projects; and the remainder, for "other" science activities.

Among the seven Federal departments and agencies sponsoring university-managed FFRDC's the Atomic Energy Commission accounted for over one-half of the funds obligated in 1967, primarily through its support to three centers: Lawrence Radiation Laboratory ($175 million), Los Alamos Scientific Laboratory ($102 million), and Argonne National Laboratory ($97 million). NASA obligated $222 million in 1967 to the Jet Propulsion Laboratory, the smallest amount reported since 1963, for its work on projects involving space exploration with unmanned spacecraft. Although this was the largest amount reported for a single university-managed FFRDC, over half of the funds ($119 million) were transferred to industrial firms holding subcontracts. Together, AEC and NASA accounted for more than four-fifths of all Federal funds obligated to university-managed FFRDC's in 1967.

Table 19.—*Federal obligations to Federally Funded Research and Development Centers administered by universities and colleges, by agency and type of program, 1967*

(*Thousands of dollars*)

AGENCY	TOTAL OBLIGA- TIONS	R. & D.	R. & D. PLANT	OTHER SCIENCE
Total, all agencies	$907,549	$800,798	$101,755	$4,996
Atomic Energy Commission	510,878	411,377	94,519	4,982
Department of Defense	135,992	135,985	7	.....
Army	6,167	6,167	....	.....
Navy	62,836	62,836	....	.....
Air Force	66,989	66,982	7	.....
Department of Health, Education, and Welfare: Office of Education	7,859	7,859	....	.....
National Aeronautics and Space Administration	223,984	221,420	2,564	.....
National Science Foundation	28,836	24,157	4,665	14

Of the 33 FFRDC's managed by universities and colleges, 26 were administered by 21 individual universities, six by four consortia, and one jointly by a university and a consortium. The latter is Argonne National Laboratory, administered by the University of Chicago until November 1966, when the terms of a new contract placed it under the joint management of the University and Argonne Universities Association.

All but $14,000 of the $5 million in "other" science activities was awarded to FFRDC's engaged in atomic energy programs. The two largest amounts went to Oak Ridge Associated Universities ($3 million) and Argonne National Laboratory ($1 million). These funds went chiefly for research training and graduate education.

The $10 million net decrease in total obligations from 1966 resulted from a rise of $17 million in research and development and declines of $26 million and $1 million in R. & D. plant and other science activities (table 20). Behind these changes in the overall level of funding are several fluctuations in the budgets of individual centers, caused by completion of existing programs and initiation and expansion of new ones. The completion of the 20-bev linear accelerator at AEC's Stanford Linear Accelerator Center in 1966 resulted in a $26 million drop in R. & D. plant support and an $8 million rise in R. & D. funds. This rise in R. & D. support was counterbalanced by an $8 million reduction in NASA's R. & D. support to the Jet Propulsion Laboratory, largely a result of the end of the Surveyor and Lunar Orbiter programs.

Among the FFRDC's showing an overall gain between 1966 and 1967,

Table 20.—*Federal obligations to Federally Funded Research and Development Centers administered by universities and colleges, by type of program, 1963–67*

(*Millions of dollars*)

PROGRAM	1963	1964	1965	1966	1967
Total	$814.1	$862.4	$895.3	$917.6	$907.5
Research and development	668.9	732.3	744.1	784.2	800.8
R. & D. plant	138.9	122.5	141.7	127.6	101.8
Other science activities	6.4	7.5	9.4	5.8	5.0

AEC's Argonne National Laboratory led with an increase of $10 million, $6 million of which was allocated to construct a 12-foot bubble chamber to be used with a zero gradient synchrotron in high-energy physics research.

More than 90 percent of the $102 million obligated for R. & D. plant was reported for AEC-sponsored centers, with about 78 percent going to Lawrence Radiation Laboratory, Argonne National Laboratory, Stanford Linear Accelerator Center, and Brookhaven National Laboratory. These centers received funds for R. & D. plant ranging from $16 million to $25 million.

TRENDS IN FEDERAL SUPPORT—INFLUENCE OF LARGEST CENTERS

For the period 1963–67, total support to FFRDC's grew at an average annual rate of nearly 3 percent. However, the trend of total Federal obligations to all FFRDC's was heavily influenced by the relatively stable funding of six FFRDC's receiving more than $60 million each in 1967 (chart 3). This group is composed of Jet Propulsion Laboratory, Lawrence Radiation Laboratory, Los Alamos Scientific Laboratory, Argonne National Laboratory, Lincoln Laboratory, and Brookhaven National Laboratory. FFRDC's combined showed a more rapid rate of growth during the period.

These large centers received $691 million in 1963 and $727 million in 1967. The $36 million increase represents an average annual growth of over 1 percent—a figure well below the nearly 10-percent average annual increase for the other FFRDC's—from $123 million in 1963 to $180 million in 1967. It is noteworthy also that these six large centers were in existence throughout the period; the "other" group includes nine centers established after 1963.

Although less than one-fifth of the FFRDC's accounted for more than four-fifths of Federal funds in 1967, it is likely that the next few years will see a continuation of the trend toward a wider dispersion of Federal allocations. As the newly formed centers develop and new ones emerge, they will claim an increasing share of total FFRDC obligations.

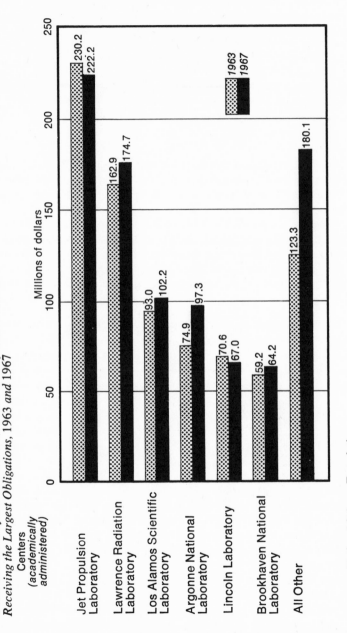

Chart 3: Federally Funded Research and Development Centers Receiving the Largest Obligations, 1963 and 1967

Centers
(academically
administered)

Millions of dollars

1963
1967

Jet Propulsion Laboratory — 230.2, 222.2

Lawrence Radiation Laboratory — 162.9, 174.7

Los Alamos Scientific Laboratory — 93.0, 102.2

Argonne National Laboratory — 74.9, 97.3

Lincoln Laboratory — 70.6, 67.0

Brookhaven National Laboratory — 59.2, 64.2

All Other — 123.3, 180.1

SOURCE: National Science Foundation

Appendix G

THE U.S. FISCAL YEAR 1970 BUDGET FOR NATIONAL DEFENSE
(In millions of dollars)

| PROGRAM OR AGENCY | OUTLAYS | | | RECOM-MENDED BUDGET AUTHORITY FOR 1970 [1] |
	1968 ACTUAL	1969 ESTIMATE	1970 ESTIMATE	
Department of Defense—Military:				
Military personnel	21,954	23,665	24,164	24,384
Operation and maintenance	20,578	22,106	21,841	21,941
Procurement	23,283	24,337	23,435	23,241
Research, development, test, and evaluation	7,747	7,545	7,805	8,174
Military construction	1,281	1,508	1,370	1,949
Family housing	495	630	625	618
Civil defense	108	82	72	75
Revolving and management funds and other	2,091	−1,945	−690	
Military trust funds		2	1	7
Deductions for offsetting receipts	−164	−140	−152	−152
Subtotal, military [2]	77,373	77,790	78,471	80,238
Subtotal, excluding special Southeast Asia	(50,826)	(48,978)	(53,074)	(57,212)
Military Assistance:				
Grants and credit sales [2]	601	548	551	610
Trust fund [2]	53	62	−22	−202
Subtotal, military and military assistance [2]	78,027	78,400	79,000	80,645
Subtotal, excluding special Southeast Asia	(51,480)	(49,588)	(53,603)	(57,620)
Atomic energy [2][3]	2,466	2,451	2,571	2,438
Defense-related activities:				
Stockpiling of strategic and critical materials	19	20	21	21

PROGRAM OR AGENCY	OUTLAYS			RECOM- MENDED BUDGET AUTHORITY FOR 1970 [1]
	1968 ACTUAL	1969 ESTIMATE	1970 ESTIMATE	
Expansion of defense production	51	180	69	
Selective Service System	57	70	70	70
Emergency preparedness activities	12	12	11	11
Deductions for offsetting receipts: Proprietary receipts from the public [4]	−116	−135	−200	−200
Total	80,516	80,999	81,542	82,985
Total, excluding special Southeast Asia	(53,969)	(52,187)	(56,145)	(59,960)
Expenditure account	80,526	81,002	81,543	82,986
Loan account	−10	−3	−1	−1

[1] Compares with budget authority for 1968 and 1969 as follows:
  1968: Total, $79,228 million (NOA, $79,229 million; LA, −$2 million [sic])
  1969: Total, $79,523 million (NOA, $79,527 million; LA, −$4 million).
[2] Entries net of offsetting receipts.
[3] Includes both Federal funds and trust funds.
[4] Excludes offsetting receipts which have been deducted by subfunction above:
  1968, $1,127 million; 1969, $1,120 million; 1970, $1,144 million.

SOURCE: *The Budget of the United States Government,* Fiscal Year 1970, p. 73

Appendix H

THE ARMED FORCES OF THE UNITED STATES (1969)

Summary of Active Forces

	ACTUAL		ESTIMATED	
DESCRIPTION	June 30, 1961	June 30, 1968	June 30, 1969	June 30, 1970
Military personnel (in thousands):				
Army	859	1,570	1,534	1,508
Navy	627	765	771	772
Marine Corps	177	307	313	315
Air Force	821	905	869	861
Total, Department of Defense	2,484	3,547	3,487	3,455
Selected military forces:				
Strategic forces:				
Intercontinental ballistic missile squadrons:				
Minuteman	..	20	20	20
Titan	..	6	6	6
Atlas	5	..	..	..
Polaris submarines/missiles (in commission)	5/80	41/656	41/656	41/656
Strategic bomber squadrons:				
FB-111	..	..	..	5
B-52	39	34	30	24
B-58	6	6	6	6
B-47	80	..	..	..
Manned fighter interceptor squadrons	42	24	19	19
Bomarc interceptor missile squadrons	7	6	6	6
Army air defense missile battalions	49½	20¼	15	14½
General purpose forces:				
Army divisions	11	18	18	18
Army maneuver battalions	124	218	217	218
Army aviation units	67	212	235	235

275

	ACTUAL		ESTIMATED	
DESCRIPTION	June 30, 1961	June 30, 1968	June 30, 1969	June 30, 1970
Army special forces groups	3	7	7	7
Warships (in commission):				
Attack carriers	15	15	15	15
Antisubmarine warfare carriers	9	8	7	6
Nuclear attack submarines	13	33	41	47
Other	328	328	299	279
Amphibious assault ships (in commission)	110	157	157	141
Carrier air wings/groups (attack and ASW)	28	23	21	20
Marine Corps divisions/ aircraft wings	3/3	4/3	4/3	4/3
Air Force tactical forces squadrons	93	144	147	138
Airlift and sealift forces:				
Airlift aircraft squadrons:				
C-5A	..	..	..	2
C-130 through C-141	16	44	44	41
C-118/C-124 and C-7	35	17	12	7
Troopships, cargo ships, and tankers	101	130	124	124
Addenda:				
Active aircraft inventory (all programs):				
Army	5,564	10,465	11,622	12,018
Navy	8,793	8,491	8,594	8,452
Air Force [1]	16,905	15,327	15,058	14,993
Helicopters included in service aircraft, above	4,047	10,188	11,468	12,014
Commissioned ships in fleet (all programs)	819	932	906	895

[1] Includes aircraft provided for support of allies.

SOURCE: *The Budget of the United States Government,* Fiscal Year 1970, p. 75

BIBLIOGRAPHY

Department of Political Science
210 Barrows Hall
University of California
Berkeley, California 94720

Bibliography

CHAPTER 1

Marquis Childs, "Crisis in the Cities," *New York Post,* August 29, 1969.

C. Wright Mills, *The Power Elite,* Oxford University Press, New York, 1959, p. 276.

Robert L. Heilbroner, *The Limits of American Capitalism,* Harper & Row, New York, 1965, p. 51.

Arthur I. Waskow, *Peace and War: The History of the United States 1939–1999,* paper at American Historical Association, December 30, 1967.

Ralph P. Lapp, *The Weapons Culture,* W. W. Norton & Co., New York, 1968, p. 12.

Murray L. Weidenbaum, "Arms and the American Economy: A Domestic Emergence Hypothesis," *American Economic Review,* 1968.

Report of the Committee on the Economic Impact of Defense and Disarmament, July, 1965.

Seymour Melman, *Our Depleted Society,* Holt, Rinehart and Winston, New York, 1965.

————, "Great Society Priorities, War, Peace and the Managerial Bent," *Commonweal,* August 5, 1966.

Report of the Joint Economic Committee, Congress of the United States, on the January 1966 Economic Report of the President with Minority and Supplementary Views, U.S. Congress Joint Economic Committee, 96th Cong., 2d Sess., March 17, 1966.

James W. Fulbright in *The New York Times,* March 23, 1966.

John K. Galbraith, *The New Industrial State,* Houghton Mifflin Company, Boston, 1967, p. 393.

U.S. Department of Commerce, *Statistical Abstract of the United States, 1968* (89th edition), 1968.

U.S. Department of Defense, Statement of Secretary of Defense Clark M.

Clifford, *The Fiscal Year 1970–74 Defense Program and 1970 Defense Budget,* January 15, 1969.

James Reston, *The New York Times,* March 23, 1966.

CHAPTER 2

U.S. Department of Defense, *Armed Services Procurement Regulations,* Washington, D.C.

U.S. Department of Defense, *Defense Procurement Handbook,* Defense Supply Agency, July, 1965.

Murray L. Weidenbaum, "Arms and the American Economy: A Domestic Convergence Hypothesis," *American Economic Review,* May, 1968.

H. L. Nieburg, *In the Name of Science,* Quadrangle Books, Chicago, 1966.

John Joseph Kennedy, *Description and Analysis of the Organization of the Firm in the Defense Weapon Contract Industry,* Ph.D. Dissertation, Ohio State University, University Microfilms, Ann Arbor, Mich., 1962.

The Wall Street Journal, February 7, 1967.

Walter Veith, "Configuration Management," *Mechanical Engineering,* Vol. 89, No. 2, February, 1967, pp. 20–25.

Clark R. Mollenhoff, *The Pentagon,* Putnam Publishing Co., New York, 1967.

Martin Meyerson, "Price of Admission into the Defense Business," *Harvard Business Review,* July–August, 1967.

The New York Times, July 11, 1968.

Merton J. Peck and Frederic M. Scherer, *The Weapons Acquisition Process,* Graduate School of Business, Harvard University, Cambridge, 1962.

U.S. Department of Defense, "An Introduction to the Defense Supply Agency," Defense Supply Agency, January, 1968.

The Washington Post, September 3, 1968; May 3, 1969.

Sanford Watzman, "The Feast at the Pentagon," *The Nation,* December 25, 1967.

Paul Hannah, "Government Buying Erodes Management," *Harvard Business Review,* May–June, 1964.

Department of Defense, *Brief of the Organization and Functions,* Administrative Management Division, Office of the Assistant Secretary of Defense (Administration), April, 1968.

Melvin Laird (Secretary of Defense writing on nine weapons projects), *The New York Times,* June 11, 1969; June 21, 1969.

(The following are two unpublished manuscripts on file in the Engineering Library of Columbia University, New York.)

Ira J. Epstein, "Quality Aspects of DOD Contracting," January, 1967.

H. R. Alexander, "Cost Control in Defense Procurement in the U.S.A.," January, 1967.

CHAPTER 3

U.S. Department of Defense, Statement by Secretary of Defense McNamara, *The Fiscal Year 1969–73 Defense Program and the 1969 Defense Budget,* January 1968.

U.S. Department of Defense, *Defense Procurement Circular,* No. 62, July 10, 1968.

American Machinist, June 20, 1966, p. 23.

FCNL Washington Newsletter, Friends Committee on National Legislation, Washington, D.C., January, 1963.

The Budget of the United States Government, for fiscal years 1965, 1966, and 1967, U.S. Government Printing Office, Washington, D.C.

Business Week, April 9, 1966.

The New York Times, January 8, 1968.

Emile Benoit, *The Monetary and Real Costs of National Defense,* paper to Annual Meeting, American Economic Association, January, 1968.

U.S. Office of Emergency Planning, "The National Plan for Emergency Preparedness," Executive Office, December, 1964.

Report of the Committee on The Economic Impact of Defense and Disarmament, Washington, D.C., July, 1965.

National Aeronautics and Space Administration, *Background Material, NASA FY 1969 Budget Briefing,* January, 1968.

U.S. Department of Defense, Office of the Secretary of Defense, *100 Companies and Their Subsidiary Corporations Listed According to Net Value of Military Prime Contract Awards, Fiscal Year 1967,* November, 1968.

U.S. Department of Defense, *Military Prime Contract Awards by Region and State, Fiscal Years 1966, 1967, 1968,* November 12, 1968.

U.S. Congress, Joint Economic Committee, Subcommittee on Economy in Government, *Economy in Government,* Washington, D.C., 1967.

U.S. Congress, Joint Economic Committee, Subcommittee on Economy in Government, *Economy in Government Procurement and Property Management,* Washington, D.C., 1968.

The New York Times, June 25, 1967.

Business Week, September 30, 1967; October 12, 1968.

The Wall Street Journal, May 16, 1966.

U.S. Department of Labor, *Monthly Labor Review,* September, 1967.

National Aeronautics and Space Administration, letter to Seymour Melman, August 5, 1968.

U.S. National Science Foundation, *Reviews of Data on Science Resources,* No. 14, April, 1968.

American Machinist, March 25, 1968.

The New York Times, August 5, 1968.

New York Post, August 5, 1967.

The New York Times, September 15, 1968.

Business Week, October 12, 1968.

Ralph Lapp, *The Weapons Culture,* W. W. Norton & Co., New York 1968.

U.S. House of Representatives, 89th Cong., 1st sess., *Report of the Select Commitee on Government Research,* December, 1965.

"Federal Research Funds: Science Gets Caught in a Budget Squeeze," *Science,* Vol. CLVIII, p. 1286.

The Economist, August 20, 1966, p. 706.

"Social Sciences: Expanded Role Urged for Defense Department," *Science,* Vol. CLVIII, November 17, 1967.

Douglas M. MacArthur, "Current Emphasis on the Department of Defense's Social and Behavioral Sciences Program," *American Psychologist,* Vol. 23, No. 2, February, 1968, pp. 104–107.

"Anthropologists' Debate: Concern Over Future of Foreign Research," *Science,* December 23, 1966, pp. 104 ff.

"Military Research: A Decline in the Interest of Scientists?," *Science,* Vol. CLVI, April 21, 1967.

Science, February 2, 1968.

"War Catalog of the University of Pennsylvania," *Ramparts,* August, 1966.

H. L. Nieburg, *In the Name of Science,* Quadrangle Books, Chicago, 1966.

Harry R. Biederman, *International Trade and Cooperation in Aerospace Products,* Ph.D. dissertation, Columbia University, New York, 1967; published as *Development Planning Report No. 80,* Lockheed Aircraft Corporation, Burbank, California, April, 1968.

Hearings by the House Committee on Foreign Affairs on the Foreign Assistance Act of 1964, Part IV, p. 510.

The Washington Post, March 23, 1969.

U.S. Senate, Foreign Relations Committee, "Arms Sales and Foreign Policy" (a Staff Study), 1967.

Executive Office of the President, U.S. Office of Emergency Preparedness, *Stockpile Report to the Congress, July–1968,* May, 1969. (See this for details of $6.8 billion commodity inventories.)

CHAPTER 4

The New York Times, March 13, 1966; January 14, 1968; June 21, 1968.

U.S. Department of Defense, *500 Contractors Listed According to Net*

Value of Military Prime Contract Awards for Research, Development, Test and Evaluation Work, Fiscal Year 1968, Office of the Secretary of Defense, Directorate for Statistical Services, November 29, 1968.

U.S. National Science Foundation, *National Patterns of R&D Resources, Funds and Manpower in the United States, 1953–68,* Washington, D.C., 1967.

U.S. Department of Defense, *Military Prime Contract Awards by Region and State, Fiscal Years 1962–1967,* Office of the Secretary of Defense, Directorate for Statistical Services, December, 1967.

U.S. National Science Foundation, *American Science Manpower 1966,* Washington, D.C., December, 1967.

U.S. National Science Foundation, *Federal Support to Universities and Colleges, Fiscal Years 1963–66,* Washington, D.C., 1967.

U.S. National Science Foundation, *Federal Support to Universities and Colleges, Fiscal Year 1967,* Washington, D.C., 1968.

Viet-Report, January, 1968 (special issue on "The University at War").

"Themis: DOD Plan to Spread the Wealth Raises Questions in Academe," *Science,* April 7, 1967.

Business Week, December 16, 1967.

American Machinist, November 8, 1965.

St. Louis Post Dispatch, September 17, 1967.

"LBJ's New Budget: Another Tight Year for Research and Development," *Science,* February 2, 1968.

Clark Kerr, "The Frantic Race to Remain Contemporary," In Morison, R. S., ed. *The Contemporary University: U.S.A.,* Houghton Mifflin Co., Boston, Mass., 1966.

The New York Times, July 11, 1966.

U.S. Congress, Committee on Government Operations, *Conflicts Between the Federal Research Program and the Nation's Goals for Higher Education,* Washington, D.C. 1965.

The New York Times, August 14, 1966.

"Federal Labs: White House Study Urges Closer University Ties," *Science,* January 26, 1968.

The Nation's Engineering Research Needs, 1965–1985 (Engineers' Joint Council) 345 East 47 St., New York, N.Y. 10017, May, 1962 (summary and subcommittee reports).

Michael T. Klare (compiler), *The University-Military Complex, a Directory and Related Documents,* The North American Congress on Latin America (P.O. Box 57, Cathedral Park Station, New York, N.Y. 10025), 1969.

CHAPTER 5

The New York Times, November 20, 1967; December 25, 1966.

Arthur M. Schlesinger, Jr., *A Thousand Days,* Houghton Mifflin Co., Boston, Mass., 1965.

Theodore Sorensen, *Kennedy,* Harper & Row, Publishers, Inc., New York, N.Y., 1965.

Robert S. McNamara before Subcommittee of the House Armed Services Committee, Statement by Secretary of Defense, October 25, 1968, on U.S. Strategic Forces.

U.S. Congress, House Armed Services Committee, *Statement of Secretary of Defense Robert S. McNamara before Subcommittee No. 2 of the U.S. House Armed Services Committee on the Fiscal Year 1967–71 Strategic Bomber Program,* January 25, 1966.

The New York Times, November 28, 1965; August 16, 1968; March 3, 1967; November 1, 1966; September 25, 1967; February 19, 1968; August 17, 1968; October 9, 1967; October 26, 1968.

Herald Tribune (Paris), July 12, 1967.

The New York Times, November 8, 1966; November 13, 1967.

Washington Post, January 16, 1968.

Murray L. Weidenbaum, "The Federal Budget and the Outlook for Defense Spending," presented at the Fourteenth Annual Conference on the Economic Outlook, University of Michigan, Ann Arbor, November 18, 1966.

U.S. News and World Report, November 28, 1966.

Business Week, January 14, 1967.

U.S. Congress, Senate Committee on Armed Services, *Hearings on the Fiscal Year 1969 Department of Defense Budget,* Feb.-March, 1968.

The New York Times, January 2, 1967; February 21, 1967; February 23, 1967.

The Congressional Record, June 24, 1968, p. S7647.

"A National Shelter Program: Its Feasibility and Its Costs," A report by a group of independent specialists. Reprinted in S. Melman, *No Place To Hide,* Grove Press, 1962.

The New York Times, May 7, 1968.

U.S. Congress, House of Representatives, *Report No. 1645, Authorizing Appropriations for Military Procurement, Research, and Development, Fiscal Year 1969, and Reserve Strength,* 90th Cong., 2d Sess., July 5, 1968.

Jerome B. Wiesner and Herbert F. York, "National Security and the Nuclear-Test Ban," *Scientific American,* October, 1964.

The New York Times, August 17, 1968; October 25, 1967; April 14, 1967; October 25, 1966; October 27, 1966.

"Chemical and Biological Warfare: The Research Program," and "Chemical and Biological Warfare: The Weapons and the Policies," *Science,* January 13, 1967, and January 20, 1967.

Martin M. Kaplan, "Communicable Diseases and Epidemics," *Bulletin of the Atomic Scientists,* June, 1960.

Milton Leitenberg, "Biological Weapons," *Scientist and Citizen,* Special Issue on Chemical and Biological Warfare, August–September, 1967.

Tsutomu Watanabe, "Selected Methods of Genetic Study of Episome Mediated Drug Resistance in Bacteria," *Methods in Medical Research,* Vol. X, 1964.

Michael T. Klare, "A Directory of University-Conducted Research on Chemical and Biological Warfare (CBW)," *Viet-Report,* November, 1967.

Nigel Calder (ed.), *Unless Peace Comes,* The Viking Press, New York, 1968.

The New Republic, April 5, 1969, p. 8.

Robin Clarke, *The Silent Weapons,* David McKay Company, New York, 1968.

Seymour Hersh, *Chemical and Biological Warfare,* Bobbs-Merrill Company, New York, 1968.

On low-cost production of fissionable uranium-235, *Business Week,* December 14, 1968, p. 136.

CHAPTER 6

Congressional Record, April 19, 1968, p. S4290.

American Friends Service Committee, *The U.S. in Vietnam,* Philadelphia, Pa., 1966.

Science, February 23, 1968.

Congressional Record, address by Senator George McGovern, April 25, 1967.

The New York Times, June 12, 1968; December 1, 1965; December 16, 1966.

Business Week, December 4, 1965.

The New York Times, February 20, 1968.

Viet-Report, June–July, 1966.

U.S. Department of Defense, Office of the Secretary of Defense, "Address by Robert S. McNamara before the American Society of Newspaper Editors," Montreal, Canada, May 18, 1966.

Armed Forces Management, July, 1966.

Statements of the Secretary of Defense on Defense Program and Budget for 1967 and 1968.

Conor Cruise O'Brien, "The Counter-Revolutionary Reflex," *Columbia University Forum*, Spring, 1966.

The New York Times, June 24, 1966.

Business Week, March 2, 1968.

The New York Times, March 3, 1968.

The New York Times, December 11, 1966; July 10, 1968; November 13, 1966.

Barry Kramer, Associated Press Dispatch, in *Cedar Rapids Gazette*, April 3, 1968.

The New York Times, June 19, 1966; September 20, 1966.

The Wall Street Journal, January 29, 1968.

The New York Times, December 22, 1967.

Jack Robertson, "The Tin Ears of War," *The Nation*, June 10, 1968.

The New York Times, November 16, 1966; January 25, 1967.

New York Post (editorial), December 6, 1967.

The New York Times, August 18, 1968.

Armed Forces Management, July, 1966.

John S. Tompkins, "Night Eyes for GI's," *True Magazine*, May, 1967; *Electronic Design 21*, October 10, 1968.

The New York Times, January 8, 1967.

The "Weed Killers," *Viet-Report*, June–July, 1966.

Business Week, September 14, 1968; December 20, 1966.

The New York Times, May 7, 1967.

U.S. Agency for International Development, *Index to Catalog for Investment Information and Opportunities*, November, 1966.

CHAPTER 7

Seymour Melman, *Our Depleted Society*, Holt, Rinehart & Winston, New York, 1965, chap. 1.

U.S. Arms Control and Disarmament Agency, *World-Wide Military Expenditures and Related Data*, Research Report 67-6, Washington, D.C., December, 1967.

Merton J. Peck and Frederick M. Scherer, *The Weapons Acquisition Process* (Graduate School of Business), Harvard University, Cambridge, 1962, chap. 1.

U.S. Congress, House of Representatives, Committee on Government Operations, *The Conflicts between the Federal Research Programs and the Nation's Goals for Higher Education*, 89th Cong., 1st Session, House Report No. 1158, 1965.

W. L. Abbott, "The New Coalitions," *The Nation,* December 23, 1968.

The New York Times, November 30, 1968; November 14, 1968; June 26, 1968.

M. Weidenbaum, "Shifting the Composition of Government Spending: Implications for the Regional Distribution of Income," Peace Research Society: *Papers,* Philadelphia, 1966.

Business Week, October 12, 1968.

Conor Cruise O'Brien, "The Counter-Revolutionary Reflex," *Columbia University Forum,* Spring, 1966.

R. L. Heilbroner, "Counter-Revolutionary America," *Commentary,* 1967.

Robert G. Sherrill, "Pentagon Loot," *The Nation,* December 23, 1968.

The New York Times, May 7, 1969.

The Washington Post, January 26, 1969; December 8, 1968; December 9, 1968.

Richard A. Stubbing, "Improving the Acquisition Process for High Risk Electronics Systems" (Distributed by Clearinghouse for Federal Scientific and Technical Information, Springfield, Va. 22151), January 30, 1969.

Richard F. Kaufman, "Billion-Dollar Grab Bag," *The Nation,* March 17, 1969.

Barry M. Goldwater, "Arms and the Man," *Barron's,* April 21, 1969 (from the *Congressional Record,* April 15, 1969).

See dispatches on the Pentagon in *The New York Times,* May 15, 1969; June 12, 18, 21, and 27, 1969, on major inefficiencies and waste in weapons production.

CHAPTER 8

Terence McCarthy, "What the Vietnam War Has Cost," *New University Thought,* Summer, 1968.

Newsweek, July 11, 1966.

Hearings before the Joint Economic Committee, 90th Cong., 1st Sess. (especially Volume II), 1967.

The New York Times, May 10, 1967.

Christian Science Monitor, June 29, 1967.

The Wall Street Journal, May 25, 1967.

The New York Times, June 11, 1967.

W. Adams and J. B. Dirlam, "Big Steel, Invention and Innovation," *The Quarterly Journal of Economics,* May, 1966.

The Wall Street Journal, August 25, 1967.

New York Post, April 12, 1968.

The New York Times, February 18, 1968.

American Machinist, January 1, 1968 and November 18, 1968 (the *Tenth American Machinist Inventory of Metalworking Equipment,* 1968).

The New York Times, September 18, 1966.

U.S. News & World Report, November 7, 1966.

Boston Globe, February 20, 1967.

New York Post, September 1, 1967.

The New York Times, February 9, 1967; March 5, 1966; October 16, 1966; September 28, 1967.

Business Week, October 16, 1965.

The Brain Drain into the United States of Scientists, Engineers and Physicians, a Staff Study for the Research and Technical Study Subcommittee of the Committee on Government Operations, U.S. House of Representatives, July, 1967.

The New York Times, November 9, 1965; August 1, 1966.

The Wall Street Journal, August 30, 1967.

The New York Times, July 24, 1966; July 6, 1966.

Newsweek, July 11, 1966.

The New York Times, May 20, 1966; May 26, 1968.

The Wall Street Journal, March 6, 1968.

The New York Times, July 28, 1966.

Hunger: A Report by the Citizens' Board of Inquiry into Hunger and Malnutrition in the United States, Beacon Press, Boston, 1968.

The New York Times, November 10, 1967; July 12, 1968.

The New York Times, July 28, 1966; October 8, 1968; September 11, 1966; September 7, 1966; June 26, 1968.

The New York Times, January 29, 1967.

The Economist, September 28, 1968.

The New York Times, July 12, 1968; October 6, 1966.

The Racial Gap, 1955–1965; 1965–1975, in Income, Unemployment, Education, Health, Housing, National Urban League, New York, June, 1967.

New York Post, November 16, 1965.

The New York Times, February 26, 1966; March 13, 1966.

The Wall Street Journal, January 5, 1966.

The New York Times, October 2, 1966.

Science, September 27, 1968.

The New York Times, January 12, 1967; March 23, 1967; December 13, 1966.

U.S. Arms Control and Disarmament Agency, Economics Bureau, *World-Wide Military Expenditures and Related Data,* Calendar Year 1965, Research Report 67–6, December, 1967.

U.S. Arms Control and Disarmament Agency, Economics Bureau, *World-Wide Military Expenditures and Related Data,* Calendar Year 1966, Research Report 68-52, December, 1968.

The New York Times, April 4, 1967.

Carl E. Taylor and Marie-Françoise Hall, "Health, Population, and Economic Development," *Science,* August 11, 1967.

The Economist, September 28, 1968.

Paul G. Hoffman, "The Rich and the Poor: 1966," *Saturday Review,* September 17, 1966.

The New York Times, October 2, 1966.

Michael Harrington, *American Power in the Twentieth Century,* League for Industrial Democracy, 1967.

Hamza Alavi and Amir Khusro, "Pakistan: The Burden of U.S. Aid," *New University Thought,* Autumn, 1962.

Report of the Committee on The Economic Impact of Defense and Disarmament, U.S. Government Printing Office, July, 1965.

Business Week, October 26, 1968.

George McGovern, *A Time of War/A Time of Peace,* Random House, New York, 1968.

The New York Times, December 18, 1968; March 15, 1966.

J. L. Clayton, "Vietnam: The 200-Year Mortgage," *The Nation,* May 26, 1969.

CHAPTER 9

The New York Times, October 25, 1968; December 19, 1968.

The Washington Post, November 4, 1968.

The New York Times, November 3, 1968.

Statement by Secretary of Defense Clark M. Clifford (at Pentagon), October 25, 1968.

T. J. Farer, book review of R. S. McNamara, "The Essence of Security," in *The Nation,* November 11, 1968.

The Washington Post, August 16, 1968 (article on guns and butter).

The New York Times, October 6, 1968; November 3, 1968 (on future arms policies).

U.S. Department of Commerce, *The Commerce Business Daily,* April 29, 1965.

J. J. Stone, *The Case against Missile Defenses,* The Institute for Strategic Studies, London, 1968.

U.S. Department of Defense, Office of the Director of Defense, Research and Engineering, "List of Major Projects Terminated during the Past 15 Years," January 5, 1968.

The New York Times, August 17, 1968 (on base closings).

The New York Times, July 24, 1966 (on underdevelopment).

The New York Times, June 26, 1968 (on military budgets after Vietnam.)

"The Slow Retreat from Stalin," *The Economist,* July 2, 1966, pp. 18–19.

The Economist, August 17, 1968 (on the cost of ABM to the Russians).

R. L. Heilbroner, "Making a National Foreign Policy Now," *Harper's* September, 1968.

The New York Times, February 16, 1968 (on secret study by the Pentagon on U.S. hegemony).

James W. Fulbright, "The War and Its Effects," *Congressional Record,* December 13, 1967.

Richard Barnet, *Intervention and Revolution,* World Publishing Company, New York, 1968.

Department of Political Science
210 Barrows Hall
University of California
Berkeley, California 94720